Mereo Books

2nd Floor, 6-8 Dyer Street, Cirencester, Gloucestershire, GL7 2PF
An imprint of Memoirs Books. www.mereobooks.com
and www.memoirsbooks.co.uk

Ston and the Bright Bar: 978-1-86151-970-2

First published in Great Britain in 2020
by Mereo Books, an imprint of Memoirs Books.

Copyright ©2020

John Hedge has asserted his right under the Copyright Designs
and Patents Act 1988 to be identified as the author of this work.

The address for Memoirs Books can be found at www.mereobooks.com

Mereo Books. Reg. No. 12157152

Typeset in 11/15pt Century Schoolbook by Wiltshire Associates.
Printed and bound in Great Britain

JOHN HEDGE

STON

and the

BRIGHT BAR

GROWING UP IN TWO
CONTRASTING ENGLISH WORLDS

For Gill and my brothers David and Bryan

CONTENTS

—⋈—

PART I - THE BRIGHT BAR

PART II - STON

THE FOUR PILLARS

HOME AND AWAY

FINAL TIMES

PART III - AFTERWARDS

PART I

THE BRIGHT BAR

Chapter 1

To Begin With

This story is about my family and me during the first 17 years of my life. That life evolved in two very different environments. We moved to a village pub, the Red Lion in Buckinghamshire, soon after the Coronation in 1953, and my parents ran it until 1965. My brother David and I went to the local schools until in 1959, for reasons which will become clear, we were both sent away for a very particular boarding school education; I was 12 years old and my brother 10. We went to the Royal Masonic Schools, Junior and Senior, known to everyone who went to them as J Ston and Ston. The Masonic schools were financed entirely by the contributions of Freemasons and provided for the sons of brothers in need. Almost every child sent to the schools went there because their Freemason father had died. Mine had not died, but by the time it was decided that we should go away to school he was most certainly in need.

The Masonic schools were in Bushey, Hertfordshire, just 33 miles and two buses away, though to us at the time the distance seemed immense. For years we alternated between term times of institutional rigour and holidays back at home surrounded by the smells and sounds of the Red Lion. It amounted to living two separate lives. The only similarity between those lives was that neither was very private, so that you tended to hang on to the things which mattered most inside your head. The six transitions there and back for three terms a year marked the seasons, and however often you made those passages the adjustment back to school or the pub was never easy and always took a day or two.

Before our move to the pub we had lived in the village of Waddesdon, in a house bought with the help of my grandfather. He had come to live with us after my grandmother died quite suddenly after what was supposed to have been a routine operation. My father, apple of his mother's eye, had served in India as an RAF Armourer in the war. My mother came from a large working-class Manchester family. She had been serving in the Land Army in rural Buckinghamshire. They met while he was on leave, and theirs was one of the many cross-country relationships which came out of the war, so that fewer people married the boy or girl next door.

My parents married in 1946. I arrived in 1947 and my brother David in 1950, so we were both early members of the baby boom generation. We had lived in rented houses in Aylesbury before the move to Waddesdon and they were very proud of the new house. They were in their late 20s by the time we moved to Waddesdon. My father worked for the County Council, and my grandfather took on a part-time brown coat stores job at the newly opened rocket establishment at Westcott, a bus ride away. My mother looked after us all. That was what she did, and that was the invariable custom of those days.

My father, John Victor, loved sport, especially football and cricket, and drinking, especially large amounts of beer. Service life in India had offered plenty of all these things, but after the war and marriage active sports and active drinking curved away in opposite directions. Within a few years of coming back from

India he married, lost his beloved mother in a botched operation, became a father and had his own grieving father move in. He had lost his hair in India, and was prematurely bald, but he was tall, strong, and for the moment still relatively slim and athletic. He had been a demon fast bowler in local cricket before the war and had the press cuttings to prove it. He had been the kind of centre forward in football usually described as bustling, and good with his elbows. A man in his prime certainly, but prone to bingeing on nights out.

He celebrated my birth so fully that he managed to get my chosen names registered the wrong way round, so that the chosen Anthony John became John Anthony, and the cause of recrimination for ever afterwards. Until much later I never saw him drunk, but my brother and I both knew about the falling down and bed-shitting episodes from the next day's arguments.

My father was certainly accustomed to having his own way. He had grown up as a favoured elder son. Seen as the clever one, he had more attention paid to his education than his younger brother. This meant that while my grandparents moved round Buckinghamshire and Oxfordshire from one small business to another, usually with limited success, my father spent most of his secondary schooling boarding with his aunt Win and her brother Cecil in Newport Pagnell. This meant that he could attend Wolverton Grammar School. Both places are now part of modern Milton Keynes. He had happy memories of his life with his uncle and aunt and of his school days, going each day on the local train, and he was an avid reader of the Gem and Magnet school stories, so that years later his ideas about our going away to school seemed to draw a great deal on the fantasy Edwardian world of Frank Richards and his character Billy Bunter.

My mother, Dorothy, was the second of a family of 10. I cannot remember my grandfather Williams, who came from Bagillt in Flintshire. Apart from serving in France in the Manchester

Regiment in the First World War he had always worked as a bricklayer. After a serious accident he developed cancer and died in his fifties in 1951, so that my mother, like my father, lost a parent at a very early age. One of my earliest memories is of being taken to Manchester by her when she went to his funeral. There were many hours on slow trains and the next day I remember being dragged around endless shops on a hot summer's day while she struggled to find black mourning material to wear for the funeral. Everything was still in short supply because of rationing, and Manchester seemed very big and very crowded.

My mother's family lived in Beech Road, Chorlton. My grandmother, a tiny woman, was clearly in charge, and always busy, in a hair net and pinny. She had a very broad sense of humour, and was very direct with everyone, but she was also very kind to us and proud that my mother and her older sister Jessie were now having the first of a generation of grandchildren. Granny Williams had certainly had a hard life. She had lost all but two fingers from one hand in a munitions accident in the first war, but managed to smoke her Woodbines using it. The family had seen some of the second war from the air raid shelter in the garden. One of the jokes my mother would always tell was of her father looking out of the shelter at the sky and telling them all 'it's OK, it's one of ours' only for there to be huge explosions seconds later. At Beech Road there was always a crowded family life – lots of young aunts and uncles, going off to work and giving us comics and toys. It was warm and welcoming and friendly. We did not go very often; visits were rare, and it was a long way on the train, but they were really special because of that.

My mother must always have missed home. She told us many stories about growing up and her different brothers and sisters. She had suffered mastoiditis as a primary school child, then commonly a cause of child mortality. She had been in hospital and had an operation. She became the favourite of the surgeon and his wife, who had wanted to adopt her. You can see from an early photograph what a pretty little girl my mother was. The idea was rejected very quickly, of course, by her mother, my Granny Williams.

One of my mother's memories of school was of being part of the Manchester Children's Choir, which sang *Nymphs and Shepherds* in the famous concert of 1929 at the Free Trade Hall. She must have been very young at the time but still remembered the tune and some of the words. She later passed what everyone then called 'The Scholarship' but did not go to Whalley Range High School because of the costs involved, especially the uniform. This was a common story then, though it may also have been to do with avoiding airs and graces. Certainly Granny Williams did not like airs and graces – she never really took to my father with his perceived fancy manners and 'southern ways'.

My mother was beautiful as a young woman. The photographs of her in Land Army uniform and at a Masonic Ladies Night with my father confirm that. She had long dark hair, the high Williams cheekbones and blue eyes. I adored her. She was the centre of my world.

So, there we all were in Waddesdon, well housed and settled. Rationing was still going on and I can remember helping to gather wood, and it being taken home in the pram, but things were getting easier. I had just started school, and in the early stages I was taken there rather unwillingly, sometimes by my grandfather. I can certainly remember the Coronation ceremonies, receiving a mug and book about the new Queen, and the village bun fight on Coronation day itself when it seemed to rain endlessly. The question is, how and why did we go from all this so soon into a public house? The answer really lies with my grandfather, Victor, or 'Old Vic' as everyone called him, to distinguish him from my father, John Victor.

Victor had grown up with Win and Cecil in Newport Pagnell, the eldest of three. He went into service on leaving school and worked with horses. He started as a junior coachman and worked his way his way up to become head groom in various great houses in Scotland and Norfolk before the First World War. When it started he joined the Norfolk Yeomanry while his brother Cecil, still back at home, joined the Oxfordshire and Buckinghamshire Light Infantry and served on the Western Front before catching a whiff of gas poisoning and being invalided out. Victor worked first with horses and later with camels in Palestine, so he never went to France. He returned safely and married after the war. My grandmother, Emily Barnett, from Wootton in Oxfordshire, came from a farming background, but she too had been in service.

In the inter-war years and through the Depression they went through a succession of small shops and pubs. These included the Horse and Jockey in West Bar, Banbury, which is still there. In one of them my father got into big trouble by cavorting about on the roof with his friend Vernon Scannell, later famous as a poet. At one stage Victor was Secretary, in effect licensee, at the Wendover Working Men's Club. This ended unhappily – his handed-down advice to my father was 'Never work for the working man'. Both he and my grandmother always represented the traditional, solid, unwavering Edwardian servant class commitment to Conservatism and the Monarchy.

Victor had certainly been a wheeler and dealer – a wild rover, with waistcoat and watch chain, while his brother and sister remained all their lives in North Bucks. He certainly made money from the black market in the War. My father told me that his method was to buy up leftovers from other publicans, and pass the mixture off as mild ale, probably with some added water

I remember him as a short, stoutish man, looking with his glasses bald head and round face rather like Billy Cotton the bandleader. He knew horses very well of course, and went racing sometimes. I can just remember a day when my parents went with him, and they came back with stuffed toys for us and tales of the young Lester Piggott. When I can have been no older than six or seven he borrowed somebody's pony and put me on the back, taking me precariously down the lane and then onto the green. He wanted me to be a 'natural' and I did my best, but I fell off and had a bang on the head so that my mother was cross with him, and in turn, though he said nothing, I knew that he was disappointed with me

Victor was a substantial drinker. There was always drink around, and one way or another it had been a major part of his life. He came, of course, from an age when nobody questioned drinking very much if you could manage to keep one foot in front of the other.

The last pub they kept was the Falcon at Aylesbury, a small place in one of the cobbled streets near the station, now long gone. I can just remember the gloom and the fruity smell of afternoon in the empty bar. This must have been when I was very young, three going on four perhaps, and not long before my grandmother Emily's death. Photographs show her as a handsome, rather proud-looking woman, and she seems to have been the most determined keeper up of 'standards' within the family, though she never seemed to exert enough influence to enable them to settle down for long, and this restless streak was later handed on to my father.

Emily had a rather fierce reputation as a landlady. Once she was asked in the bar by some customer to cheer up and give him a smile. 'You can't be laughing all the time', she told him. The family story was that she had once walked out of a Max Miller performance at the Holborn Empire. This may or may not have happened, and no witnesses survive. Even if she didn't, it seems clear that she would have approved of anyone who did.

Her death, in her late fifties, changed everything for Victor and for my father. More fatalistic attitudes prevailed then, and people had lower expectation of long life for most, but her death was sudden. She was being operated on for cancer and died on the operating table. My father always afterwards assumed an unexplained and unchallengeable negligence, but could do nothing about it. In those days doctors, and especially surgeons, really were untouchable to ordinary people in a godlike way, so that little was ever explained and you had no option but to live with what had happened. He was still in his 20s when this catastrophe happened, and ill prepared for it. I only came to realise many years later how deep his sense of loss and longing had been and for how long those feelings affected his life, especially when facing problems.

My grandfather acquired surprisingly significant cash savings through his erratic career, and helped both his sons buy houses. In the early 1950s you could buy a house for a few hundred pounds. My first contact with that kind of money apparently was as a four-year-old. I took the cash box with the money for my uncle's new house and ran off down the street with it, pursued by my grandfather and parents. I didn't get far.

Having bought the Waddesdon house, sweetly named 'Sun Rising,' my grandfather came to live with us. After a quiet interlude, probably too settled for the old rover, he was clearly behind the brilliant idea that the family should sell up and take on a village pub. He and my mother would work during the day, and my father would keep up his administrative job in the County Council Architect's Department and then become Mine Host in the evenings and weekends. With my grandfather's business track record, my father's love of convivial excess, my mother's complete lack of experience and two small boys, this seems to me to have been not only a complete triumph of hope over experience but also a rejection of safe respectability. What after all could possibly go wrong?

Chapter 2

COMING TO THE
RED LION

We moved to the pub in the late summer of 1953, not long after the Coronation. When the moving day came the furniture went separately and we travelled in behind by the Red Rover bus to Aylesbury and then the 82 bus to Oxford, which went through Haddenham. It was a sunny day and all I recall after the long journey was being allowed to ride my red tricycle round and around the patch of grassed garden at the front of the pub, underneath the big sign with a huge painted Red Lion, which squeaked on its hinges in the breeze. I seemed to be there for hours, and was largely left to myself. No doubt a great deal of work to take the place over was going on inside.

Haddenham was a large village and had a number of pubs. The Red Lion looked out onto the Green and St Mary's church, with its duck pond in front. Just round the corner was the Green Dragon, and nearby in Station Road was the Rose and Thistle. Elsewhere in the village, if you wanted yet more choice, you could use the Sun, the Crown, or the Wagon and Horses. All of them had their regulars, and most were primarily beer and spirits houses. Wine for other than special occasions was still regarded as rather cosmopolitan and not really a pub drink at all. The Red Lion had the best setting, I always thought, and on a summer's day with a blue sky and white clouds the whole scene might have come from an 'Under an English Heaven' calendar.

To a five-year-old the Red Lion seemed vast and mysterious. There was a big oak front door leading on one side to the public bar with its wooden floor and tobacco-yellow walls and ceiling. I realised when I was a few years older that this was not the original colour and that the staining was an accumulation from the smoke of endless pipes and cigarettes. Later on, once in a blue moon, an effort would be made to wash them down, but this made little real difference to the patina.

While it was out of bounds to us, supposedly, during opening hours, you were never far from the bar's rumble of conversation, the chink and plonk of glasses and the clatter of dominos. As time went on we often went into the bar in the afternoon shade and played darts or just sat around. There was a bench seat which ran around most of the room. Soon after we arrived my father put up pictures from a sale; the usual pub items with prints of horses and old English life. The bar had an open fire, lit for the autumn and winter, and this was a cosy place to sit on a winter morning before school.

On the other side was the Lounge Bar, which had carpets, sofas and more delicate seating, much of which must also have come from salerooms. The overall impression was of chintz and a rather dusty decorum. We came to know the Lounge as a quiet place with few customers, and they were often those who needed to speak in whispers or wanted to share their anxieties with one or other of my parents. This was where my father would speak with our village PC when he came to call routinely and enjoy a complementary rum and black. It was also the place where several regular mournful individuals would come for the facility of solitary soaking.

The lounge had an old upright piano, which my father sometimes played to accompany singsongs. He had been able to play an accomplished jazz piano, and though he no longer played regularly he could bang out most tunes very well, with some occasional virtuoso stride playing. Normally, though, the lounge had a peaceful, almost sombre atmosphere, and it remained like that until some years later when, in an attempt to boost trade and attract younger people, my parents decided to place a jukebox there. This did not please everybody, but it certainly brightened up the atmosphere. They would never have stood for it in the public bar where talk, opinions, darts, dominoes and the freedom to have a good moan were what mattered.

Behind the counter was the bar, the 'bright bar', as I thought of it, and it immediately fascinated me. It was surrounded by fairy lights and had spirit bottles and optics full of glinting liquid at the top. There were many mysterious bottles with bright labels – whisky, gin and brandy of course, but not vodka in those days. There were some more exotic drinks like advocaat or cherry brandy and the old standbys of medium sherry and ruby port. Below the bottles stood hundreds of glasses and then below that, on the bottom shelves, all the different varieties of bottled beer and 'minerals'. To the right was the till, and the chink of coins going in and being handed back was all part of the bar's soundtrack.

There was always a Schweppes Racing Calendar on the wall. Every month featured a horse and jockey notable from the previous year. In that first year of 1953 it would certainly have included the previous year's Derby winner – as the calendar would have put it, 'Tulyar, Charlie Smirke up'. They all looked much the same to me apart from the different jockey colours.

Most men drank draught beer or spirits, and women sherry, port or bottled beer. The old beer engine lasted through all the years we were at the Red Lion. The pump handles connected to pipes, which went three or four steps down to the cellar behind the public bar. The cellar was the publican's engine room to which under no circumstances could the customers have access. It was the back stage of the show. It was where barrel changing under pressure happened, with plenty of heaving about and swearing, especially on a busy night. The privacy of the cellar certainly helped in the conjuring which licensees sometimes had to do. Even as children we knew my father's standard trick, which went as follows:

The customer, holding up slightly cloudy pint of mild with the usual bits floating in it.

'Thaas a bit cleowdy Jahn!'

John: 'OK Fred (or Bert or Harry), give it here.' Descends to cellar, counts to 10 and returns to the bar. 'That better Fred?'

Fred, holding pint up to the light: 'Thaas bewtiful Jahn, thanks and 'ave one for yerself, and your good laydy'.

When we first came to the Red Lion, although my father had lived in pubs at various stages of his childhood, he now had to learn the trade in more detail, helped by my grandfather. This included knowing how to clean out the pipes without poisoning anyone, how to tap barrels properly, and ordering so that the place did not run dry. For my grandfather, who had done it all before and had always gravitated back to the trade this must have seemed an opportunity to hand on what he knew, but also to have a last and unexpected chance to make it all work alongside his son.

Almost all pubs in those days were tied houses, belonging to breweries. The landlord was the live-in licensee, required to stock only the brewery's products, though you had other suppliers of soft drinks and tobacco. There had to be enough accommodation for families. The Red Lion had been rebuilt in the 1930s, and most of our rooms were upstairs. Behind the bars, though, we also had a hallway leading to a back living room attached to a small kitchen. My brother and I spent much of our childhood in that back room, a few yards away from the door to the bar, and our parents would usually look in on us every few minutes. It was pleasant enough with a fire and chairs, and later the following year (1954) our first TV. It could be lonely though, and outside school hours everything fitted round the pub routine and its unchanging hours, so that there was little time left for conventional family life.

We usually had the back room to ourselves, but from time to time other people were invited in. This was sometimes favoured customers and friends of my parents, and usually to see something on TV, normally football or boxing. Occasionally we were joined by a customer's child or children. This was not welcome, and really did feel like an invasion. I was very shy and remember the agonies of trying to sit behind a comic without speaking and peeping out now and then to check, as the long silence went on, whether a little girl in plaits, probably equally shy, was still there. A stand-off like that, without either side blinking, could go on for some time, punctuated occasionally by parental checking and the offer of lemonade and crisps, which we had plenty of.

Upstairs were three bedrooms, a large living room, which had a windowless box room, and a bathroom. We hardly ever used the upstairs living room, which had comfortable armchairs, a large dining table and four dining chairs with plush seats. For want of use, it was usually, the only tidy room in the house.

My brother and I shared the middle bedroom. It looked out onto the side street, Gibson Lane, and once we had been sent upstairs to bed we often looked out onto the street and watched the various comings and goings. This was all entertaining and fun, but later on as night came I was always afraid of the dark, and for this reason liked the hubbub coming up from the bar below. Even then the big old wardrobe on the far side of the room, with its large mirror casting strange reflections, seemed frightening. You had to look and check though, to see that nothing had changed. Compulsively your eyes were drawn there whether or not you wanted to look. Sleep always came in the end.

My parents had the big front bedroom, which looked out onto the green, and my grandfather had the back bedroom, next to the bathroom. We knew very well that we were not allowed to go into it, and he could be gruff at times with us.

I discovered fairly soon that you could get out of the bathroom window onto the flat roof of the cellar. From there you could see right down over the garden and down the lane and I imagined often that I was the captain of this big ship, the Red Lion, and at the wheel about to sail off down Gibson Lane.

The back door of the pub led to a small back yard with a big coal bin. If you climbed onto this, you could see through the top window into the Ladies' at the back of the lounge. One of our naughtier childhood games was to climb into the bunker and look at women sitting down to pee. We never saw anything much, as skirts were pretty full in those days and many of the women were of considerable size. We were certainly curious, but not very conscious of what we might be looking for, beyond knowing that it was 'rude'

The pub car park with a chain fence was where we played our games against a big garden wall, made out of crumbling wychert. I did not know until I was older that this was a method of building unique to the area, using chalk and white clay mixed with straw and any available rubbish, so that you could sometimes see embedded bits of bottle in it. Haddenham became famous for these walls, which were topped with broad red tiles, but we paid little attention and thumped ours, already rather the worse for wear, with cricket balls and footballs.

There were three garages on the car park, wooden and quite large. Two were let and one was used largely as a store by my parents, though in our early times at the Red Lion my father had an ancient Triumph Gloria pre-war tourer. He had passed no test but drove it anyway, encouraged by my grandfather, until eventually, while we were all out in it, miles from home, a big end went and we limped back, to an accompaniment of recrimination from the front seat and tired weepiness from the back. It never went again, and probably for the best, as my father was not a great driver but a considerable drinker.

This tour of the Red Lion and its surroundings is almost complete. The remaining feature was the garden. This was quite large, with shrubs and vegetables and currant bushes. In the early years my grandfather did the gardening and he taught us about weeding and what to leave alone. He also kept a few chickens in a sizeable wire enclosure with a coop, and we had eggs from them. I remember when the baby chicks arrived and we had them all squeaking and jostling each other on sheets of paper in the back living room. He hatched a few from our own hens, as well, and I can remember him in his brown overall showing us a little beak pushing its way out of the egg in his hand. I can only have been six or so and it did seem marvellous.

Church End had shops either side of the pub, so almost everything was bought from these neighbours. Cartwright's, the grocers, was on one side with its tins and bacon slicer and across Gibson Lane Percy Ing, the butcher. Just down from there in Station Road was a newsagent's, not far away there was a bakery, so you never had to go far. Most people did not have cars and if you wanted anything else it was the bus to Thame or Aylesbury. There were no supermarkets yet and people tended to shop more locally and more frequently.

So that was the Red Lion and its immediate surroundings. Across the road was the C of E Primary School which we were to attend – as brief a walk to school as anyone could expect – and then in the background the church itself. We were to live for the next 12 years around the bright bar. We arrived when I was five and left when I was 17, and in my mind's eye I can still walk very inch of the place, for better or worse. It went on being a pub for many years after we left, but in modern times it has become a private house and is now, no doubt, changed beyond all recognition, through the view across to the church, the pond and the green is really just as it always was

Chapter 3

THE SCHOOL
ACROSS THE ROAD

———⋯⋈⋯———

S t Mary's Church of England Primary School was a classic
redbrick village school, built in 1902. At the front end of the
roof was a brick bell frame, rung every morning as we all arrived.
The school had one big classroom cum hall, where the infants were
taught, and two other classrooms for the older age groups. There
were three teachers, one for each class, with the Head teaching
the top class. Outside was a playing area and the toilets. For the
boys this was simply an open-air urinal. There was a garden area
right at the back, which was for some time cultivated and later
given over to grass. Later on in my third year there, as we all
dug or weeded one spring afternoon, I was entrusted with a fork,
but managed carelessly to puncture the sandal of the boy next
to me, narrowly missing his toes but causing great alarm. There
cannot have been more than 60 or 70 pupils at St. Mary's and the
connection with the church across the green was very strong.

Just before our move we had acquired a dog, a small black woolly mongrel, bought, I think, as a sweetener for the move. He was called Mack, after a friendly Red Rover bus conductor we knew from the Waddesdon days. My brother and I loved him dearly, though he was never properly trained and had an outlaw existence around the village. Though tied up at home for much of the day, he was a terror when allowed to roam.

I have two abiding memories from the Infant's Class at St Mary's. One is of hearing our dog bark continually through the day, and hoping very much that the teacher was not going to mention it, which thinking back was very kind of them. The second was hearing a bible reading with a reference to publicans and sinners, and thinking that this was not very good news for my father.

I had not found it very easy to transfer, at five years old, from the Waddesdon school. There I had gradually settled and overcome the anxiety about being separated from my mother. Now it all came back, and home being just across the road seemed to make no difference at all. I must have been a solemn and preoccupied little boy at that stage. Though an early reader and quick learner I found all changes hard to cope with, but could not explain why I was so anxious. I was in dread, for example, of being pushed up early into the next class because of my progress, and at times refused to go to school.

My parents worried, I knew, and asked the advice of a children's doctor in the village. Dr Patterson rented one of our garages and was a kind white-haired old Scotsman who drove a small, low-slung and rather beautiful ancient Alvis. He talked to me, asked me to read something to him, and told my parents that they should not worry, and that I would come through it in time. It was the usual advice of the time, and not much more than 'give it time'. To some degree he was proved right, but for a long time yet I found the mornings especially difficult. I developed a ritual which lasted for ages. I had written down a little script of assurances which I had convinced myself must be asked of my mother in exactly the same way each school day before I left. Behind them lay a dread of more change and my mother not being there. It was a powerful and demanding ritual, and although it eventually subsided it must have lasted for at least another year.

I did eventually come to enjoy school very much. In the playground in the ice of winter we would make a huge slide, and if the cold days continued it would get wider and increasingly glassy, eventually becoming a small motorway of ice which went the length of the playground and could propel you at speed into the brick wall of the boys' toilets. Children's games were extremely gender specific – boys played a lot with Dinky lorries and created construction sites in the dust, and girls played house and hopscotch and skipping. We did have a wider range of organised activities – races, jumping, and of course country dancing. We must have been one of the last generations for whom this was practically part of the curriculum. It was generally very inclusive, and we did practise a lot, so that in the summer we would 'strip the willow' and all the rest of it to gramophone recordings in the hot sun. It became so hot once that the disc began to melt, and the music became slower and slower before growling to a halt.

For boys keen on football and cricket, our small school, with no playing field, was less good, and I never played any games on a proper pitch until I went to secondary school. Instead we used the village green. This was quite small, and surrounded by roads, though there was still not much traffic, so this was no great hazard. It all meant a rather constrained approach, and more often than not we played rounders – inclusive and coeducational, but dull if you dreamed of fast bowling and hitting the back of the net.

At Christmas and Easter we would put on plays on the church itself, helping to set up a stage. The costume was always the standard dressing-up box approach to Palestinian dress, with plenty of flowing robes. On several occasions I was, of course, the Innkeeper in nativity plays. One of my parents usually came, while the other stayed behind the bar at the Red Lion. The connection between the school and St Mary's church across the green was very close. Our assemblies often involved the Vicar and we all sang the well know hymns with gusto. I remember trying to hold on to a fart once during a hymn, trying to time it so that the sound would be covered by a loud part of the singing. I got the timing wrong so that it came out loud and reverberating between verses. Though I hoped not to be noticed and sang on hopefully, my hot red face must have given me away even apart from the noise. It was a fart to remember, but nobody said anything, so it must have been assumed to be accidental rather than malicious.

Our teaching was quite rigorous – plenty of chanting of tables and mental arithmetic, but nothing beyond arithmetic, so that geometry and algebra came as later unpleasant imponderables. We wrote stories and did endless 'comprehension' exercises. History and geography tended to be about facts and lists. I was already a very keen reader – anything from comics through to classics, which you could buy in the cheap Regency editions for two shillings from the local paper shop. I enjoyed books from the travelling school library and remember especially liking the William books, read warm under the quilt on an icy winter night.

Both my parents were very committed to education and my father particularly saw my 'getting to the Grammar' as the big goal. He worried too about the implications for my brother David, two years younger, who had been diagnosed with brittle bone disease. He had a bad leg with a bow in the shin and he had lost a good deal of school with various fractures and spells in hospital. My father bought for both of us a set of encyclopaedias – 'The Book of Knowledge', which came in eight volumes and was kept in pride of place in our upstairs sitting room. I endlessly dipped into it. The spines had strange titles – 'Boo-Cro' and 'Org-Ser' for example. It took me some time to work out that this just denoted the alphabet spread of each volume. I loved the pictures and colour plates – I remember tracing out a big diagram of the internal workings of a steam locomotive. In fact we all worked at general knowledge in those days. It was a big thing and there was plenty of kudos at school in scoring well.

We all knew our teachers very well. Mrs Bryant, the infant teacher, was an Anglo-Indian lady married to a blind musician called Bocker Bryant. I always assumed that Bocker was his first name, but have never come across it again since. He would occasionally play the piano for assemblies and special days and we would watch in awe as he gazed ahead with unseeing eyes while playing effortlessly on the school's upright piano. Mrs Ing, who taught the middle class, had the kindest voice I can remember from all my school days. Ing was a fairly common name in the area but I cannot think that she was related to Percy the butcher next door to us, whose loud voice and fierce manner made him a scary individual to us as children. I remember that most days ended with Mrs Ing reading to us, and I can still remember being spellbound by each daily episode of the Hobbit over one autumn term in the warm glow and fading light of the afternoon classroom.

Our head teacher changed during my time in Mrs Ing's class, when I must have been eight years old. Miss Bevan was Welsh, brightly dressed and with a big jowly face and bright red lipstick. She had been kind and helpful to me and my parents over my early difficulties, but the following year she left, never to return. She died, I think, of cancer, though in those days this was not the kind of subject discussed by anyone, let alone by parents to children. As with most things, though, my father leaked information wherever he went and to everyone he knew, so that of course I found out. Though this was knowledge without understanding, I knew instinctively to say nothing at school about it. There, nothing was said, though it was generally understood that she had died. This went unmarked, unmentioned and unexplained in line with the taboo and tradition of the time, but it now seems very strange to me that for a C of E school there was no kind of service or even special assembly. Nobody said anything to us, though she had been much loved and had taught there for a long time. In those days the general assumption with children was that they should not be expected to know about these things unless it was unavoidable, and that everyone would be best served if the normal routine of life continued as seamlessly as possible. This did not stop you feeling sad, but you had no way of asking questions or showing how you felt about it all.

For a time we had Mr Burnham as temporary head (kind, Ford Pop driving, with a small moustache and a smoker of post school cigarettes), and then Mr Warry arrived. A short, slim bespectacled man in his 30s, and married with two small children, Mr Warry was always immaculately dressed – usually a blazer and flannels man. He had huge energy and walked incredibly fast. He had taught previously in a town centre school in Reading, and St Mary's was his first headship. He had the impact of a whirlwind, which was exactly what he intended.

I found change as hard as ever, and did not like the new regime at first. My father was somewhat collusive in my resistance. My father, ever the anti-puritan, saw it as too clean-cut and crisp, with what seemed to be an excess of zeal about the church side of things. Though meant to be supportive I could see that this was neither fair nor helpful. Actually once I got used to it and settled down, I was soon able to bask in the glory of being one of the three 'cleverest' achievers, with Jacqueline and Janet in a top class of very mixed abilities, all of us aware that the dreaded 11 Plus would soon arrive

In Buckinghamshire this examination was used to send children in one of three directions – the Grammar School for the higher scorers who were reckoned worthy of an academic education; the Technical School, for those who scored a bit lower and were regarded as likely to benefit from schooling with a technical emphasis, and the all-through school at the other end of the village for everyone who scored lower still. This was actually the largest group, and children who had started there at five years old stayed until they left at 15. For the St Mary's children who were to go there it meant transferring to a place which was by no means a Secondary Modern, was quite small and had very few facilities.

The 11 Plus was highly competitive. It felt like that and cast a great shadow of expectation and potential doom for at least a year ahead. It was officially dressed up as a consistent way of assessing suitability for different types of education. In reality everyone concerned, pupils, parents, teachers and the village, saw it as a matter of success or failure, with the Grammar School as the real reward and the Technical School a kind of second prize. It was unfair and very divisive, taking no account of different development speed and largely dependent on teacher performance. At least there we were much luckier than most. However in a mixed ability class of 11 and 12-year-olds it was inevitable that more attention was paid to the 'better bets' in a kind of informal streaming, so that the process started earlier than most people realised. Parents behaved in different ways, of course – many believed in coaching for the tests, and my father bought a small book of crammer exercises, which I was expected to work at – and did, in a desultory way. Others took their children into private education, but most just accepted the decision.

After the 11 Plus exam life went on towards the end of the school year, but I contracted pneumonia during the summer term and missed most of it. I remember getting overheated playing football on the Red Lion car park and waking up early the next morning with a pain whenever I breathed in. My mother, who generally took a strong line about going to school, said that it would wear off if I went. It did not and by the time I got home at lunchtime I had really bad chest pain with every intake of breath, and was sent to bed. I stayed there for weeks. I was visited by the Vicar, who lent me a copy of *The Ascent of Everest*, which regrettably he never got back, and I only heard the 1958 World Cup, in Sweden, on the radio, which was a big disappointment. By the time I was getting better the 11 Plus results had come out and I had passed for the Grammar – it was all rather an anti-climax.

The reality of course was that the selective system cut right across our friendships in the village, so that as well as being unfair educationally the 11 Plus had a big impact socially. I remember going to a Christmas party held by Mr Warry after my first term at the new school, and going on about it to the friends who had not made it. Mr Warry quietly suggested to me that I should not go on too much about it, as other people were not getting these opportunities. I remember my ears going red with shame, but it was hardly my fault.

As I look back on the years between about eight and 12, I remember just being very fond of school, happy in it and settled. I can call up most elements of it even now – the cosy late afternoons of the Christmas terms with a party at the end of it, full of blancmange and jelly and iced cakes of all kinds. I remember the smell of tea-leaves and disinfectant used by Mrs Clarke the cleaner to sweep the place through every day, and those small school smells of bottled milk, ink and clean books. Life had begun to be much more unpredictable and at times very unpleasant at home in my final two years at St Mary's and school came to be something to rely on, and sometimes a refuge from the pub across the road.

Chapter 4

OUR LIFE IN THE PUB

Ｐeople who have grown up in pubs know that for children
they can mean a strange mixture of loneliness, freedom and
excitement. It may well mean that the sitting down together side
of family life is very limited. Your parents are there but busy
with other people, with whom they have to be prepared to be
friendly, welcoming and the providers of a willing ear, or at least
the appearance of willingness. There were times when I really
envied the calmer and more highly organised homes of friends,
which ran to a different and less public rhythm, and lacked the
pressure of evenings geared up to opening at six and lasting until
long after we had gone to bed. For my brother and me, there
were compensations. A degree of show time went with pub life,
as well as an ever-ready supply of lemonade and crisps. From
time to time there would be the added excitement of a special
visitor. I can remember Laurence Olivier and Vivien Leigh being
served with drinks in our front garden, on the red and cream
seats my father had placed there. They did not stay for long and
I remember left half their drinks, and apart from hearing his

unmistakeable voice this is the only thing I can remember about their visit.

On another occasion while visiting nearby friends, the actor Dennis Price came to the pub several times. I saw him from my view at the side door of the public bar. He stood very tall in his grand actor's overcoat with the locals gathered, holding court. My mother was recovering from pneumonia in the local nursing home and my father, now drinking more heavily, was trying to look after us and run the pub. On his second visit Dennis Price handed my father a huge bouquet of flowers for my mother – whom of course he had never met. A case, I suspect, of one grandiloquent piss artist spotting another.

From time to time we also had much more unassuming people who had something special to share, and my father, to his credit, usually made sure that we were introduced to them. One of these was Jimmy Dimmock, who had scored the winning goal for Spurs at the age of 20 in the 1923 FA Cup final. He carried the medal around with him and showed it to us. We had a number of Irish customers and I remember one of them bringing in a shinty stick to show us, and telling us about the game and about Ireland. The regulars could also be generous to us. There were football programmes on Saturday nights – often from three or four different clubs, and always one from Luton Town, then the nearest League club. As mentioned earlier we were sometimes allowed to hang around the daytime bar and customers could be good for ice cream money in the summer, and firework money from October onwards.

For all the developing family tensions, there were other attractions for us in pub life. Our birthday parties were usually popular. They usually took place after school in the empty public bar. Our guests could all play bar billiards and use the table football with its whirling handles and clunking goals. Since my mother could open the machines, we had all the games for free. You could even play darts, though David and I with plenty of after school experience could usually beat everyone easily. And again of course there was always plenty of pop.

David and I got plenty of practice at those pub games. By the time I was 11 I could play darts well, and have never subsequently had that kind of dead-eyed certainty which comes with plenty of practice. We had an endless challenge match, which went on month after month. Once the new game of bar billiards arrived the competition spread to include that as well. As we had access to the key of the machine, we could recycle the game as often as we wanted. Pool has completely taken over in modern times but for a time bar billiards almost rivalled darts in the pub games world. If you have ever played it you will remember the delightful jeopardy of trying to angle your last ball so accurately against the cushion that you scored maximum points while avoiding the front black peg, thus losing your whole match score. I can remember my brother David at eight years old becoming master of the cheeky 'in off'. Plenty of practice enabled him to make half the balls on the table disappear at once and rattle through the different holes on the table using a cue nearly as tall as he was.

We would often be left to get on with activities on our own in the afternoons. This was fine when you had friends to knock around with, and we certainly had the run of the village, or at least our end of it. At other times though it could feel dull and isolating. My father would be at work and my mother, faced with the morning and evening sessions in the bar and seven late nights a week on top of looking after the family, would tend to go to bed in the afternoons. In the early days my grandfather would sometimes take us off to Aylesbury, but he died in 1954, putting even more pressure onto my parents. It was after that, in the same year, that we got our first television, earlier than most people. We watched a great deal, perched in front of the huge Pye box with a 14-inch screen. At that stage with 1 BBC channel only you had often to put up with what was called 'the interlude' – usually some unexplained paint-drying theme which lasted until the next programme was due. The best remembered of these was known as 'The Potter's Wheel'.

We liked the early children's television and some of the programmes had a long subsequent career. Andy Pandy and his friends all lived in a basket. The Flowerpot Men had their strange voices and graceful Weed. Rag, Tag and Bobtail concerned the adventures of a hedgehog, a mouse and a rabbit, whose world, even by 1950s standards, moved along very slowly. After school there was each day a cowboy series, of which the most memorable were The Cisco Kid, a Mexican Robin Hood and his amusing sidekick, Pancho. The Lone Ranger, with a white horse and cloud of dust, had a more serious companion, Tonto. All this fuelled the main street game of boys then, which was Cowboys, not always against Indians. Everyone had cap guns and rifles and galloped along furiously whipping their hands against their thighs to get some speed going from their imaginary horses.

Because of the pub hours and our parents only checking us occasionally, we also saw things not really meant for children later on in the evening. I remember best a documentary series called 'They Come by Appointment'. This started with ominous music and was about people who had gone to see a consultant about a serious medical problem and then undergone some harrowing and life-threatening procedure. On the whole, though, most television, in those days, was very bland. There was no need for a watershed because what you could say or show was so circumscribed, and the hours of broadcasting were by modern standards very short. The arrival of ITV as a second channel lightened the mood a good deal and the jingles for early ads were sung endlessly by schoolchildren – 'the Esso sign means happy motoring', and 'You'll wonder where the yellow went (charming!) when you brush your teeth with Pepsodent'.

Many households, of course, still did not have TV, and more serious people often regarded getting access to TV as a sign of loosening moral fibre – and this sounded severe and chilly to those of us who loved the early game shows and comedies like The Army Game. Whatever the snootier part of the population thought, this was really, whether anyone liked it or not, the beginning of a mass common culture, which had never been possible to the same degree before. This was the start of the TV catch phrase, and there was really no way of escaping from it.

For the main weekend staples we would sometimes be joined by favoured customers – especially the Saturday evening football highlights programme. ITV had Sunday Night at the Palladium, which we usually watched, and which came in three sections – novelty acts, comedians and singers leading up to the big star final performance. If this was someone really big we always had visitors – I remember Johnny Ray and Guy Mitchell. My mother was a big fan of both. I remember her having nights out, rare for her, to see them at the New Theatre in Oxford.

We did other things as well, of course. I always read a lot, and we always had comics. In the early years this was the relatively high-minded Hulton Press *Swift* and *Eagle*, with Dan Dare and co, but I moved on to the comics like *Hotspur* and *Wizard* with long stories in small print, and a great emphasis on impossible wartime heroics. The war, just a decade or so on from 1945, remained a strong focus in daily life. Most parents and most of the pub customers had taken part in some way. It had often shaped their lives and attitudes and continued to be a major theme of public bar debate, so not surprisingly novels, films and comics all reflected British heroism and German brutality. Children growing up in the 50s were handed down an extraordinarily stereotypical set of ideas about Germany and Germans of the 'Gott in Himmel Die Engländer' variety, which took most of us a long time to escape from, and sadly some never have! Interestingly, and depressingly, it was accompanied by a casually anti-Semitic tradition which also persisted in everyday English life.

For a long time we had a train set upstairs in the big sitting room which we added to with bits of pocket money. I was also keen on the cheap plastic aeroplane kits which Airfix introduced. They were so cheap that you could buy a new one most weeks from Baker's the toyshop in Aylesbury. They reflected the war preoccupation in that most were 1939-45 fighters and bombers. I would string them with cotton in impressive diving positions from the ceiling in our bedroom. Soon afterwards I started trying to paint them with the enamel colours which had just come in. This was harder and required more patience, but could look really good if you got it right. The smell of plastic cement and Humbrol was literally a heady mix, as you sat there, tongue hanging out in concentration and tried to keep each colour in the right place.

Our back living room had a Utility dining table. It had a solid wood block appearance, and a dark rather scratched veneer. For most of my childhood when there were family meals together this is where we had them. We usually had a cooked breakfast, and came home across the road from school at dinner-time to a hot meal as well. My mother was a good cook and very particular about this. We had an evening meal early, before my father came home, and his food was usually reheated on a plate. If he didn't want all of it, you sometimes got some of this as well. My mother always believed in feeding us up, and that proper meals should have meat and gravy. She was a traditional cook – great at pies, stew and dumplings and all the rest, but we seldom saw much salad. This regime, and easy access to lemonade and crisps, meant that I became a rather tubby child. The St Mary's school portraits of the time make this all too clear, with my round face, short haircut and gappy smile. David, for all his having to put up with a bad leg, had the same diet but managed to avoid getting fat – he would probably say that this was because I made sure I got hold of most of the food!

The business of the pub went on in its routine but often entertaining way. The draymen from the brewery would roll huge barrels on and off their wagon and throw them about with deceptive ease. The weekly tobacco delivery included all sorts of strange products. There was twist tobacco, for example, a strange plaited shape in silver foil, and Digger Shag, a rolling tobacco made by Players with the picture of a grizzled prospector in a strange hat on the packet. It was fascinating to rummage in the big cardboard box and count up the different types of cigarettes – Players, Kensitas and Turf, which had a picture of a flying horse on the packet. There was no sense at all then of tobacco being harmful, and my father was unusual in never having smoked. My mother was more typical. Coming from a large working class family she had smoked since she was 14 or 15, and all her life stuck to un-tipped Players. In the end smoking played a big part in killing her.

The tobacco box always included small round silver boxes of snuff. My parents let us use one of those boxes if we were bunged up with a cold, and we would sit there, me and the Brittle Bone Kid with clear heads and brown handkerchiefs as we sniffed and sneezed the stuff for all we were worth. It was years later before I realised that this was actually powdered tobacco.

We were usually off to bed at sensible times, but on light spring and summer evenings we would lean out of the window and listen to the talk of people below outside the pub. Lying in bed we could hear the usual sounds from the bars downstairs – a subdued clank and chink of glasses, and the jingle of cash in and out of the till. Behind those sounds, the rise and fall of public bar conversation went on. We were used to it and it did not keep us awake. On high days and holidays, though, my father would play the piano and everyone would sing – there was usually an Irish tenor who would take the solos and would always sing 'Kathleen' with huge poignancy and feeling. There was sometimes a whistler. In those days, when Ronnie Ronalde was still famous, everyone knew 'If I were a blackbird'. So we heard all those songs and the choruses which everyone knew to join in with. Many of them were old music hall tunes and none of them current. Many years later I realised that I could still belt out all the words as if they had gone forever into my brain by osmosis through the kippered ceiling of the bar.

Earlier in those bright evenings we had often played cricket or football in the pub car park, on and on until the light faded and you could no longer see the tiny rubber ball we used. Often we had gone down late to the station to watch the trains thunder through to Paddington one-way and Birmingham or exotic sounding Birkenhead in the other. There was always more to train spotting than collecting numbers and names. The station was virtually our second home, and there was something magical especially in the evenings. You could look north after the ringing of signal bells, and then the big signal would clank upwards. In the distance you could hear a gathering noise and then see a big King or Castle rocking over the crossing half a mile above the station. It would roar past and then 10 seconds or so later, as the train faded towards Risborough, there would be a silence like no other before the evening birdsong returned. In the dusk a little later, when other trains came past, you would see a glow from the firebox and the shadow of the crew. Later, and left with a kind of yearning for faraway places and who knew what, we would head for home and the lights of the pub. Much later, in bed, in the silent darkness you listened to the so slow clank and knock of a goods train in the night.

For all this, over time and for reasons which may be becoming clear, family life became more tense and stressful. My father's drinking and my mother's exhaustion were less easily contained within the family, and conditions at home deteriorated. There continued to be a family sit-down dinner on Sundays after morning closing, and as time went by this often became the most anxious time of the whole week. My father could be argumentative, but it usually took time for rows to develop. As any children who have been through these situations know, there are often a few minutes at the beginning of a bad row when you cling onto the hope that it will be fine this time and will not develop but recede. You pray that this time, just for once, it will stop quickly and they will be nice to each other. And this never happens. However much you try to stop them rowing, it never happens. A wrong word is said, or an earlier grievance, parked by the need to be nice to the customers, resurfaces. Soon, the row is established, and within a few minutes it has a life of its own. There is then the endless circular replaying of recrimination and threat, accusation and mockery, with nothing new said and nothing new heard, so that it all has a wearisome and scripted quality.

As children we picked up the tension, and I can remember so well the misery of wanting it to stop so desperately that your mouth went dry and your stomach tied itself in knots. I would pick up the tension and as the older child I would try to say things to make them stop, but if you tried to intervene, perhaps trying to calm my father by ingratiation, or tried to change the subject, you found yet again that the juggernaut of the Sunday row was not for turning. If you took sides, as I often did, to try and defend my mother, then you ran the risk of a mouthful yourself. Sometimes there was physical hitting but more typically the pain was inflicted by the slights and taunts which my father reverted to when half cut. The fact that these arguments did not usually involve physical violence in no way diminishes their significance, or the way that they stuck painfully in your memory for a very long time afterwards, and through to later life. In the end they would just subside, often into Sunday afternoon snoring, but they had by then soiled the day in a way which made you glum and wretched.

Chapter 5

MY GRANDFATHER'S DEATH

—◁✕▷—

I was eight years old when my grandfather died. My brother David had just started school, so it happened in his first term, in late autumn. It was my first direct experience of death. I could just remember being taken to my grandmother's grave in the cemetery at Aylesbury when I was four years old, or thereabouts, and the smell of flowers on a damp day. I had been told that Granny was in the sky and like any child I would look to see, but of course saw only the clouds.

Grampy, as we called him, had his stroke while we were having tea in the back living room. It was late afternoon, and a long time before my father would come home from work on the bus. He sat in the red armchair, as he always did, with his head against the linen cover. He was eating cheese with tomatoes, and as always plenty of salt with them. He was talking with my mother, but all I can recall was the moment when the talking stopped, I think. A second before everything was normal, and then in an instant he had changed. One arm was hanging down by the side of the chair, and his eyes stared ahead. His head was at an angle, and his mouth sagged at one side. He had flecks of white on his lips. I was scared to the pit of my stomach.

David and I were bustled outside 'to play' and after that things must have happened very quickly. My grandfather, short and stout, must have been hard to move, and I do not know what control he had left, but my mother must have managed somehow to get him upstairs We had no phone and the doctor was at the far end of the village, so she must have used the phone at Cartwright's, the grocer's next door, to call him and tell my father. I do not know why, but there was no ambulance with ringing bells. Coming back into the house, once the doctor's car had arrived, I remember there being a great deal of clattering up and down the stairs and the creaking of the landing to and from my grandfather's bedroom.

My father came home and went straight upstairs. Time seemed to go very slowly. No one said anything to us, and although my mother tried her best to be reassuring we knew from her face that she was very worried about whatever was going on upstairs.

I went outside again, on my own this time, and walked round and around the car park as the dusk fell. Lights began to come on in houses down the lane and in the pub. I was still very scared, but it was easier to be outside than in the strange unaccustomed tension of the atmosphere inside. I had for the first time that lonely feeling that something very bad indeed was happening, but not knowing exactly what it was, what would happen next, or what I should do. People were walking past on their way home from work. To me it seemed incredible and wrong that ordinary life was going on as normal when something huge and strange was happening to us. I could not understand it. I really could not understand how that could happen.

I always remembered those feelings and came to understand eventually that they were quite normal for children faced with unexplained family disasters beyond their control. It has always seemed extraordinary to me, though, that not only was there no issue of taking my grandfather away to hospital, but that my parents opened the pub that evening. It was never discussed afterwards and must have been either a sense of obligation or a way of hanging on to normality – who knows? More than 60 years have passed, and both attitudes and practice have changed. The doctor perhaps decided that, since there was no question of survival, the best course was to allow Victor to die at home rather than in a hospital bed or on his way to one. As to the pub opening, I suppose my parents felt that the brewery expected this and that they must do it . We make very different assumptions these days about both our own actions and the expectations we have of others. It was normal then to keep your feelings under control, at least publicly, and carry on regardless. Death without benefit of A and E, and dying at home, were not unusual. Today we all have massively different expectations about illness, treatment and indeed age. My grandfather was only 68, but that was actually just above the average age in Britain for male deaths in 1955.

That evening went on longer than expected for me. My brother was taken up to bed as normal, but I remained there in the back room watching TV and hearing the comings and goings through the hall, from the bar, and up and down the stairs, as my grandfather lay in the bedroom at the back of the pub over the cellar.

I heard things I was not supposed to. My Uncle Francis arrived and I heard my mother's angry words thrown at him as he went up the stairs: 'Too late. You're too late – you never bothered before and now it's too late'.

I knew perfectly well that my mother had carried most of the burden of looking after the old man. For all his Edwardian jauntiness to the outside world, at home he could be grumpy and fault finding. I realised some years later how much the lack of help or even contact from Francis had been an issue for her, and one which my father had never addressed. They were cruel words, nonetheless, and like most shocking outbursts had come from a well of tiredness and frustration. Though Francis never mentioned it again, those words were never really forgotten or forgiven. The architecture of most family histories is like a rambling Gothic house of many rooms, and those words stayed on in ours as a kind of everlasting and ugly gargoyle. There was reference to them in arguments between my parents for many years – usually by my father. My uncle had never really had regular contact with us, and this did not change. If he did come, there was always an awkward coolness between him and my mother.

So, my grandfather, horse expert, veteran of the Camel Corps, and erstwhile publican, died that evening in his own bed. He had been with us first at Waddesdon and then the Red Lion for four years, and survived my grandmother for not much longer. I cannot remember whether I slept well or not that night. I was told the next day that he had died, and we were kept off school. My father and mother did not, or could not, explain what all this meant, and while they must have been upset, there were no tears in front of us.

My father must have known that I was anxious, given my history of 'nerves', and from time to time I was described as having 'too much imagination', as if this was a generally rather unhealthy state. So when I asked where my grandfather was, my father tried to reassure me. I was not to worry because 'Grampy is in the church'. I had been in the church plenty of times and knew it quite well. Where would they have put him? The following evening I looked over the green to the church in the moonlight and wondered. Was he in the vestry where the bell ropes were? Or on the pews? I knew from school about Jesus and Nazareth, and the hymn we used to sing at the end of a school day about 'shadows of the evening.' Was that where he was now, in the shadows of the evening in church? For all the surfeit of imagination I was supposed to have, I found it hard to think how this might be, and so, while I really wanted to believe what my father said, the fact is that I didn't. I suppose he must have been with the local undertaker, Frank Wilson, one of the lounge bar customers, but I knew, with the certainty of an eight-year-old, that he was still in his room at the back of the pub above the cellar.

Both the insight of children and their capacity for anxiety was certainly underestimated in those days, and my parents were not alone in failing to see that false reassurance tends to fuel fear rather than alleviate it. My parents certainly wanted to spare me, I suppose, and may not have felt able to explain what was going on, but they would have done better to try. It is said very often that now most people are so distanced from the practicalities and details of death that it is has become a taboo subject. For all that it may have been closer to everyday life in those days, I am not sure it was actually very much different then. There was a general assumption that children should be shielded and protected from these things, with the result that, like me, they still worried but had no reliable information which they could trust.

For the next few days we did not go to school, although the pub still opened and closed in its usual routine. There was a strange and curiously peaceful atmosphere, but I still thought that my grandfather was in his room, and going to the bathroom upstairs meant going past that door. I put off going, and when I had to I rushed in and out again, trying to avoid even glancing at the door for fear that it might somehow open to reveal him lying there. I did not feel able to tell David about this fear or my suspicions about the room. I did not want to scare him, so I did not dare say anything and kept my feelings wrapped up inside.

A few days later the relatives arrived for the funeral. They included the likes of Aunt Nell from my grandmother's side of the family in Oxfordshire. We had hardly ever seen her before, and she was an almost legendary figure. She seemed very ancient, though she lived on for many years after that, and certainly reached her 90s. Aunt Win, being as proper about everything as usual, was there with Uncle Moss. They all crowded up the stairs, and I followed behind without being noticed, As I got to the top someone realised that I was there, and a kindly relative gently ushered me back down the stairs, but not before I got a glimpse of the big long black box, bright with silver fittings, which seemed to fill the whole of my grandfather's' room. So, I thought, I had been right to worry. He had been there all along, and that big box must somehow have been taken up there on the quiet.

We were not taken to the funeral, and I do not remember a reception afterwards, so this must have taken place somewhere in Aylesbury. We went to the cemetery but much later. He had been buried next to my grandmother, but no one suggested that they were both now in the sky.

I do not remember missing my grandfather particularly. He had seemed to me as a child rather a distant and stern figure in some ways, and he seemed closer to my brother David. This may have been because of his bad leg, but also, I think, because David was less awkward and more outgoing. Selfishly wrapped up in my own feelings, I never paid much attention to David's loss of his ally, or the confusion and pain he may have felt. To Grampy I may have seemed an irritating and oversensitive child, whose parents were over-attentive and made too much fuss. I was older before I realised the implications of my grandfather's death for my father and mother. The whole pub project had assumed his presence, at least for longer than two short years. My parents were still only in their 30s, and with two children they now faced running everything on their own, with my father still keeping on a full-time job. It was also clear later on that my father, prone to heavy binge drinking and volatile emotionally, had now lost an important restraining hand only four years after losing his beloved mother – the granny we had hardly known.

We both received something to remember Grampy. David received his pocket watch, though it was kept for him until he was older. It had always fascinated him, but I do not know whether he still has it, or whether he used it ever. I received his old black fountain pen, and this too was only given to me later when I was seen to be ready for it. I had it later on at Boarding School, but the barrel broke. I kept the pieces for years as it seemed wrong to throw them away, but that is what must have happened in the end.

This was not the only legacy. For years afterwards I had a real fear of that room with the brown door and Bakelite handle next to the bathroom. To me it seemed very likely to be haunted. I was generally scared of the dark anyway, but this was a more specific and persisting fear. For a long time the room was left empty with the door shut. I dreaded my parent's telling me to sleep in there. In fact they put David in there for a time and he did not seem to have the same troubled thoughts. I marvelled at his courage in coping with this, but did not tell him so for fear of rocking the boat and then being told that it was my turn.

Later on and in the safety of daytime, I dared on a few occasions to explore the room, always with one eye on the door just in case. The only signs of my grandfather were his little Masonic case, which was locked, and a mysterious white Bakelite tub with a black lid, which unscrewed to reveal hundreds of fragments of soap saved up in the frugal Edwardian way, just as Aunt Win saved newspaper for spills to light the fire.

I had dreams as well. There was an occasional recurring nightmare. It lasted until my later teenage years and is the only childhood dream I can now remember. It was always the same. I am walking alone in moonlight along the upstairs landing towards the bathroom door. A yellow light appears under the door of my grandfather's room and the door very slowly begins to open of its own accord, I rush to the stairs but make no progress, however hard I try to run. I dare not look back and at the last moment I am able in desperation to jump off the top stair into the darkness below.

My grandfather Victor was born in 1887, and was already 13 years old when Victoria died. He was in service soon afterwards. By the time of the First World War he was in his late 20s, and had looked after horses for great families in town and country during the long summer of Edwardian England. He had an exotic time with the Camel Corps in the heat of Mesopotamia and came home to marry a farmer's daughter and have two sons of his own. He ran business after business and while nothing seemed to last for very long his version of the licensed trade was enough to help his boys make a start in life. He did not live long enough for me to know him really well, and I would love to have his heard his tales at first hand. His legacy for me amounted to no more than my father's second-hand stories, an old fountain pen, those childhood terrors, and a very persistent bad dream which lasted until I was almost grown up.

Chapter 6

AROUND THE VILLAGE AND BEYOND

If I had been a shy and unconfident child in my early years at St
Mary's, then I became much more sure of myself as time went
by. Ours was a large village to roam around in. As well as the
lanes with their battered wychert walls, we also had fields and
woods, and of course the local station with its friendly porter.
Children were generally left to their own devices in the 1950s.
This is more than misty nostalgia and a selective remembering
of sunny days, and suggests a number of assumptions then made
by parents and children alike, about play, risk and responsibility.
Although having television at home was now beginning to be
common and there were a few more cars, the life of a village like
ours, certainly from a child's eye view, had a good deal which was
unchanged from the 1930s. When you read about William and
the Outlaws, walking along dusty roads and getting into scrapes,
you could still identify their village as pretty similar to your
own. We might be singing the early ITV jingles about the Esso

sign meaning happy motoring and Double Diamond working wonders, but we were also climbing trees, experimenting with small fires, quietly trespassing, and generally messing about.

It is assumed by some people nowadays that this was all possible because adults took a more collective responsibility for children then, but it probably had more to do with a more casual and less informed attitude to risk. However much our parents fussed over us at home they shared this view of a predominantly benign environment. There were certainly busybodies who might tell tales to your parents, especially about apple scrumping or ploughing through gardens to retrieve balls without asking, but on the whole, outside school hours, adults just left you to it. We were told not to talk to strangers, but strangers were scarce, and probably did not want to speak to us anyway, or so it seemed. Parents always seemed to regard traffic, the countryside and our wanderings dawn to dusk as having very low risk. There was no sense that there might be men around who contemplated unspeakable acts, and such things were simply not talked about. We know now, of course, that they were there all along and that the chief risks were from the adults closest to you. That must have been as true of our village as anywhere else, but the very idea would have been beyond belief then.

There were more obvious hazards, of course. All children then were expected to plough gradually through all the familiar ailments, now largely avoided through vaccination. We all got mumps, chickenpox, measles, whooping cough eventually, and all the miseries of itching and aching which came with them.

The great fear for most parents was that a child should get polio. It was the great scourge of the early to mid-1950s, and the epidemic of 1956 led to a surge of panic. Not long afterwards this was only resolved by the introduction of the Salk vaccine, which we all trooped into the clinic at Pebble Lane in Aylesbury to be given.

Our big village had two ends, and you pretty much kept yourself to your end. Philip, John, Robert, Alan and the others knocking around in a loose knit gang were from the 'Bottom End', where our school was. We generally kept away from the 'Top End'. This was where the other, bigger school was, together with the main village playing fields, but we did not use them, as this was 'Top End' territory. It was also where most of the village's council housing was, and in those very class-conscious times the Top End was seen as rough. In fact many of my parents' customers walked down the village to make the Red Lion their local and we knew them quite well, so our juvenile snobbishness, rather reinforced by my father, was certainly misplaced. It was all reinforced by the schools – very few Top Enders came to St Mary's C of E. All of this meant that the children at both ends kept to their territories, and, and although there were no pitched battles there was not much crossover or contact.

One of the few places where Top and Bottom End boys met each other was in the Wolf Cubs. I joined later than most of my friends, mainly because they were in it and I sensed that I was missing out. John, whose family owned the Beehive Stores just along the road, and Philip, who lived in Station Road, were already old hands. They had plenty of badges and experience, and took me along. Once I had my dark green jersey, the cap and a purple and green kerchief I began to feel part of it. My mother sewed on the various insignia. I only learned about sewing much later and never did get the badge.

During my first year in 1957, when I was nine, we went to the Jubilee Jamboree at Sutton Coldfield in August. Special stamps had been issued to mark this 50th anniversary of scouting. On the day our coach was very late and it took hours to get there, but it was exciting and impressive. We met scouts from all over the world. It was like an atlas come to life. I was especially impressed with meeting scouts from Fiji who had made an amazing structure with poles and ropes. At school we had gone to London to visit the Commonwealth Institute, but this had seemed rather dull. Now I had a first real experience of the wide world.

Though I had not joined for the treat, and began to learn the basic knots and skills, I never really persevered with the cubs or scouts once I had started at Grammar School, which was a real shame. I never did get any badges. In reality things soon began to go badly wrong at home and soon afterwards we were sent off to boarding school, where cubs and scouts did not feature as an option.

In my primary school years of knocking around the village the members of our group did not change much. Some did leave the village, and occasionally this was because their families migrated. I remember the Coggins family and their boys – Terry, who was my age, and his younger brother Ralph. They lived down Gibson Lane and I knew their parents and their granddad. He was left behind once they moved to Canada. It all seemed to happen very suddenly, and I remember their cleaning out the house and getting rid of absolutely everything but their suitcases before they went to start a new life. Many people were doing that in those years.

Later on, after my father had become ill and people were gossiping about us, I thought the idea of Australia and a new start was very exciting – based, it has to be said, on pictures from Lyons tea cards (1959 again) which I was collecting and which made all of it, jacaranda to sheep shearing, look wonderful. I mentioned it to my mother, but she was too busy coping with a tough daily grind to give my 'sweep it all away' solution much attention, so we never did become the assisted migrants or £10 Poms that I had hoped we would, but plenty of people did.

In the summers of the 1950s many families did not go away on holiday, and we never did. This may have been for financial reasons, but was mainly to do with being tied to the endless routine of the pub. Seaside trips were often made on a day-long coach excursion. For people from landlocked Buckinghamshire those trips were very popular, and we went on one or two every year. They were usually provided by a local firm, Walls Coaches, which picked up from various villages at the very early start of a long day. If the weather was good you were lucky, and if not you had to make the best of it as it was a one-shot experience. I wrote a poem about it some years ago and this still sums up my main memories of those trips. 'Coachwork by Duple' was the message on the cigarette stubber attached to each seat. It took me ages as a child to work out that coachwork was the seats and fittings and Duple was just the name of the firm.

We'll have some days out and not go away

So up at six and cold, there in the dawn
To start the coach trip to the Sunday Sea.
Avoid the hanky with the dab of spit
And put off shaming fears of being sick –
Someone was always sick by half past ten
The cig smoke and the engine fumes to blame
The peeling of an orange the last straw
Though this was good fun if it wasn't you.
And then at last the seaside. Four whole hours
Of sand and chips and sand and wind and sand.
By some old law of bus trip time and tide
The sea was always out and far away
Saving itself it seemed for paying guests
As if it owned a boarding house itself.
Then in the sunset trail back to the bus,
The mothers bearing brick red arms and bags
The fathers, bright on beer at two now tired,
The kids still screaming lemonade and chips.
Then rolling home, some merry and some sad
Not getting back until the dark had come.
That was a day trip to the somewhere sea
When I was little and my father said
'We'll have some days out and not go away'.

There were other village events through the year, which children looked forward to, and they were our main calendar markers. The two I remember best were both in the autumn. First came Haddenham Feast, in September, when the fair came to the village. In those days it all took place on the Green and its borders, including the edge of the pond by the church. We knew the day the fair would arrive, travelling on from Thame Show not far away. When that day came children would wait on the walls outside the grocer's, next to our pub, to watch the bright lorries and their trailers, the caravans and generators, come into sight along Station Road and growl slowly up the hill past our school towards the Green and an appointed place. The whole business of unloading and assembling was riveting to us, and we would watch for hours.

The fair meant several nights of great business for the pub, which was the nearest to the action and used also by the show people, including the elderly Mr Pettigrove, who was always very friendly towards my father. He was the Fair's presiding elder and had a big traditional roundabout, with a message round the top which proclaimed 'Pettigrove's golden galloping horses, pride of the 20th Century.' The man himself, portly and squinting through his spectacles, always wore a dark suit with a collarless shirt and watch chain, topped by a weathered trilby hat. I saw him in the bar once, taking his money from his pocket – a huge wad of notes, since the Fair dealt only in cash.

We went at least once every year and always did the dodgems and bumper cars, getting increasingly confident and aggressive in our driving year on year. You paid your shilling to the young man who jumped onto the back of your car and somehow glided round without getting bumped. We always went on Pettigrove's gallopers too. As well as the horses there were ornately painted great dragon boats and as you came round each time you passed the ornamented clashing organ belting out the music, surrounded by chipped cherubs and glass mirrors – a world of red and gold and clashing mechanical cymbals.

Much later on and into my teens I became old enough to help behind the bar, washing glasses, and had the feeling that we were part of the show ourselves. On those nights, despite all the problems which had developed by then, we all pulled together in the heat and smoke of the packed bar, and that was a good and warm feeling. I can still remember the noise and exhilaration of it all. At the end of the feast, after the church service on the dodgems, the fish and chips and the whole village out in the evening together, everything was packed up and they were off to the next place. The show folk usually kept themselves to themselves. The people who lived in a big maroon caravan which stayed outside the school usually sent their kids to ask us for water and we often helped them with it. Theirs seemed an exotic life, but not one which they wanted to tell us much about.

Bonfire Night followed not far behind, though the gap seemed longer to us as children. We started to look forward to it soon after the Fair had gone. Over the weeks David and I would spend all our pocket money on fireworks. Any extra scrounged from parents or sympathetic pub customers helped us get together a good collection, a few at a time. They were sold then much more widely. All our local shops stocked them and would sell them to us as children quite willingly. We kept them uncovered on the big dining table in the upstairs sitting room, counting and fondling them each time we made a new addition – rockets, Roman candles, golden rain, Vesuvius and all the rest. In the run up to Bonfire Night, with other village boys, we let off bangers and squibs to great effect around the village, to the annoyance of some, but happily tolerated by most people.

Occasionally, when the fireworks were handled too much, small amounts of powder would escape. I remember being fascinated by the grey dust and what I might do with it. I looked it up in the Book Of Knowledge, so I understood the theory, but

I wanted to follow this up with a practical experiment, so I went one stage further and placed the insides of a banger round the metal edge of the water butt near the pub's back door. I threw a lit match which went out, tried that again, and then just stood over it and dropped a match onto it. The whoof of smoke and flame singed my eyebrows, but nothing else happened, so I was very lucky.

We were friends, around that time, with a boy called David Parker, who lived round the corner. He had a big brother who showed us how to make bangers explode in their water barrel with entertaining depth charge results.

When Guy Fawkes Night eventually arrived, there were really two celebrations. The first was when we eventually persuaded our father to set off our fireworks. This was usually in the pub car park, but sometimes in the garden. My father had usually been drinking by this stage, so he would take a carelessly cavalier approach to any kind of instructions provided on the firework. He would seldom retire immediately having lit the blue touch paper, and would always return to a firework which seemed to have gone out. The consequences were often very entertaining but sometimes worrying too. He would heroically hold a Roman Candle in each hand and stand there in a pose while coloured balls of fire shot round him and into the smoky air. My mother often made parkin, which we liked very much, but she left the fireworks to the old man.

The second celebration was the lighting of the huge bonfire on the Green, which had been put together over several weeks, mainly by the young men of the village. It was an amazing sight for us as children, and you could hear the crackling and see the flames from a long way off. Most of the village came, and again it would make for a good night at the pub. These days there would no doubt be a committee, grants and sponsorship. It would certainly not be allowed to happen on the Green now, but then it just happened by unwritten tradition year on year.

We always worried about our dog on 5th November. The lawless Mack would always manage to escape and continued his outlaw existence around the fire. Sometimes people would tell us that he was running around with a firework in his mouth and we were scared that he would be hurt, but somehow he always came back none the worse for wear, so my father and he shared the same luck, at least with fireworks.

Apart from classroom contact and parties, we did not have much to do with girls, and no conscious awareness of sexuality or the yet-to-come exciting mystery of the difference. As a group of village boys we were not always well behaved. There were rivalries, and I am still ashamed even now when I think of the way a few others and I spent a period tormenting young Harry Makepeace. We were all about 10 years old. Harry came from a large family, and his dad was a ganger on the railway. He was a quiet boy, interested in country things and not very outgoing. It was a case of bullying the outsider, and since he would not fight back we had power over him, and thought ourselves smarter. I do not think we hit him, but we chased him and he fled. This happened quite often for a time, and he found himself more than once up a tree and surrounded until we decided to let him be. One of the really unfair things about this was that all of us knew his brothers and sisters and had been invited to birthday parties at his house up by the old station, now long gone. The truth is that we enjoyed a vindictive pleasure at his expense, but Harry said nothing, or if he did he was probably told to face up to it. That was often the advice given in those days, and sadly still is sometimes. I am still ashamed when I think of it.

We often went to the local fishing place called Pond Close, or 'Ponnee' as the 'little ol' boys' called it. This term was used by everyone in the Bucks dialect to describe almost anybody else – as in 'All they little ol'boys loike ter toddle off down Ponnee for a bit o' fishin.' 'Toddling off' was another old Bucks expression simply meaning to go off somewhere. Some of the regular customers were anglers at Ponnee, and spent hours catching roach and tench. Although there was said to be a big pike in the inner depths, I cannot remember anyone catching it. My father decided at one stage to try his hand at fishing and acquired a rod and tackle, but he was surprisingly reluctant to handle the one dark green tench I remember him pulling out. He fiddled around using his handkerchief and eventually let it back into the water. His fishing life did not go any further, so no skills were ever passed on to us.

Ponnee with your friends was a great place for tree climbing and pond dipping, but it had a wild magic about it as well. When I was just a little older I remember once coming back alone from Pond Close along the path back to the village in the late dusk of a spring evening. On either side the hedges were full of pink and white roses, and all around on the breeze you could hear the last birdsong of the day. I looked up at the moon and experienced a kind of aching longing, with an almost sexual excitement at the thought of all that might lie ahead, whatever it was going to be.

Chapter 7

A FEW CRUSTED CHARACTERS

Growing up in a village pub inevitably meant a degree of being on show. As well as your parents, teachers and friends, you also lived in view of the Red Lion regulars. There were daytime and night time regulars. Some managed to be both. The whole essence of being a regular was that your pub time, what you drank and where you stood or sat all had a set pattern and rhythm. For the longest serving, this had the relentlessness of tidal flow or the orbit of a small planet.

We were of course not supposed to be in the bars when the pub was open. However, at school lunch times, weekend mornings and early evenings the atmosphere was more informal, so that, providing we were reasonably quiet about it, the rule was not enforced very firmly, and we were often in the public bar. David and I would hear the stories, the moaning, the bragging and the jokes as the regulars drank their pints, smoked and took their time about it. Almost all were older men, with enough time available for darts and dominoes. They would sometimes let us play and David, even from the age of six or so, was especially favoured as an early evening crib dominoes player of precocious talent, sitting in the public bar like a small trusted apprentice among the flat caps and pints and moving his matchsticks along the board with the best of them. Some of these old boys were there so regularly that they became woven into the pattern of our childhood.

I do not remember being exposed to any serious or obvious drunkenness at those times. There was generally less tolerance then of bad language, and I do not think that this was simply at the times when we were around. Certainly I have no memory of much swearing beyond a few bloodies and buggers. I do remember as a nine–year-old picking up the 'f' word from somewhere, but not, I think the pub. It represented then, though I did not know it, the nuclear option among swear words. Thinking it was just mildly colourful, I once used it in front of my father. I know that I pronounced it 'focking', so there may have been a forgotten Irish source, though I cannot think who that might have been. My father shouted at me to ask where I had got this filth from, and slapped me round the face so hard that I was more shocked than hurt, as he never normally hit us.

Whenever I think back to the long-serving regulars I always recall Topper first. I do not know the origin of his nickname, or what his real name was. He was just always Topper Hopkins. He seemed to me from the age of five until we left the pub when I was 17 always to have been old. He was the porter at the station about half a mile away down the road. Haddenham Station, on the line between Paddington and Birmingham, had no more than half a dozen stopping trains a day, slowly plying between Princes Risborough one way and Banbury in the other direction. Topper would time the pub visits between trains. He came down the hill and along to us on an old bicycle with a leather bag over the cross bar for empties. He would always greet my father in the old

Bucks way – 'Ow be ahn John?' A pint or so later and he would be back on the bike to the station. I never saw him hurry, and I never saw him cross.

Topper never wore a railway cap and his uniform was the usual railway jacket, waistcoat and baggy trousers. He wore these whatever the weather, and when, much later in the early 60s, British Rail issued new-style uniforms, his looked much the same as the old one after very few days. Topper was short and slightly bent over, with a face rather like a wizened Mr Punch. He usually had a sliver of fag on his lip. We spent a good deal of time down at the station, so were often able to see him in action. He would occasionally actually have to porter luggage. With the kind of grander old lady who tended to ask for this service, his approach was to lace his slow efforts with much forelock tugging and madaming. This usually produced a gratuity from the client and a sly wink at us from Topper. Years later, after we had gone away to school, we always tried to come home by train, and Topper would always be there when we got back to Haddenham Station. He was always the first person we saw back in the village.

He was once in the national papers because his son, Frank, had been appointed stationmaster and they were supposed to be a unique father and son team – a kind of inverted seniority. It seems strange now that a station like that should have had, at that time, a porter, station master and signalmen. Many of the local boys frequented the station. There were echoing empty waiting rooms to explore on the two long platforms, and the exciting rush of through trains every few minutes, which rattled the windows as they roared through. Above all there was the chance to roam around without anybody bothering you. Topper was very tolerant. He would sit in the weighbridge building in the station yard in front of a warm stove, and around him there would often be a kind of informal youth club. Beeching shut down more than the station when the cuts came.

Several of our regulars were our local shopkeepers. In our early years at the pub the butcher just across the lane was the one we saw most of. His name was Charlie Ing, mentioned earlier, but everyone knew him as 'Buckle', probably because of his big leather belt, but no one really knew for sure. He was a fierce-looking man, usually in a white coat and bloodied apron. He had a long boiled-looking face with horn-rimmed glasses over a big purple drinker's nose and sparse grey hair plastered back over his scalp. He had huge red hands.

Buckle was always kind to us, as the landlord's children, but seemed scary and unpredictable nonetheless. He was certainly an angry and impatient man, said to hurl his cleaver occasionally at any passing dog which had hovered unwisely at the shop door. I was often sent across the road to collect our meat, so I would often see Buckle setting to with that cleaver with impressive violence. He would complain endlessly to my father about the expectations of customers: 'Leg o' lamb, John, leg o' lamb, they all want bloody legs o' lamb. They must think all the bloody lambs got twelve legs'.

My mother used to complain that late on Friday nights, when both Buckle and my father had had plenty to drink, they would go to the shop and my father helped him make the sausages. This involved sitting round buckets of boiling water squeezing sausage meat into cases while Buckle's dog ends and ash fell into the bucket, along with the damp sawdust and who knows what else.

Buckle was known to be a bully and a wife beater in those days when interference would have been regarded as taboo. His wife was a small and extremely respectable-looking woman with a quiet voice and polite ways, so they seemed an improbably ill-matched couple even to me as a child. He usually hit her in the face in drink and temper so that she had to face the world with her black eyes and bruises, and he went on doing so for a very long time. She sought my mother's help on at least one occasion, but in those days things hardly ever went any further and people did not interfere, or feel that this was even a possibility. Buckle and his wife moved away in the end and someone else took the butchers over, but the new butcher never came to the pub, or at least not to ours.

There were many other regulars, including a number of couples, who always came to the Red Lion together. I remember especially Ron and Ethel Bridges, who lived on the other side of the church in Flint Street, a lane which led onto the Pond Close path. Ron often went up to Stamford Bridge and brought us back the Chelsea programmes, and they were both great darts players, helping to run the Pub teams and the Christmas Club, so the Red Lion was a huge part of their lives. I remember how Ron and Ethel dressed up for darts matches, and how my mother made sandwiches for the two teams. In the early years at least our parents were very selective about who they let past the bar door and into our family life, but my mother and Ethel became very close friends, and after my youngest brother Bryan was born in 1960 she became his godmother. Ethel was a loyal friend throughout the years soon to come when things would go badly wrong, and my mother often needed her help and reassurance then. Sadly, as will be clear later, a time came when she felt she could go no further, but for the moment that was all in the future.

My mother, still only in her thirties, was already working too hard for her own good, and she was sometimes worn out, which explained her pneumonia and the nursing home episode. Tired or not she was always soft hearted and was often very kind to customers she thought needed help. I can remember when she shared a lunchtime stew so that a young Irish farm labourer had the dinner she thought he needed. Then there was old Mr Mathews, who lived on his own and seemed lonely. He was one of the elders who loved to play domino cribbage in the bar with David. My mother invited him for Christmas Night one year. I remember him arriving at the dark back door of the pub on that one closed night of the year in his old dark suit and collarless shirt. He had a big white moustache and a chuckling, wheezy laugh.

Of course, we got know the men who made regular deliveries to the Red Lion. The regular brewery draymen in those early years were a strange pair to look at. I never knew their names, but they were an odd couple. The short, round one had fair curly hair, with a red, smiling face, and his tall mate had the look of a poor man's Boris Karloff, with a long cadaverous face, weathered-looking tombstone teeth and huge hands. They heaved both full and empty wooden barrels about with little apparent effort, holding them against their leather aprons and then dropping them down onto the waiting racks in our cellar. They always had a couple of pints each regardless of who was driving, once they had loaded the empties onto the lorry. This must have been repeated at each stop so that their daily intake as they drove around Buckinghamshire must have been staggeringly high in those days before the breathalyser, when there was less traffic, and all you had to do was walk the white line in the police station if anything went wrong. Then and for years afterwards brewery workers were always given plenty back at the yard as well, so that one way or another I doubt that they lived into very old age.

When I was about 12 years old we acquired a jukebox, which was proudly placed in our lounge bar, gleaming and neon-lit. Once you had put your sixpence in the slot and made your selection it operated a fascinating clunking mechanism to pick up the record and take it to the turntable. My parents clearly wanted to attract more young customers, but some of the older regulars did not like it much. The Juke Box could certainly shatter the dusty peacefulness of the lounge with its usually unplayed piano and atmosphere of chintz. The records were changed gradually every three weeks or so by someone we knew as Juke Box Johnny – a friendly man who arrived in a station wagon full of records and spare parts. Johnny always stayed for a cup of tea and a chat and he would let us have the discarded records. Although the middles had been knocked out, you could still make them work on our Dansette by using Plasticine to fill the middle in. I remember soon after it arrived endlessly hearing the two Elvis hits of the moment – 'Wooden Heart' and 'His Latest Flame'. Both tunes can still take me straight back to Juke Box Johnny from Surrey, who was fun and friendly and gave my father members' enclosure tickets for a game at the Oval one summer, and we saw Bill Alley from Somerset make a century.

In those days even sizeable villages like ours had an intimacy which is now rare. People knew each other, and roles and reputations tended to become fixed. This could easily be regarded as comfortable and comforting if you chose to wear nostalgia goggles, but, in reality, it could be cruel and limiting. This was obvious even within our small community of regular customers. Old age did not necessarily give you any immunity either. I remember Mrs Cook, an ancient relative of Ron and Ethel's. She was certainly sharp-tongued and a sour, endless complainer about everything. She also had a reputation for tightness, sitting for hours over a single drink. But people felt able to be startlingly rude to her face, as well as making endless jokes about her general witchiness when she was not there. My father was much more likely to join in than my mother, but it all went on well within our hearing and understanding. There seemed to be two basic rules for the licensed trade. The first was that you could discuss anything with customers apart from religion and politics. The second was that if you ran with anyone it should be with the hounds and not the hare.

Another of the scapegoats was a scruffy and dirty man called Fred Stratford, who occasionally showed up in an ancient and filthy belted raincoat with straggling grey hair spiking out in all directions from a battered and greasy trilby. He was always the butt of jokes, not only for his appearance but also because of his supposed rudeness and moaning. My father could be a bullying showman in situations like this, particularly after a few pints. Still a relatively young man, and very strong, he once threw Fred Stratford out of the side door of the pub with such force that he fell against the wychert wall on the far side of the lane. On another occasion a number of the men sat Fred in a chair in the pub car park and with my father's encouragement gave him a haircut with garden shears. I never knew what happened to Fred Stratford. He would come back occasionally and then eventually disappeared.

I expect things like this happened, in those times, in other village pubs and that ours was not that unusual. If it did happen it relied upon the kind of rallying recklessness which men like my father provided. My mother, always uncomfortable with this kind of behaviour, was just not listened to. Strangely, and despite this kind of thing the Red Lion retained a generally respectable image. This was partly achieved through my father's charm offensives with the local well-to-do and better-off customers when required, and partly the low profile of our village policeman, who believed in leaving well enough alone.

The man we knew for longest, from the day we arrived until he died years after we had left, was Henry Webb. Though he always seemed to operate in a solitary way, Henry was related by marriage to a local builder, and part of a sizeable wider family. He worked a smallholding outside the village up a lane called Bag Hill, or 'Bagull' in the Bucks accent. Henry was of indeterminate age, had a lean grizzled face, always with stubble, and usually had a roll-up on his lip. He never took off his grimy flat cap and always wore a countryman's leggings, a collarless shirt and boots, which were always filthy. There was a place to the right of the public bar where Henry always stood, and the wooden floor around it was always ingrained with a residue of cow shit. Over time this had become so embedded that the toughest daily mopping never quite got rid of it. Henry had a soft voice and a gentle way. He knew about animals and wild flowers. He identified snapdragons for me once. He never altered his routine, and he was an alcoholic.

Henry would call in for a drink, always mild beer, in the morning on his way out, on the way back, and then again in the early evening. In the afternoons, when we were closed, he would knock at our back door with two big empty bottles and ask for them to be filled so that he would be topped up until the early evening. After a certain age, no older than nine or 10, my brother or I would go into the bar and pull the mild into the bottles if our parents were not around. It was always two slow long pulls and then a bit more He must have paid later. It was outside licensing hours of course. My father once asked him what would he say if the village policeman asked him what it was. 'I should say it was a drop o' cold tay' said Henry, though of course the froth would have given the lie to that, so it was a good job it never happened, and was unlikely to, given the law's low profile.

When our dear old rogue of a dog Mack got a growth in the throat years later it was Henry who took him in his arms and despatched him without pain and without the need of a vet. We were by then away at school. I was very sad, but at least it had been Henry. He could not read or write, and sometimes asked for help with forms. Once a year, going to Thame Show, he would turn up looking slightly smarter than usual and ask my mother to do his tie for him. He usually had the old Schweppes racing calendar at the end of each year. For all his slowness and whiff of cow muck, Henry was never ridiculed in the same way as Fred Stratford. He had a place and was a fixture.

A few times we went up to Bag Hill and saw him with his cows and big bins of mangelwurzels. He kept himself going for alcohol up there with plenty of home-made wine and I know that later on my father sometimes joined him up there.

Henry did go on to hospital in the end. It must have been hell for him. He died, inevitably, from his drinking. He was not an old man, and none could remember his being a young man.

It was rather as if Henry had lived his whole life in middle age.

So there are some of the crusted characters from the old days when I was a child and growing up with my brother in the Red Lion. They cannot have been a cross-section of the life of the village 60 or so years ago, and they were a curious lot of people for my brother and me to grow up with. Most of them were kind to us, and they were never boring.

Describing it now, the pub and the village may seem nearer to the 1930s than to modern times. The early 1960s were beginning to see bigger changes, but by modern standards not very rapidly. Much that was traditional about the old life of the village endured, and there were plenty of characters. For all the picture box image of the pub on the village green and the warmth of good friendship and familiar faces, there was that underbelly of cruelty and stigma which was also part of village life. We were soon to know much more about that from direct experience.

Chapter 8

MY FATHER'S ILLNESS

$\rightarrow\!\!\!\!\!-\!\!\!\!\infty\!\!\!\!-\!\!\!\!\!\leftarrow$

It will be clear to you having read this far that my parents were beginning to have problems, both individually and in their relationship. Using the main landmarks from my childhood s perspective, I know that the main crises took place over a two-year period in the late 1950s, when I was 10 to 12 years old. For a child that is a long period, and although a series of things seemed to go wrong and be painful, life went on. Even years later as an adult, I found it hard to get the sequence of events clearly sorted out in my mind, or how one problem affected another. The effect, as things worsened, was that a life of bright days with occasional clouds turned into a kind of foggy gloom, lit now and then by brighter interludes which never lasted long enough to point up a horizon.

I came to understand later how things began to deteriorate after my grandfather died. The responsibilities of the pub and my father trying to keep his full-time job going made my parents' plan much harder to sustain. Little by little my father's heavy drinking got heavier, and my mother seemed to become almost permanently exhausted. One of the big challenges of family life lived in public houses was to keep family and business separate, and when problems developed there was consequently a great temptation to try to carry on as normally as possible, to avoid those problems becoming public property. In the longer run that clearly becomes impossible. In the shorter term, despite everything that was going on behind the scenes, my parents tried very hard indeed to present a united front as landlord and landlady of the Red Lion.

My mother became ill first. The pressure and drudgery of maintaining the pub and looking after us led, in the end, to her becoming extremely run down, and she got double pneumonia. She went to the local nursing home and my father looked after us. We did not go to visit her, I think because she was supposed to have complete rest. We were very worried about her and scared too, but we did as we were told and tried to be brave and helpful. We sent cheerful cards, letters and drawings. It moved me to tears many years later when I found one of them with her things, after her death.

For the time she was away we had to put up with my father's inept attempts at cooking, which mainly relied on a variety of tins and potato crisps. On Sundays, though, we were sent next door for Sunday lunch to Bert and Edie Cartwright, the brother and sister who kept the grocery shop on the corner. Edie especially was very kind, and old Bert, one of my father's regulars, tried to talk with us in his gruff way, but we were both shy, and a bit daunted by the solemn politeness and small talk of over the roasted meat and vegetables.

It was obvious to us that my father drank more heavily during this time and did not bother much about his own food, though he had put on a great deal of weight. I remember things getting sufficiently serious that his brother Francis came over to see him. This was rare, given the falling out over my grandfather, so he must have thought the situation was serious. I remember, with my ears wide open as ever, hearing some of my uncle's perfectly sensible, if bossy, advice to his troubled older brother – 'pull yourself together, eat properly and stop drinking all that stuff' seemed to be the brunt of it. Easy to dish out advice and then leave him to it of course, and Francis did just that.

Once my mother came home care was taken for a time, but the old routine quickly re-established itself, though my father's drinking now became worse than ever. Increasingly he drank whisky – then an expensive commodity, even if you were the landlord. He now seemed to lose all control, and for all my mother's frantic attempts to hide bottles and plead with him to stop, he could not. He became dependent on a huge daily intake, business-wrecking in its proportions. I can remember his efforts to hide the bottles, so that the flat cover over the lounge bar service area was scattered with empty whisky bottles. There were many more angry arguments, with shouting and accusations.

It is desperately hard for children to understand addiction. You have a sense of how a parent used to behave, and now their behaviour seems scary and unpredictable. My father could be tearfully sentimental and clinging, but then become almost instantly angry with a red face and bulging eyes. However much you longed for 'normal' behaviour you never got it. It meant that for much of the time he just seemed not to be our father, and that felt very lonely. We loved him but became scared of him and what he might do next. You tried to take some responsibility, however hopelessly, for an out-of-control parent who would not listen, at the same time as worrying about your mother.

As a child, however bad this becomes, you have a bigger dread of it escaping outside the family so that everyone else finds out. This seemed a real danger, as father was capable of becoming loud, abandoned and very rude in his most florid moods. In a village, and with school just across the road, this other set of prevailing anxieties was very real and very tiring, You could not say anything to an outsider and in any event, although many people must have known what was happening, no one asked, as was the custom of those tight-lipped times. I sat with our old dog, told him about it and cried to him, but no one else.

Part of the uncertainty was that my father could sometimes be a happy, Rabelaisian drunk. I remember him more than once declaiming Shakespeare late at night across the Green from the bedroom window. It was usually the Friends, Romans, Countrymen speech and he seemed to know an impressive amount of it. My mother hated this public display, but it was amusing, and as a child you struggled with conflicting emotions – shame and anxiety, certainly, but finding it oddly impressive and funny as well.

At other times, he could be aggressive and threatening, or sad and lost himself. I remember him threatening my mother and grabbing hold of her. I tried to push him off, but was wearily batted away. Once I saw him on his own in the upstairs sitting room, crying bitterly for his own mother, and in a world of his own. I now see that she had died only seven years before, and that he had never really got over her loss. I was shocked at his tears, as I had never seen him cry before. It made me sad in a way that I can still recall.

A physical crisis came, inevitably. He suffered initially from a kidney stone and I can remember his cries of pain from the front bedroom with the windows open on a summer day. It was another of those times you get as a child when the rest of the world seems to go on as normal while yours is scarily frozen. He was soon sent on by ambulance to Stoke Mandeville Hospital with jaundice and liver trouble. A friend of my parents who worked with my father took us to see him at least every week in his car.

Once over the yellowness of his jaundice, he seemed more cheerful. He was in hospital for some time, and that long summer must have been incredibly demanding for my mother, but at least things were calmer. Apart from visits to the hospital, we never left the village. The summer holidays were long and empty. We were left a great deal to our own devices, and at the back of it all was anxiety about money and what would happen. The signals about this were clear enough from snatches of conversation and the level of disorder through the house, as my mother struggled to do everything and keep the pub going. She managed somehow. but it must have required heroic powers of resilience.

After some weeks my father came home, and although there were several relapses he was determined not to drink. For the landlord of a pub who had been drinking strongly all his adult life this must have taken great courage. He had given up his County Council job in desperation during the worst of his drinking, so having abandoned the security of superannuation and the day job, it may have been economic necessity that kept us clinging on at the Red Lion. Beyond that, though, neither he nor my mother ever seemed to see any choice beyond staying on. Even now I am not sure what this represented – whether fear of the unknown or a doubt about what else he might be able to do.

Though his drinking had stopped, his mood swings continued. There were days of black depression when he seemed locked into himself and incapable, almost, of moving. Soon afterwards, after a visit by the doctor, he was taken into hospital again. This time he went to St John's, the County Psychiatric Hospital, for assessment. St John's was in the village of Stone three or four miles away. Nobody ever called it St John's – it was just known as 'Stone'. My father had started his working career there, in a clerical job, just before the war. He had played cricket for the staff team, and was written up in the local paper as a demon fast bowler. Now he was there as a patient. What being in Stone meant to local people was that you had 'gone mental' and the assumption usually was that once there you would stay, and that was that. People were scared of it, and scared of having much to do with anyone who went there. In every part of the country, then, you only had to mention the name of the local psychiatric hospital to conjure up those ideas of hopeless and incarcerated loonyness. We may still be concerned now about the stigma of mental illness, but then it was utterly profound and based on the deep wells of an ignorance which amounted to folklore. Some people identified Stone as somewhere you went if you were 'simple', and others thought it was where you had to go if you 'went mad'. Clearly there was plenty of depression around in those days – we all knew that the landlord of the Green Dragon round the corner had killed himself in his car with the exhaust fumes, but no one talked about it as mental illness. Even we, as children, picked up the unpleasant connotations of failure and lack of moral fibre.

The fact that someone in the family had gone into Stone meant notoriety and gossip. As children we were not spared this at all. I can remember several children taunting me about my father being in the loony bin, and saying 'my dad says you'll have to leave the pub soon'. While I was angry and wanted to lash out I don't think I did, but it was very unpleasant and confusing. Sadly, no one explained anything – even my mother. With hindsight, I realise how new this all was to her as well.

My father's diagnosis was of manic-depressive psychosis, known now as bipolar disorder. The alcohol had masked this underlying condition and when the booze stopped, the illness rushed in. We were to learn more about it in bits and pieces as time went on, including the treatments being used for it in those pre-lithium days. I can certainly remember the chasm between the manic episodes, when he could carry on loudly and embarrassingly in the street about any subject, regardless of the audience, and those desperate silent depressive phases when he would be incapable of anything.

I remember the first visit we made to the hospital, travelling on the Number 82 Aylesbury bus and getting off at the unaccustomed stop just outside the hospital. We were apprehensive about what we were going to find and what it would be like. For my brother and me it meant entering a place we knew everyone was scared of. It was the classic scary old institution, with a clock tower and red brick buildings set back from the road and a huge Victorian chapel to one side. We were to get to know it well over the coming years, though I did not realise that at the time. My father, in his own clothes, was in a new unit, away from the rest of the hospital, called Beacon House – presumably to celebrate the new approach to services after the big Mental Health Act of 1959, but I knew nothing of that at the time.

It seemed important to be there and to be loyal to our father but we had no idea what to expect of him and what else we might see. The hospital, in those days, had plenty of people who looked and seemed very strange. Some of them had probably been there for most of their lives. In the hospital café and around the grounds there were whiskery old ladies with staring eyes, old men with oddly-shaped heads and people who suddenly shouted strange things to no one in particular. We were told not to stare, but it was hard not to, and of course we did. Soon enough, as we went back more often, it became clear to us, even as children, that there was nothing really to be afraid of. Although my father was undergoing some intensive treatment it was reassuring to see him. He and my mother seemed close. They would always kiss at the end of the visit, which I liked.

In the coming years my father had a number of admissions to Stone, always after crises at home. The term 'revolving door' sums it all up. It seems now to me to be a remarkable feat of courage and endurance that my mother went on managing to keep the pub going, despite all the problems and money worries. My father showed courage too, in trying to sustain his role as Mine Host despite being a sober alcoholic and having a major mental illness. They remained at the Red Lion and stayed with each other through everything. Was it love and commitment, or fear that change might have even worse consequences? I do not know, but sense that it was a combination of both. It seemed to me, years later, that neither of them could really explain how stuck fast and mutually dependent they had become.

My brother and I learnt over time something of my father's condition and the treatments involved. It is worth saying that no one to my knowledge ever offered us as children information, advice or support of any kind. His illness was not mentioned, and school continued as normal. I do not know whether people felt sorry for us. It was just never talked about. While this bred a kind of fierce, quiet loyalty and self-sufficiency, there should surely have been more than this, though I expect things may not have changed that much even now. I remember one solitary visit from a social worker who came to see my mother. The man, sandy-haired and in a blue blazer, ignored us and we never saw him again.

Over time and many admissions, my father clocked up a long experience of ECT and was also one of that generation of patients who road-tested the drugs of the great therapeutic revolution of the late 1950s and early 60s. He spent most of his time at Stone in the newer therapeutic unit. After a while I knew more or less what ECT was and the whole idea of being wired up and shocked on purpose seemed terrifying to me. He tried to explain how it felt and that he was OK once the effects had worn off, but it still sounded very frightening. Part of that scarinesss was the sense that you did not seem to have much choice about it. It seemed that you had to have it or be seen as resisting treatment. It was, after all, the orthodox approach of the day, and the doctor was God.

The drugs which my father took in hospital had to be continued when he was at home – sodium amytal, largactyl and others, so that we became accustomed to the array of pills and liquids on the shelf at home. At times he would not take them, or overuse them, and to find him slumped and incoherent was often the first sign that we could expect another admission soon.

Everyone is affected by the mental illness of a family member, and sometimes that impact is very profound, and it can be long-lasting for children, especially if nothing is explained and you are left to make sense of it on your own. At least in the treatment of bipolar disorder there have been huge advances, and to a degree some increase in popular understanding of mental illness, though the stigma lives on. In those days, even as a child, you knew that an illness like this was not one to talk about. For all the treatments and for better or worse, my father retained a spark of resistance and challenge. Though that sometimes caused him and the rest of us problems, his spirit survived through all his mental health travails.

If you drive through Stone now there is little to see of the old hospital apart from that institutional Victorian chapel, which has been retained through some strange notion of architectural merit. The whole Victorian complex and the various huts and annexes are gone and the land, as with many of the old county hospitals, has been sold for new housing. It is easier to sweep away the buildings than the stigma, of course.

My father was at home when I learned that I had passed the 11 Plus which he had been so determined I should succeed in. But a few months later, when I had to start catching the bus to Aylesbury and the Grammar School, he was back in Stone. He had told me that he would wave to me on the first day from the hospital gates. He was there, and it seemed important to wave back as best I could, whatever anyone else might say.

One of the consequences of my mother struggling to cope on her own was that I did not get all the bits of kit required from the inordinately long list provided by the school. One of these was a white woodwork apron. The teacher was an unpleasant, angry man and it was clear that I would have to have an apron. My father made me one from a kind of khaki cloth in his OT sessions. It stuck out from everybody else's, but I wore it with a kind of fierce loyalty. It made me feel better, though I discovered very quickly that I would never be much of a woodworker.

Chapter 9

THE BIG PLAN

I did not much enjoy the two terms I had at Aylesbury Grammar School. After all the uniform buying and the new routine of getting to and from school with a bus pass I struggled to find my level, both academically and physically. By then a rather overweight and wheezy child, I found rugby and cross-country running a real trial. There was also the business of being a very small fish in a much larger pond after the high status of being at the top of St Mary's. I did not find the transition from the village primary school to the Grammar School at Aylesbury very easy. In those days there was no real preparation for the transition. I had never even seen the new school before, let alone visited it, and one of the main consequences of the 11 Plus was that from a small primary there might be no others 'going up' that you knew. Three of us had passed that year, but Jackie and Janet were going to the new Girl's High which was just opening, so that I was the only one going to the old Grammar, now a single-sex school.

Lack of preparation meant that some of what lay in wait was scarier in prospect than it actually turned out to be – mass changing for games and PE and the compulsory showers afterwards turned out to be not so bad after all, providing of course that you had remembered your kit. Nor did the low-level bullying of new kids on the bus turn out to be that terrible, once you realised that they weren't actually going to throw your stuff out of the upstairs window.

My mother, struggling on her own with the pub, had struggled to get the long and expensive list of uniform and equipment sorted out. This included the black blazer with its bright new red and white badge which marked you out as a new arrival. Despite all her efforts, though, I was still missing several items when term started. My father had sorted out the woodwork apron, but not games shorts. Told to get some by a tough-talking games master, I took the problem home and my mum put out an alert to customers. This produced a pair of vast and anciently faded blue shorts. They would have looked baggy on Stanley Matthews but were the only option after the money for kitting me out had been spent. On the next games day I hitched them up as best I could. Since most of the others were also anxious about their first contact with the game of rugby I got away without too much ridicule, but it was the moment when my pub car park sporting image of myself met reality. I can still remember the burning shame inside which came with looking odd and different when you least wanted to.

The afternoon double games session at the playing field quickly became something I dreaded each week. Although very tall for my age I was certainly overweight, with a wheeziness left over from my bout of pneumonia a year or so before. I also had little actual experience of organised games. These days children are introduced carefully to rugby, but then it seemed mainly to be about chaotic charging about with the ball usually a long way off. There was the added misery of being shouted at if you were seen not to be running hard enough – though where to and what for were not very clear, at least to me.

My size meant that I seldom escaped attention, and once I was actually slapped round the face by the middle-aged bully running the session, for some misdemeanour I did not understand. I was told to run round the field for the rest of the session. I gasped and grizzled as I slowly trudged round on my own. My mother, always determined to defend her own, wrote to complain the next day. I was left alone after that, to my relief, probably on the basis that I was a hopeless case, and I made little sporting progress. However, I did not escape the annual cross-country race, again undertaken with no preparation or explanation. I came almost, but not quite, last. I walked when I could and came across several others who were in the same gasping and stitch-ridden state. We tried, over the last bit on the school field, to look as if we had all been running all the time, if very slowly.

In the classroom life was very different too. I had been used to having one teacher who spent the whole day with us, and now my first-year form of 30 or so stayed in classroom 20 for most of the day, to be visited by a variety of masters for the different subjects. It was my first contact with French, taught by a tall man with a red nose and an exaggerated style of pronunciation. He would arrive for the day on a bike with a beret and long raincoat, so that all he seemed to lack were the onions over the crossbar.

I enjoyed the new experiences of science subjects and more advanced geography and history. The English lessons were disappointing. I had always enjoyed the subject, and because I read a great deal it came easily to me. The sour-faced, prickly, middle -aged man who taught us had a high-pitched and world-weary manner – he was essentially rather 'camp', though the term had not been invented yet. To drag through syntax and grammar exercises seemed dull and uninspiring, so it seems clear that while no one forgets a good teacher, you remember the poor ones just as clearly.

The two biggest challenges for me were woodwork and maths – subjects in which my need to learn at my own pace was most obvious. My father was the least practical man imaginable. He struggled always with practical tasks, however basic, so that I had no real experience of tools. Now, once a week for two afternoon periods, we all went to the woodwork shop and an older man in a brown coat shouted instructions from the front about the individual project, which we all did in common. It was a footstool with a woven top. His orders included plenty of dire warnings about the cardinal sin of inappropriate use of chisels.

Most people made reasonable progress, but as with the cross-country I found myself with several fellow incompetents, loitering at the back. I stayed there and tried to draw no attention to myself by appearing to be busy. This meant sawing away, fairly indiscriminately, at bits of wood with a serious air and acting the part of woodworker. It says a lot for his teaching and my youthful acting ability that I got way with this for the whole of the two terms I was at the Grammar School, despite my size and the khaki apron.

The problem with maths was more difficult. At Primary School I had not really gone beyond arithmetic, which I was very good at. Suddenly, I was now plunged into a world of basic algebra and geometry. After a few weeks, though I tried hard to understand, I seemed unable to keep up. The teacher, a youngish man with straw-coloured hair, glasses and big front teeth, was cheerful and informal, and this should have helped, but didn't. I was too nervous to say that I did not understand.

His way of checking that we were making progress was to have frequent tests, and he was sufficiently trusting that we were allowed to mark our own exercises and homework. This meant that if you were the necessary few rows away from him, as I was, and quick with a pencil, you could cheat – always being careful to give yourself a realistically modest score for credibility. I was always anxious about this and relieved when it was done and I had escaped again. I could so easily have been caught, and learned later, after I had left, that a boy in my class had done the same, been caught and although not expelled had been punished severely.

The result was, sadly, that in both woodwork and maths I learnt more about escaping attention and fiddling than joints and equations. I feared the exposure of my real ignorance when the maths exams came, and I managed only 20%, but to my relief this was again not so bad as to attract individual attention.

My report after the first term was reasonable – better than I probably deserved. Nonetheless I was struggling to keep up. Trying to cope with homework in the back room at the pub along with the usual family tensions was hard, and I remember often feeling tired. My father was back at home by now and seemed to feel that I was doing well enough. My parents had so much to cope with, and my father had invested so much in my getting to the school, that it seemed impossible to say anything about how difficult much of it was.

My going to the Grammar meant that for the first time David and I were in separate schools. He may well have been pleased to be free, at least at school, of a bossy and opinionated older brother. David at that stage already loved football and Manchester United in particular. His brittle bone disease had meant a life of many fractures, with dashes to the hospital, always followed by long periods with an itchy plaster and restricted activities. By this stage his left leg, the most frequently fractured, had developed a pronounced bend in the shin, protected by a leather guard. He coped with everything bravely and patiently. There was never any self-pity about David, who remained up for pretty well all challenges. I came to realise later how remarkable this was, but I suppose I took it for granted at the time. It was known that when he was older there would need to be major orthopaedic surgery.

At the age of nine he was a determined trainspotter, and had an encyclopaedic knowledge of football and other sports.

He loved bacon sandwiches floating in brown sauce, and had excellent skills at all pub games, especially cribbage, where he held his own with the old boys in the public bar. There was no doubt that he had lost a good deal of schooling, though, and my father, for all his quixotic behaviour and rollercoaster moods, was always concerned about our education and getting the best he could. For me it had been getting to the Grammar, but what about David, who had lost so much schooling that his 11 plus prospects were not very good?

It was early in my second term at Aylesbury that the great Royal Masonic School idea occurred to my father, who was beset with his financial problems and mental illness. He had been a Freemason, following his own father, for many years. Although not a regular attender he would sometimes go off to Lodge in a suit with that little suitcase, which we had always been told we must never open on any account. Others who grew up with a father in the Masons will remember that warning. Some children may have chosen, or been sufficiently scared not to look, but most of us did take a peek. What you usually found was a rather sumptuous apron and a little book, so it was normally an anti-climax, but I have heard of others who made more exotic finds, especially if the parent concerned had used the case as a more general hiding place!

My father had received support in his illness from some Masonic friends and they must have told him about the schools. He soon decided that if at all possible David and I should both go to them. I could be expected to cope and receive yet further advantages. For David, it was seen as a more fundamentally important opportunity. Finally, and surprisingly, my mother had become pregnant, and although I had not thought much about this, and knew even less about what to expect, I suppose it must have represented a real commitment to the future, whatever the problems of recent times had been.

So for all these reasons, going away to the Masonic Schools

became the Big Plan. Once my father had the idea firmly in his mind and arrangements began to be made, it became for him the solution he wanted to find for everything – the Masonic magic bullet. We were not involved at all in the decision, and I think my mother had little say in the matter. He dealt with any possible resistance by selling it to us on the back of vivid and tantalising descriptions of what life would be like and the fun we would have. It was an effective approach. Though I had begun to make friends at the Grammar and had learned how to cope in my own way, there were enough continuing anxieties, including a possible Maths nemesis, for me to be willingly carried into dreams of an exciting future away at school. He painted pictures of potential sporting glory, merry japes and camaraderie. In reality this was based on the kind of fantasy school life which was informed by his own reading of school stories. His images of boarding school were based more on the Gems and Magnets of his youth than any direct knowledge, investigation or experience.

My father's favourite book as a boy had been *Tales of Whitminster*, a collection of school stories by Ascot R Hope. I still have the copy he gave me to take away. It was actually a school prize given to my Great Uncle Moss for good attendance at Elementary School! Whitminster was the archetypal Public School setting for fun and games with an Edwardian air of sunshine, cloisters and 'doing the right thing in the end'. I think my father hoped that the main elements of this world would still be available for us, even if he had not had the chance. He was also a fan of the Greyfriars stories, and no doubt wanted us to find Bob Cherry, Harry Wharton and Billy Bunter in a school life of structure and purpose funded by the Masons. My father had no doubts at all. He just knew that it was all going to be marvellous and a great success

My own expectation of boarding school became quite high, so my father did succeed in carrying me along with the plan. I knew that we would first be going to the Masonic Junior School in Bushey in Hertfordshire. I had no idea how far away that was. Although in fact it was only 30 miles or so, I did not know that then, and it seemed a long way from home in any event. My own expectations from reading were taken from the Jennings and Darbishire books, then very popular, which described the light-hearted escapades of two friends in what sounded generally a very benign prep school, where everyone had nicknames. Would it be anything like that? I didn't know, but hoped so.

For a time it all lay on the horizon, beyond immediate concern, but one afternoon towards the end of the spring term I was taken into a classroom on my own to do some tests to assess my educational level. At that point it became real, and although I was uncertain about what was ahead it seemed exciting, as well as providing a feeling of escape. I went home on the bus that day already feeling a distance from this routine and knowing that everything would change soon.

My mother was less sure, and as the day approached she became anxious and occasionally tearful. I can see looking back how much she had already coped with and how much change she was now facing. She was pregnant, and from her point of view being asked to accept our going away. My father had worked hard at persuading her, though I think that in reality she had been given little say, and was now expected to fall in with everything. She tried with great loyalty to do this, but it was plain to see that she had her doubts.

Little of the reality was explained to us in advance. I had never spent time away from home, and David had only had his hospital stays. Despite that we did not fret much in advance. The arrival of wooden tuck boxes, which had our names and initials stencilled onto them, was another step closer to the day. As we were starting in the summer term, there was the prospect of playing proper cricket for the first time, and since we would begin later than the local schools, we had a slightly longer holiday. This added up to a strange phony war period when no one else was around. But then the time seemed to gallop along faster and suddenly, or so it seemed, the day itself arrived.

I remember not sleeping very much the night before we went. We were ready quite early the next morning, packed up as instructed, with our bright new tuck boxes. My father and mother were coming too, and we were to be taken by my father's Masonic friend from the village, Jock Lucas. He ran a small garage and chauffeuring business, so we were to go in his large black Austin Princess. I hoped desperately not to be sick from nerves, and the smell of petrol and leather seats.

We all got in, my father in the front with Jock, and David and I in the big back seat with our mother, already putting a brave face on, and trying to reassure us. Off we went slowly through the village and then onto the main Aylesbury Road. I remember as if it were yesterday the route, the car smell and the quietness. Very little was said, and nothing about the matter in hand.

I may not have recognised it at the time, but this really was the end of one life and the beginning of another. I had made one jump recently from the small comfortable world of a village school to the Grammar where I had begun to cope despite the struggles at home. This was a much bigger change. What on earth would it be like?

Chapter 10

The Masons and the Royal Masonic Schools

—⊶◇⊷—

Since much of this book is about the experience of a boarding education provided by Freemasons, it is really important, given all the myths and legends about freemasonry, to inject some practical information and explanation at this point.

The very word 'Freemasonry' is enough to send some people into a self-righteous spasm. For a long time it has been the subject of very strong feelings, not usually much informed by facts. Secrecy, or the perception of it, is unpopular in modern times with everyone except the Government. Colourful writings with exaggerations of ceremony have fuelled suggestions of darkness and conspiracy. Until modern times the Masons themselves contributed to this, though they seem now to be making efforts to explain Freemasonry more openly. Even so a strange and generally hostile fascination persists.

The problem is that many Masons have used their secret world of brotherhood and mutuality to achieve personal gain, advancement or preferential treatment. You had to be invited to join that inner world, and you were only invited if your face fitted and you were willing to keep secrets way beyond ceremonial details. For small businessmen like my father and grandfather this meant personal contact, often with powerful people, and for an ambitious police officer it was a definite step along the alternative, and often faster route to advancement.

None of that is defensible in a more diverse and transparent society, and modern rules about disclosure have made an important difference. Suspicions about unfairness and special favours have continued. Perhaps that is not surprising, but we do need to go beyond the stereotypical assumptions still being made, and knowing the basics about Freemasonry's origins and history will help.

It is a very long and intricate history, as long and scholarly as the annals of some religions. It begins with interweaving strands and uncertain origins in the far-off mists of the Middle Ages. The usual assumption now made is that the original Freemasons were skilled artisans, emancipated by medieval statute from the restrictions and control of local guilds so that they could travel around to work on cathedrals and other great buildings in a way that others could not. These 'free masons' formed a common understanding guarded between themselves, with a system of secret signs and passwords so that they could recognize each other. So it was nothing to do with Gandalf and spells, and everything to do with the mutual support of the skilled technicians of the time.

Centuries later Freemasonry begins to be organised on a broader basis with the setting up of the Grand Lodge of England in 1717. A secret brotherhood was established, and its purpose seems to have been enabling men to meet in harmony, promotion of friendship, and working together to be charitable. The basic ideals are that all persons are the children of one God, that all are related to each other, and that the best way to worship God is to be of service to his people. They do not see themselves as a religion, but they are committed on a non-sectarian basis to the existence of a Supreme Being, the architect of everything. Accordingly they illustrate their moral universe with allegorical symbols from the Mason's trade, with compasses, trowels and other tools. And so, much later, the badge of the Royal Masonic Schools was a Lewis – a three-sectioned instrument with a handle for lifting stone – and the device of a square and compasses was also evident on various buildings at Ston.

The general requirement of belief in a Supreme Being has enabled most religions to take part in Freemasonry, but for centuries the Catholic Church regarded Freemasonry as a great enemy. In the European Masonic tradition, Freemasonry was associated strongly with the Enlightenment, and anti-clericalism played a big part in the French revolution. The leaders of the Italian *Risorgimento*, Voltaire, Garibaldi and Mazzini, were all Masons.

The tradition of liberal commitment and anticlericalism, allied to a fear of conspiracy, ensured that Freemasonry often suffered at the hands of Dictators, the most obvious being the persecution of Masons during the holocaust. The Nazi unit which pumped out anti-Semitic material did the same work against Freemasonry. At least 80,000 and possibly 200,000 Freemasons were killed in the Holocaust. Masonic concentration camp inmates were graded as political prisoners and wore an inverted red triangle. Hitler believed that Freemasons had succumbed to the Jews conspiring against Germany and should be eliminated. In the Spanish Civil War Freemasons were strongly allied with the Republican side. Franco banned Freemasonry in Spain soon after he came to power, and in the years that followed references to a Judeo-Masonic plot were frequently part of the Dictator's rhetoric.

Of course Freemasonry took a different path in British conditions, because of anxiety about the spirit of change in Europe, and the French Revolution. In 1799, English Freemasonry almost came to a halt when the Unlawful Societies Act banned any meetings of groups that required their members to take an oath or obligation. The Grand Master of England prevailed upon William Pitt (not a Mason) to exempt them from the Act, arguing that Freemasonry supported the law and was much involved in charitable work. The compromise was that the Secretary of each Lodge was required to place with the local "Clerk of the Peace" a list of the members of his lodge once a year. This continued until 1967, when Parliament rescinded this by now theoretical obligation.

Through 19th and 20th century Britain Freemasonry grew steadily and its status was reinforced by substantial royal involvement, so that by the time we were going away to school it had reached very high places in most walks of British society, while retaining most of the mystique and secrecy. More serious challenge and greater scrutiny were to come, but only much later.

Unlike modern Freemasonry in Europe, where women's lodges and some joint organisations have developed, British Freemasonry has remained essentially male. Though the great women's rights campaigner and theosophist Annie Besant joined in France and brought Lodges for women back to Edwardian England, 'co-masonry', as it is known, is not recognised by the United Grand Lodge even today. It seems that mainstream Freemasonry is the last surviving bastion of male exclusivity. This is certainly a contributing factor to some of the persistent dismissiveness, and may help explain why modern royal involvement has such a low profile.

So Freemasonry has a long and tortuous history, with its own scholars, schools of thought, and a literature including some tomes of inordinate length and labyrinthine complexity. In Britain, where Masons have held to their commitment to the establishment, they have also maintained a commitment to charitable work. That was what they had told William Pitt in 1799, and down the ages they have stuck to it. You can argue that this is primarily focused on helping their own, as with the Schools, but the length and extent of these mutual commitments has been a really significant and under-acknowledged achievement. It has, after all, been about more than secret ceremonies involving grown men with rolled-up trouser legs and enquiring confirmation of each other by curious handshakes.

As to the schools themselves, a girls' school came first. It was started in 1788 by a committee of ten masons looking to establish a charitable organization for daughters of Freemasons, particularly those who had lost one or both parents. At the end of their school lives, many of the girls were returned to their parents. Girls who had no family to be returned to were apprenticed or otherwise supported by the school until they could establish themselves. In the mid-1800s this institution became more obviously a school.

The boys' school had different beginnings. A charity was set up in 1798 to clothe and educate the needy sons of Freemasons, and they originally provided funding for boys to go to schools near their homes. Eventually a Masonic school in its own right was set up at Wood Green in North London. As demand grew, a decision was made to expand. A much bigger school was built in Bushey, and opened in 1903 with a Foundation Stone laid by the masonically-ubiquitous Duke of Connaught. There was further development in 1929 when a large junior school across the road was opened.

All this growth meant that by 1939 the Royal Masonic Institution for Boys, as it was known then, had 800 boys at the two schools. By the time my brother David and I arrived in 1960 they were still apparently thriving and a new broom, H.G Mullens, a classical scholar and successful grammar school headmaster, had been appointed as Head at the Senior School. He was to coax a good deal of new investment out of the Governors, and no one can really have expected at that time that the end was only a few years away.

Numbers did decline at the junior school, which closed in

1970 and eventually became an academy school. Numbers were also supposedly the main reason for the closure of Ston itself in 1977. It seems unlikely that this was the whole story. The baby boom had certainly worked its way through, and the total number of Masons was beginning to reduce together with the risk of their early mortality, which had, after all, been the main reason boys were sent there. I think there were two main factors. First Ston, despite some efforts to modernise, remained a rigid and Spartan establishment ill-suited to modern times and more enlightened attitudes. Secondly, the Governors decided that they had no faith in its future, and used the funding to support children in other schools as they had done back in the 18th Century. None of this seemed to affect the viability of the Girls' School, which broadened its base, modernised successfully and developed over the years into an extremely successful private school charging high fees, but presumably still able to educate the daughters of needy Masons.

The later story is very curious. Ston became for a time the home of the United States International University and eventually the whole site, clock tower, houses, dining hall, and everything else was bought by a firm of developers, the Comer brothers. They had a track record of turning former institutions into luxury housing and gradually turned the old place into 150 luxury flats. They rechristened Ston Royal Connaught Park, so the name of the ubiquitous Duke was to live on!

Prior to its development as a rich gated community, Ston was empty for some years and had a long period as a regular film and television set. Many times over the years I have seen it suddenly appear on screen as a hospital, prison, gothic castle, or indeed school. It was in Monty Python's *The Meaning of Life, Lucky Jim*, and many more. The dining hall was seen in early Harry Potter films and for a long time Judge John Deed held forth in a court set in Ston's dilapidated, but still panelled, main hall, or Big School as we always knew it.

Just as this second or third career was ending in 2010, Jonathan Glancy of *The Guardian* wrote about Ston under the headline, 'The scariest building in Britain?' He quoted the filmmaker Merlin Ward, scouting for a location for his 2003 film *Out of Bounds*, a psychological thriller set in a boarding school.

'It wasn't just that this vast Edwardian school was conveniently close to London and the film studios around Elstree,' he wrote, 'it was the gloriously spooky entrance tower and the sense of foreboding evoked by the surrounding buildings: cavernous, ominous, Halloween-like. I couldn't have asked for a more unnerving setting.'

Glancy's interest was in the architecture, and what the Comer brothers were planning. He notes that the original architects, Gordon, Lowther and Gunton, used a highly eclectic approach to their 'vast white stone and red brick complex'. The tower alone, he says, 'reads like an encyclopaedia of Gothic design': 'It takes an age to walk from the tower to the enormous dining hall at the far end of a cloistered quadrangle. Almost too large for the eye to take in, the hall, which will be used for big social events, boasts dark timber panelling, exposed beams and lofty gothic windows that pour light into an echoing cavern.'

Regardless of all this, Glancy prefers to build up the case for his spooky headline. He feeds the idea of the gloomy, despondent and eerie institution, with its suitability for horror settings. I hated a great deal about school life at Ston, as coming chapters will make clear. Apart from anything else, I had come, as described earlier, from a very troubled family, and never did learn to cope with the yo-yoing between a tough boarding school life with very little privacy and the endless and unshareable turbulence and chaos of home. But there was nothing gloomy about Ston's buildings. They bustled with life, and if I shut my eyes, the main images I have are of sunshine, the light through high windows, and the views from playing fields of that great tower and the cloistered houses surrounding it. You could be proud of the buildings, for sure, and to see them now and then on film or TV made for some feeling of loss, despite your better judgment. It was as if a rather grand Edwardian great aunt had taken up a later life of vaguely immoral earnings.

My last visit, with my brother, was to a final event at the chapel, some time after development was under way. We crowded the pews and sang the old hymns loudly – 'O God our help in Ages Past' and so on. We knew few of the men there. Our generation had been the least assiduous of all in signing up to the old boys and staying in touch, but it was a poignant event certainly. I remembered some happy times, and some achievements but also much that I had always hated. It is possible, though, to miss the buildings just for their own sake. If I am ever on the train going north from Euston I know exactly when to look out to the right, just before Watford Junction, to glimpse that white clock tower still standing tall on the horizon.

I have tried to explain enough about the Masons and their schools to provide a context for my account of school life and its utter difference from life in the Red Lion, but it will be clear that I am conflicted still by the whole experience. I would never have considered joining the Masons, and hated much of the commitment to settled and conventional middle-class values which they seemed to represent. I wanted nothing of the networking and would have run a mile from the social life involved. I hated much of the education they provided for me. At the same time their commitment to us was huge and generous, with no real strings that mattered. For all the miseries of school the surroundings were beautiful, and the loss of them is to be mourned as no longer available to any of us.

Once you had been to Ston and 'worn the blazer' as it were, it was part of your history and identity, whether you liked it or not. Forever after, if the subject of your schooling cropped up in discussion, or interview, you were aware that people often had strong views one way or the other about Freemasonry, and there was always a need to explain, or even justify. It was tempting in some circles just not to mention it once you knew the level of political correctness you were operating in. I have always refused to use this level of denial. Over a lifetime of campaigning and public service since then I have often taken up radical positions and fought for them, but I have never denied the generosity of the Masons and the more ignorant assumptions made about them.

PART II
STON

Chapter 11

GOING AWAY

—⊃◇⊂—

During that first leaving to go away to school I was certainly excited, but sufficiently scared that I wanted the journey to last a very long time. It certainly seemed to, and I have always remembered it as taking hours. In fact, even at Jock's careful speed it cannot have taken much more than an hour.

Eventually we rolled up the London Road in Bushey, my father excitedly pointing out the grounds and buildings of the Royal Masonic Junior School on the left. However long the drive had seemed we were still early, and it was decided that we would stop for tea.

The Copper Kettle tea-rooms, with their burnished ornaments, served as a rather polite and refined waiting room. We all sat there with tea and cakes. The tea-rooms were near the school entrance, and I now had many butterflies in my stomach. I could see the gates to this uncertain future, but actually going through them was now postponed for a final reprieve of 30 minutes.

My mother, still clearly anxious about losing us, tried to

smile reassuringly and had little to say. My father, keen to get on with things, was still telling us how exciting it would all be and how we would soon get used to it. Jock said hardly anything, but nodded in agreement with my father. We just sat there – shy and still not knowing in the least what to expect as the time ticked on towards the great depositing.

Once we finally got there, walking through the big gates and down a drive with huge pink rose beds on either side, things began to happen very quickly. We met the Deputy Head and the Matron in a large sunlit entrance hall with shining pale wood panels and a smell of polish. Quite quickly we were asked to say goodbye to our parents, and I remember how tongue-tied and shy David and I both were. We were trying hard to cope with the stress of feelings not experienced before, and in these new and grand surroundings crying and making a fuss seemed impossible. I always assumed that this policy of getting the farewells over quickly was based on an assumption that a clean, quick break was best for children. How cruel it now seems. To me, already, the village and anything familiar seemed a very long way away.

I do not think that the staff meant to be cruel, and that this approach seemed to be right to them, handed down by received wisdom, but the whole process after our parents had gone ticked all the relevant boxes for institutional induction. Almost immediately David and I were separated, without much ceremony or explanation. He went into the 'Junior' house, and I went into 'C' house. The houses were all substantial three-storey brick buildings with wide stairways up and down and a large day room with long tables where everyone sat and worked at 'prep' in the evenings. There were eight houses all in a row, linked by a cloister on one side and with a vast playground running the whole length of the houses on the other. It was a far bigger world than anything I had known before and seemed bewildering and loud, especially in the large Dining Hall and School Hall. If I shut my eyes now I can bring back those first sensations – the babble of voices, the smell of polish, the sheen of acres of wood panelling, and a rising sense of panic and desperation.

In quick succession I had a new uniform – back from long into short trousers, grey jacket, grey shirt, strange 1930s style square-ended tie in the house colours of chocolate and blue, and substantial black shoes, with plenty of nails in the sole so that they felt very clumpy to walk in. No one was unkind. Matron was a large grey-headed lady in a white coat with a parrot nose, large chin and pink cheeks, so that she looked like Mr Punch's big responsible sister. She was universally known as 'Tron'. There was an appointed place for me on one of the tables near another new boy called Saunders, who seemed very calm and accepting of it all. I wondered why and how he could cope, but that just added to my own confusion and turmoil. The food seemed OK, but it was strange to sit in that big dining hall with 40 other people at a long table with the Housemaster at the top and 'Tron' at the other. I tried to see where the Junior table might be but could not spot David. There was plenty of talk, but, shy and new, you did not know how to dive into it and so it was rather like being the odd fish out in a shoal, which somehow bypassed and surrounded you at the same time.

The housemaster was even kinder than Tron. Mr Reid was a wiry middle-aged man with a wrinkly face and short grizzled hair. I soon learned that he was the Latin teacher and was said to have been a Japanese prisoner of war. He tried to explain to me the things I needed to know about – you did not ask to go to the toilet but 'the kiosk'. This strikes me still, nearly 60 years later, as absurdly twee and silly, but that was the only term you were allowed to use. I was given a locker in the Day Room to keep my things in. My new tuck box had been loaded onto a shelf in the room kept just for that purpose. It stood out in its newness from the battered boxes and chests the old hands had. Your box was private to you and not to be moved from that room. It was explained that I would have to write a letter home on

Sunday afternoon, and that all letters were read before sending, presumably to ensure that there was no subversive thinking or complaints about cruel treatment.

I did not know what my parents were thinking at this time, already miles away back at the pub. I also did not know how my brother was faring in his separate house a few buildings away. I had enough to do in coping with my own confusion. The new activities and the sense of being processed into a completely new world over which you had little say left me with very little sense of privacy and an odd feeling of weightlessness inside. I was 12 years old and for all that I was attempting to cope on the surface, I began very quickly to be silently homesick.

The rest of the day passed in a blur. There must have been some first lessons, and then another meal, but soon enough it was 7.30 or so and time for bed. I had been used to later nights and the buzzing of the pub downstairs, so getting into a counterpaned and hospital-cornered bed on that bright summer evening in a high windowed dormitory was very strange. It was hard to sleep. There was plenty of chatter after 'lights out', but I was still unready to join in. The darkness eventually fell. All you could hear were the Metroland trains in the distance with their rattle and flash in the distance. I felt very lonely, and having held myself together all day I wanted to cry, but I held it in until I had a sore throat with the effort. Eventually and inevitably, I fell asleep.

For several days I struggled on with new experiences every day. I found that the cricket we played in teams was very different from being on the pub car park with my brother, and a good deal harder. I had my first Latin lessons with my housemaster and received my copy of the standard text book – *First Steps in Latin* by F. Ritchie, amended in ink by someone, as they all were, to *First Steps in Eating* by Cliff Richards. As I was starting from scratch I was just told to work on it from page 1 and do all the exercises. The boy behind me, a catarrhal and casually bullying boy from Newcastle, delighted in sticking compasses into me from behind – I knew the code as always was not to complain, so I just put up with it. He was from another house, so our paths did not cross outside lessons. I realised that the boys came from all over the country. There were so many accents I had never heard before.

But the yearnings and homesickness got worse, not better. I fought them, but they would not go away. One of the great assumptions about homesickness that adults made then, and probably still do, was that it is a very short-term thing and soon over. As with many things in life adults, who must have experienced these feelings themselves when they were young, have a vested interest in burying the memory of that awful loneliness and isolation, so they are not best placed to take it seriously. Strong homesickness may not happen to every child in that situation. It will depend on their own level of insecurity and the fears about home that they are grappling with, and I had plenty of both. That level of separation anxiety and distress does not respond to bland reassurances that you will get over it. It is especially tough in an institution, however kind the people in charge are trying to be, and at J Ston they tried very hard. They certainly assumed, I think, that it would just pass away in time and was best ignored. Yet I was left in a fretful and disabling daze. In those pre-child-centred days, with the long summer term of 12 weeks stretching away to the horizon, I only kept going as long as I did because I knew I was expected to keep my feelings under control. There were no phones, so talking to anyone at home was not possible. In any event the Red Lion never had a phone all the years we were there. Even for pub business they would walk round to the phone box and put four pennies in the slot.

For a day or two I thought about desperate measures, and catching one of the buses, which ran up and down the London Road, so tantalisingly close. I told my brother this in a whispered conversation when we met in the playground. I said that I wanted to run away and that he should come, but he did not want to and the moment passed. Only many years later did I find out that he was very unhappy too. He also experienced some traditionally cruel approaches to the bedwetting problem a child of nine newly away from home might be expected to have, regardless of the disability with his leg. It seems to me that David, with his experience of time in hospital and his general determination to keep going, showed much more courage and resilience than I did, but he should not have had to.

The day after, I did give way. I broke down in the games fields. I was supposedly fielding in a cricket game. I began to sob loudly and was so distressed that I could not even stand still. In the end I peed myself as well, but I was past shame by then. At the time I felt that the master concerned just ignored me, and that the other boys just got on with things, but they must all have known that there was a problem. It is a weird feeling to stand there in snot and tears and feel that your behaviour has just not been noticed. I have never forgotten the pain and misery of those moments, with no contact and feeling completely helpless. Strangely I was not teased about it by any of the boys, who must have sensed that there was something sufficiently distressing going on that it was best to say nothing. It may of course have struck a chord with some of the older hands, as many boys at J Ston had been there from the age of eight.

It had been noticed, of course. I struggled on, but a day or so later and with no advance warning, my mother and father arrived. My brother and I were brought to them in the entrance hall. I imagine they by then that they had talked with the staff concerned. They both did their best to reassure us and in particular to calm me down, but I wanted to go home. I wanted that more than anything, and I wanted everyone to know. I cried and shouted and hugged my mother, heavily pregnant by now. I called them all a bunch of snobs and went on and on until

I suppose I had shocked myself enough to run out of steam. I simply could not do any more, and just knew that it was hopeless. My parents left and we both stayed. In hindsight it must have been incredibly difficult for my mother, given her doubts about the whole business, but as ever she went along with my father's wishes, on this issue at least.

The message got through to some extent; we went to lunch at the Head's house – an apparently unprecedented thing – and our Housemaster clearly put me in the charge of two of the senior boys. So in the end I did begin to settle, and by the time of the Sports Day later in the term my parents were pleased at how I seemed. Afterwards, though, my mother always found it very hard to cope with our return at the end of holidays. While some of that was to do with the worsening of life at home for her as time went by, it was also, I know, the impact of that first sense of loss.

Looking back down the years at it all, I can see that my ugly separation from home and my extreme reaction to homesickness might not be very surprising, given the way things had been at home. There had been in the pub family life a curious and unhelpful mix of over- and under-protection. I was loved and valued, praised as clever at school and able to roam securely in the village, but there had also been anger and violence at home as well as the strange and scaring sights of the 'bin'. There had been the increasingly erratic nature of our care as both our parents struggled to keep things going. In their very different ways they were both loving parents, but neither had much insight, looking back, into what was healthy for children growing up in a public house. They certainly had curious ideas about what was healthy for children. Surprisingly for intelligent people, their approach owed a good deal to folk wisdom ('feed a cold and starve a fever') and even more to their own early experience. As well as the snuff-taking for blocked noses mentioned earlier, my father's sovereign remedy if you cut your leg playing outside was to slap on a handkerchief and give you a glass of port to drink, 'to replace the blood'.

This background meant that my father's grand plan of shipping us off at short notice and with no preparation to a large institution was actually a more drastic measure than they probably believed. Based on an institutional version of middle-class family life, the Ston universe, with its respectable euphemisms and culture of playing the game with feelings kept in check, was a rude shock to children who had never been away from home before. My father certainly saw it as an immediate answer to all the problems, and for the rest of his life he never stopped believing in his public school 'Greyfriars' fantasy. He thought that whatever else had gone wrong he had made that world accessible to us, and never appreciated any attempts to disabuse him of the realities. It was strange, though, that a man so capable of the Rabelaisian defiance of normal conduct, and one who could declaim Shakespearean speeches loudly from the upstairs of the pub across the Green while drunk, should set so much store by the kind of propriety and conventionality which marked the Masonic Junior School.

Although we did both settle eventually, going away was an unpleasant experience, and one I have never forgotten. Was it character and resilience building? Even if it was, I think there must have been better ways, and I am always amazed when I hear that people are still sending children away to school at an even younger age than David was. I am sure that schools now are less institutional, and more obviously caring. I hope so, because the old ways certainly left their mark on generations of children who, like me, have never forgotten the grossly underestimated misery of homesickness and separation.

Chapter 12

FIRST TERM AT J STON

As the weeks passed in that long summer term, I adjusted to the daily routine. I had been placed in the third stream of five. J Ston followed the old Public School Common Entrance syllabus so it took time to adjust, and some of it seemed very advanced to me. I ploughed on with my catch-up Latin exercises. The boy behind me tired of his fun with the compasses, and I pleased Mr Reid with my rapid progress.

He was, no doubt, relieved that I had settled. I soon learned that there had been big problems in the house in the previous term. Two boys had been bullying others very badly in a reign of terror which seemed to have gone unchallenged for a long time. This was possible, of course, because of the no-sneaking code, which was very powerful at J Ston. Most members of C House seemed to have been affected and survivors always referred to this period simply by using the names of the bullies. You only had to use the words 'Grundy and Jenkins' to call up a time of terror and really quite intricate cruelty. They had been expelled, but memory of them lingered on.

'Alfie' Reid, as Housemaster, must have carried responsibility for all this being allowed to happen. He was, doubtless, now taking particular care. Some of the kindest people, with their willingness to see the best and a tendency to over-optimism, can be the least likely to see bullying for what it is. In the Prep School tradition, giving boys power as prefects over others was always a risky business. Benign assumptions, limited supervision and the endless opportunities of institutional life make bullying almost inevitable. They are also the conditions in which the victims are least likely to say anything.

Now, though, C House and its forty-odd boys had come through that storm. The newly appointed prefects seemed fair and sensible, so that the atmosphere was pleasant enough, and I made friends. The daily routine with lessons, games and early nights went on steadily. There was absolutely no television, and after a time you ceased to think about it. TV was something you would only have at home.

On the long tarmac playing area that ran the length of the house blocks, each house tended to stick to its own informally agreed section. We had plenty of time there and could also roam reasonably freely around the grounds. There was also an empty house – 'A' at the start of the row – and I realised after a time that you could explore this with reasonable impunity. It included a whole floor at the top given over to a huge but derelict model railway, which seemed to have been abandoned as a project long ago. I loved it, but could not make anything actually work. I liked even then spending time on my own, and loved the small school library where you could sit and read, as well as going through the bound volumes of old railway magazines with their pictures of 1930s locomotives, and the smell of clean glossy paper.

The approach to school and house discipline at J Ston was traditional. There was a good deal of corporal punishment, and all the houses had variations on its delivery depending on the approach of the Housemaster. Several relied very heavily on beating. C House was, thankfully, more to do with occasional 'spanking' than serious caning, so there was less of a fear factor for us. In C House the general implement was a Jokari bat. Jokari was a game. It involved hitting a ball attached to a bat by elastic, and the bat itself was a sizeable wooden paddle, but to us it just meant an instrument of punishment, which really stung. The more serious option, less frequently used, was a sawn-off cricket bat. One of the places where it was most important to behave and avoid punishable behaviour was the morning assembly in the Main Hall led by the formidable Headmaster, Colonel Dark, who had been so kind to us during my first days at J Ston. For all his suggestively Dickensian name, his bark was actually much worse than his bite.

The curriculum and routine were certainly traditional. We had a half-day off on Wednesdays, but there were lessons on Saturday mornings. This was when we had 'writing practice'. We used old-fashioned penholders and nibs, dipped into inkwells. You carefully copied against the guided exercise book, and dabbed the mistakes with plentiful supplies of pink 'blotch'. This could also be rolled into inky missiles when the teacher's back was turned. For all the required effort at the time it made no difference to the long-term decline of my handwriting in later years.

My mother wrote almost every other day. My father had found an office job in a local firm, and seemed not to have been in hospital for some time. On the whole my parents seemed to be getting on better together. In July my youngest brother Bryan was born, and my father wrote to tell us. It was the first letter from him that we ever got, and it was typed, so he must have done it at work. I suppose I was pleased, but I had not much idea what to expect.

By the time of Speech Day in July, a rather grand event at J Ston, I was doing well, and had also, with the exercise and highly controlled diet, had lost a considerable amount of weight. Both my parents came to Speech Day. It was my first sight of baby

Bryan, bundled up in a shawl. He was much admired by other parents, mainly mothers at J Ston, and we basked in this reflected glory, though not quite knowing what to do or say about it all. With hindsight it was perhaps the only time I remember my mother feeling happy and at ease on a visit, with the family together and the two of us now settled. This was also the first occasion for it really to dawn on me that having a live father was a curiosity at J Ston. Saunders, who had started on the same day as us and had seemed to settle quite easily, had lost his father, like almost everyone else. He asked about my father, and I did not know quite how to explain what to say. In the end I think I just said that he had had a lot of problems with his health. As was the code at J Ston, no more questions were asked, and that was that. My mother holding Bryan looked tall and smart in a green suit and I was really proud when some of the boys said how young and pretty she was. I now realise, as I think about it, that she was only 35 at the time.

That first term ended eventually, though the way everyone slowly counted down the days made the wait seem endless, particularly on those long restless summer nights in the long high dormitory. Most of the boys went off to London stations or on buses to places all over the country. They all left early in the morning. We were being collected by car – Jock Lucas and my father again – so we did not leave until mid-morning, and were on our own in the strange peace of a suddenly deserted school, anxious to get home but enjoying the freedom of a warm summer morning, with the gardens full of roses.

Eventually we were off, and the journey seemed much shorter this time. Three months is a long time at that age, and it felt odd to be arriving back in the village. Just for a moment, the most familiar sights seemed new and different. At home, after the initial hugs and greetings, it was even stranger. After all those weeks of huge rooms and wide stone passages, everything at home, even the Public Bar, seemed so much smaller, and I kept tripping on the stairs all that first day.

It was a good summer. Everyone, including Mack the dog, was still there – Henry in his usual place by the bar and the domino games continuing. My parents, with Bryan to care for, still seemed to be getting on better. Though my father did spend spent some of that long summer in hospital, it still felt a calmer and more optimistic time. I remember them kissing at the end of a hospital visit – not a quick peck, but a proper kiss. I cannot remember seeing them do that before. I felt a mixture of embarrassment and a warm tingling of security. Children who have been through turmoil at home recognise and remember those moments as an unaccustomed and pleasant surprise. I got very used to pushing Bryan and his pram round the village, and learning to look after him in the evenings while my parents were in the bar.

This summer was also blessedly memorable because there were things to do. They included my going away camping in Scotland, quite near Edinburgh with my old Primary School, St Mary's, and meeting up again with the children I had grown up with. This meant that for now at least, all those links to the village were restored. I was happy about that, and about the very long train rides and train spotting opportunities.

We also went up to Manchester to show Bryan to my mother's family and were paraded around all the uncles and aunts. We had a good time, but it was clear on the way home, after a week away, that my father actually yearned for the big city with all its life and interest, and did not want to return to the 'swede bashers' of the village (the term we used for 'country bumpkins'), as he loudly declared when we got off the train back at Haddenham, despite the hushings of my mother.

For him I think the public bar visibility of his earlier disasters damaged forever his feelings about the pub and the village.

In that small world he could never again join in with the easy drinking and comfortable routine of the regulars. He must so often have craved what he saw as the anonymity and freedom of life in the city, but he seemed, then, unable to do anything about it. He showed courage and stamina in continuing to work during the day and be the non-drinking Mine Host of evenings and weekends. I think he lacked the confidence to break out of it until very much later, and was also, I realised when I was older, desperate not to be on his own.

At the end of that summer I was getting ready to go back to J Ston to start the year of 1960/61 year. In the days beforehand I now had feelings of real excitement and anticipation. When we left, with my father, my mother was as upset as she always had been and always would be at these partings. I can never remember a time when the separations did not cause her tears, but, sad as this made me feel, I did now have a world of my own to get back to and was keen for it all to start.

Chapter 13

A HAPPY YEAR

That year became one of the happiest of my childhood. Once back and into the routine, I enjoyed the experience of being popular and successful in that close and highly-organised world. It was that time of latency when you are old enough to be confident and busy, but not yet preoccupied one way or another with sexual development, complicated relationships, and all the urges to get on fast and become grown up. There were few outside or media pressures in those days, least of all in a boarding school. There was activity without exhaustion, responsibility without pressure, and a rolling routine into which you fitted.

Though neither top of the class nor a star at sports, I was good enough at all these things to be well accepted. I was loomingly tall for my age, had lost my podginess and was back, thank goodness, to long trousers. My brother was now a junior in the same house and I was really glad that he was there, although in the approved way of brothers at boarding school I did not pay him much heed. To everyone else we were Hedge I (that was me), and Hedge II, and all our clothes and kit were marked in this way.

Institutional life at J Ston was a curious mixture of kindness and being cruel, supposedly to be kind. The boys came from all over the country – in C House we had two brothers from the Isle of Man, a contingent from Liverpool and a good number from the North East. These included Dave Marshall, or 'Boghole'. As with most nicknames, no one could remember why he had been called this in the first place. He was small for his age, with black swept-back hair and a fantastic knowledge of pop music and football. He was centre forward for the school football team, which had other North East boys in it too. They had been together at the school for a long time and were very hard to beat. As J Ston was such a mix of accents and backgrounds it must have been odd for opposing teams, usually from expensive posh prep schools, to come up against this crew of Geordies and Scousers. How stupid and wasteful it was to break them up when we all went to the Senior School the following year, where only Rugby was allowed – though this turned out to suit me very well.

The goalkeeper in that team was a Manchester boy called Bramfitt. He and a couple of friends were keen to smoke, but tobacco was very hard to come by. They would hang about at the back of the wandering crocodile on Sunday walks around Bushey gathering up salvageable dog ends. They would mix these up and then smoke them in a wooden pipe in the House drying room. That drying room, with no windows, was always good for secret and illicit activity.

It was there that we looked in great detail at the nude magazines of the time. They were only occasionally available, and someone must have brought them back after holidays. They were closely guarded and only seen by those allowed into the secret. In the drying room we would huddle around as pages were turned. The pictures were all black and white, and usually the Health and Efficiency style of glamour – pale ladies stretching out on beaches, or pressed against a rocky background with a melodramatic, yearning expression. You would have learnt very little about the bodies of women from these pictures, as any full-frontal details were either airbrushed away or covered in gauzy material. It was exciting, but I still knew very little about the actual mechanics. I suspected that my ignorance was more profound than most, and it was from the more knowledgeable of the Drying Room boys that I picked up the real facts, or the basic ones at least. Awareness and interest began to dawn.

Formal sex education was very limited in those days. When the school cleaner and handyman – an older chap with a flat cap and milk bottle glasses – found the nude book stash in someone's locker, the owner was in big trouble. The lockers were supposed to be private, so the cleaner's motives seem very suspicious, looking back, but everyone was spoken to by Mr Reid. He duly gave us the talk on masturbation and its evil consequences, in essentially Victorian terms. If you were to believe all this then there was no doubt that the masturbator had little to look forward to but a life of exhaustion and moral decay. Fortunately, even then, that seemed rather unlikely to us.

There was no one else to ask. No one would have dared to consult our kindly old Matron about any of this. She presided over the piles of laundry in her room upstairs, occasionally descending to administer spoonfuls of compulsory malt. I suppose this was meant to be good for our general health and to keep us regular, but I could never stand the taste and avoided the process whenever I could.

We never saw television, but there was radio. This was on sometimes in the Day Room but most people managed to get a small transistor radio. They were quite new then, and although the number of stations was very limited you could at least choose for yourself. Boghole was really keen on music and Radio Luxembourg, so we all stayed up with the latest tunes. Tucked up at night in the silence of the dormitory, you could also use the tiny earphones to hear football commentaries. You had to watch out for the Duty Master's inevitable checking visit, but we were all in the same boat, so we usually managed a shared and effective early warning system.

The other popular individual pastime was dot cricket, which may still be played for all I know. Cricket was then the second national game and most boys knew a good deal about current and earlier famous players, so that you had a score book, and entered two teams which might well include yourself and Harold Larwood to open the bowling against a team with Ken Barrington and WG Grace. You used a dice, or more usually a small cardboard spinner that you could make yourself. There was a recognised code for dot balls, runs and wickets. You got some surprising results of course – Sobers caught Compton bowled Hedge 0 for example!

Our masters in the house were sometimes quite helpful if we came up with ideas of our own. I was keen on plays and theatre, though I had not seen very much yet. However I had, with increased confidence, discovered a talent for getting things going. Having got together a group of friends, we were allowed to 'do a play' in the empty A House at the end of the row. It was called, I remember, 'Shivering Shocks' and was one of those ancient spy mystery potboilers which Samuel French published in the 1930s. I don't remember where we got our set from, and the copies must have been given to us from some unopened pre-war cupboard or other. We seemed to be left to get on with it in a most unusual way for J Ston. I made sure of course that I had the lead, which involved being tied to a chair in the last act before getting myself free to solve the riddles and dish the villain.

We also managed a bit of singing. This was organised by Boghole of course and was accompanied by kazoos and paper and comb. It was a great success, and seen by all the other houses, so we did it a few times and basked in our short-term fame and success.

Teaching at J Ston was strict and traditional, but generally benign. There were exceptions though. I was very glad not to be learning Spanish. This was taught by the Housemaster of E house. He had a Spanish name and dark fierce looks with receding black hair, but I will call him Mr Blanco, since he was capable of spreading white-faced fear all around him. He dispensed beatings not only to the boys in his own house, but also to anyone else who ran in the corridors or committed other serious crimes of that sort. Victims suffered serious bruising to the buttocks, and like all bullies he tended to target the same people. There was never any real remedy to this and although one boy's mother went so far as to complain, this changed nothing and he seemed to us to be dangerously unpredictable and completely invulnerable. The truth is that all old-fashioned boarding schools harboured a minority of sadists and paedophiles. These days Mr Blanco would of course have his motives more clearly examined and probably be locked up. To beat fatherless boys of 11 or 12 as he did implies a sadism of real commitment, which can now only really be seen as perversion.

It was the lower forms who learnt Spanish – I do not know why this was seen as more suitable for them than French, but it was believed to be easier. This meant that they were more obviously at risk. No doubt this massively discouraged them from much interest in the Spanish language. I have no idea what may have happened to Mr Blanco in the longer run. It is too much to hope for, perhaps, that he encountered his own eventual Inquisition, but that is surely what he deserved. I was very glad that my brother David, because of his brittle bone disease, was spared any punishment by this man or any of the others.

There were a few other severe characters, including a heavy-handed man called Stewart who taught maths, and as well as being ever-ready to dish out retribution with a sawn off cricket bat he was prone to severe sarcasm and insult. I remember that he dismissed the whole of my class as second-rate dunces who would never amount to anything. Charming – especially from a single man in his 30s living in at a charity boarding school with no obvious interest aside from school games and beating. At least you knew where you were with him, but this was not the case with Reverend Stowe, the school chaplain. He took services on Sunday and taught RE. A lantern-jawed evangelical with Buddy Holly glasses, he held fierce views on religion and much else. He had an ability to go from beaming beneficence to ferocity very quickly if you got on the wrong side of him.

Most though were decent and friendly. My favourite apart from Alfie was our English teacher, a man called Brown, who also ran the school cricket team. Under him, quite surprisingly, I did make the school first XI in my last term, and playing in proper whites for the first time felt really significant. My nerves tended to get the better of me and I made a duck in my first match, compounding it by dropping a catch and generally proving to be a poor fielder. I did better in the match against the staff, making some runs, and then, somehow, taking a bullet-fast low catch at mid on from 'Alfie', who was a fine cricketer and legendary hitter. This was not especially popular, as he was the main attraction for everyone watching, and I stopped him very early in his display. I can still remember the shock and then the thrill of actually holding on to the ball at ankle height. It was a long way on from the pub car park.

We all took the Common Entrance exams in that last term. This was not about admission to another school, as we were all heading across the playing fields to the Senior School, but it was used to put us into classes when we got there. Common Entrance was a demanding test for 12 and 13-year-olds. Many of the boys had been there from the age of eight or nine and had more years of French, Latin and Algebra than me, so that it did take time for me to find my level, for all the extra Latin exercises. While my maths improved somewhat, my woodwork made no progress at all. Again, as at Aylesbury, the main exercise was a covered stool, and again mine never got beyond the very basic stages. At J Ston, though, this was the least scary of subjects. The teacher, a heavy smoker, was supposed to have been the builder of the abandoned railway layout in A house. By now, however, he seemed to have little enthusiasm and spent a good deal of the time outside in the corridor with a cigarette, merely barking instructions from time to time. My general incompetence was barely noticed.

We saw our parents at mid-term, when we all received what was called an 'Exeat'. This was a written permission to go out and was for set hours. You had to be back by the early evening, so when our parents came we were always keen to be off. A popular choice was the Ruislip Lido not very far away, but my father, who was usually the one to come, took us to a football match at Watford once, and several matinees in London. There was always a great comparing of notes when we all got back. It was reassuring to hear directly about home, though my mother always wrote at least once a week. Though the homesickness was long gone, you did miss your parents.

The unmentionable dread of the boarding school child, which you could never bring yourself to speak about, was to be summoned to the Head's office to have the news broken to you that a parent had died. I don't know why we always assumed that it would be a summons to the Headmaster and there must have been some folklore about this, but it was not an unrealistic fear for most of them, who had already lost a father.

During that year the holidays back at home were reasonably settled. Bryan was christened and everything seemed quite settled for once. The final summer term at J Ston was the happiest of all my time away at school. As well as playing for the school I won a form prize, and was taken down to Watford to choose a book by the Deputy Head, Mr Blackwood, an urbane and friendly man, able to set you at your ease, demonstrating again what a mixed bag the J Ston staff were. I chose a Patrick Moore book on astronomy. Though not much of a mathematician, I was in love then with dreams of space and other worlds.

The final treat of that term was a trip to the 1961 Russian exhibition at Earls Court. This was a very big event at the time and the first major cultural exchange since the Cold War began. This was the Russia of Gagarin and going into space, but the Hungarian uprising had been only a few years before and we all lived whatever age you were with general fears about the bomb and nuclear disaster. I do not remember much about the exhibition apart, of course from the space stuff, and Sputnik. I brought back masses of printed handouts and magazines, but it was, as always, great to have a day away from school.

So, by the time I came to leave J Ston I had become used to the boarding life, and although another even bigger change was coming up I knew that I would be making that shift with many boys that I knew and liked. 'Going up' had all the usual myths and stories attached to it, but you knew you would be doing it with friends and not on your own. The summer holidays were generally fine as my parent's calmer period continued, and of course my baby brother, 13 years younger than me, still needed a good deal of pram pushing around the village. Things had changed, though. Although the pub regulars remained largely the same, my own connections with the village were less sure and the links with my primary school friends were slowly and steadily slipping away. There was no single moment when this happened and I wish looking back that I had made more effort to hold on to the people I had grown up with, but I didn't really know how to do it and gradually from then on it just happened.

Chapter 14

OVER TO STON

—◦⟨✕⟩◦—

It is now the late summer of 1961. I am 13 years old. The summer holidays are nearly over, and I am beginning to get ready to go to the Senior School, to Ston itself. I know that my brother and I will be parted again as he will be staying at J Ston for another year. I have been to Ston a few times, to take swimming lessons last year, but otherwise I have no definite idea of what to expect, beyond the usual tales and warnings broadcast by those with older brothers. Though there is not much accurate information available, and we have had no real preparation, I am not particularly anxious this time. This is not just because I am getting used to school changes – this is the third move in two years – but because the senior group from my class and house at J Ston will go through the same experience together. All moves are easier when you are not on your own. We all know that this is to be a very different and much bigger change. We face a rite of passage, though none of us could have called it that.

For the first time I travelled to school on my own by Green

Line bus. I can remember very well walking through the high gates and looking up at the tall, beautiful tower with its flagpole on top and gilded clock faces on each side. Though built just into the 20ᵗʰ century, the Royal Masonic School was designed to seem older. It had many towers and ramparts, with shaded cloisters and broad fields. It was the complete embodiment of my father's imagined idyll of a public school. In the autumn sun he might have imagined Harry Wharton complaining to Bob Cherry about the Fat Owl of the Remove and the price of tuck.

In just a few days we all came to know the layout of the place. Even now I can visualise every inch of it. I was to be there for four years and although, as will become clear, there was a great deal which I hated about Ston and what it represented, I never doubted its beauty. On winter evenings, when your breath smoked and your feet clattered along the paved cloisters on some errand, it had a magical and almost mediaeval atmosphere. On summer afternoons, if you playing cricket on the main field, 'The Table', you looked towards the main buildings and the clock tower and saw an Edwardian picture of sunny calm and opulence. This then was the Royal Masonic School. Provided by Freemasons for the sons of dead or distressed brothers it represented their faith in endurance, order and obedience. It was summed up in the school motto 'Audi, Vide, Tace' or Hear, See and Be Silent, and in the lines from Ecclesiasticus, which we were to hear intoned so often in chapel – 'Let us now praise famous men and our fathers that begat us'.

There were eight houses, each with about 50 boys, set in pairs at the corners of a large quadrangle. All had a similar layout on three levels. On the ground floor there was a day room, washroom, and changing room. Above were two floors of dormitories with the younger boys at the top. The dayroom had lockers on two sides and long tables for evening prep. The layout may have been the same but each house had a very different culture, with varying approaches to discipline, and they all inevitably reflected the attitude of the Housemaster, who was absolutely the most important figure in your day-to-day life.

I was assigned to Headmaster's House. I suppose this was because it was next to the book-lined rooms of the Head's home, between the clock tower and us. In fact we had no special relationship with Mullens, a diminutive Classics scholar who outside chapel and formal gatherings was hardly ever seen without his pipe. Bald and portly, he might have been John Betjeman's more serious older brother. All the other houses were named after Masonic luminaries, all of them associated with the school – Keyser and Connaught, Derby and Devonshire, Leas and Burwood. We were never told anything much about these Edwardian grandees, but they certainly reinforced the Masonic identity of the school.

The new intake in those baby boom years was big enough that some of us, myself included, did not go straight into our assigned house. We went instead to the Overflow, a little way apart from the others, at the back of the school, in what must have been an old sanatorium building. Though this seemed disappointing at first it was certainly more modern and comfortable than the main houses. It also gave us a gentler introduction to the steep hierarchy of older boys and the complexity of house rules. We did games and activities with our parent houses, and ate with them on the long refectory tables. Otherwise we studied and had our free time in the main room of the Overflow, a large chalet style building with plenty of big windows. Boys from the different J Ston houses were not always transferred together to their new house at Ston. I was lucky again that Paul Griffin and I from C House were both attached to Headmaster's house, and both in the Overflow. It made a world of difference, especially if you were shy and awkward, and I was certainly still both, to have a more confident friend alongside.

The Overflow housemaster was an older man, J R Wards, who taught Latin and Spanish. He had a walrus moustache and a shambling manner, with a habit of tugging at his collar, harrumphing as he did so as if it was too tight. He had four prefects to run the daily routine, each assigned from a different main house. They were generally strict and we got used very quickly to writing lines and sides of composition on impossible subjects for mainly technical transgressions. For example we were supposed to polish all footwear to a gleam, including our slippers. I failed to do this, and can remember trying to compose four or six pages on 'The inside of a tennis table ball'. This was good for the imagination, but not for your prose style. It was certainly tough going for those who struggled with the pace of routine or were less good at English so that there was unfairness about it, too. It was an onerous regime but not especially brutal – unlike the stories you heard from form mates in the main houses.

Headmaster's House itself was run by a younger competitive and ebullient character called David Harvey Hector Beams, who features strongly in later chapters. He taught geography, was an officer in the Cadet Corps, and gloried in physical activities. The house had a name for being rather rough – physical and rather *laissez faire*, rather than merely hearty. It was fine if you liked rugby and so on, but if you were more timid or not very sporty it could be an intimidating place.

The Head of House was also the Head of School. His name was Harvey Postlethwaite. He was in his final year and went on to have a legendary engineering career in Formula One racing before dying of a heart attack at the age of 55.

We did our lessons in a block of classrooms which adjoined the main hall, or Big School as it was called. Many years later this long room with dark wood panels and high windows would become a favourite set for film and TV productions with its echoing Gothic atmosphere. Outside, in the corridors, the walls were covered with painted but peeling honours lists of schoolboy glory from long ago. They were painted out several years later in a belated redecoration project. Keen by then on Gothic reveries and the Romantic poets, I felt that this was a great shame.

Science went on in a separate block, on one side of the cloisters, so that you had to walk though it to get to the Refectory from our house. It usually had the old-fashioned 'science' whiff of gas mingled with a hint of formaldehyde. There was a chemistry laboratory with tiered seating and Bunsen burners, but I remember best the Biology laboratory, with various curiosities in glass cases. The most shocking of these was known to us as 'the bottled baby.' This was a fully formed foetus with tiny ears and nose and the remains of an umbilical cord. It seemed to me, even at the age of 13, that this was an extraordinary and obscene 'exhibit', always visible, but never referred to in any lesson, and never explained. This may have been fairly common practice 50 years ago – certainly Lindsay Anderson makes his heroes find one in the film 'If', when they are rummaging in the dark spaces below their Big School. At least theirs had been taken off display. There was a kind of unspoken awe about it, and it was never trivialised with a nickname but always remained 'the bottled baby'.

The early weeks of that first term involved a whole series of new subjects and new routines. There was a chapel service each morning to start the school day and matins on Sunday, so we saw plenty of the chapel. The new joiners all had treble or alto voices, but we now joined in with the booming male voices of the older boys.

There was an early reconnection with the rugby which I had so loathed at Aylesbury. Now, with a red and black hooped house shirt and a fair degree of physical confidence, I found that I could catch and run well and began to enjoy the game. I was less keen from the start on the Cadet Corps, which was compulsory and dominated Tuesdays until lunchtime. For the first couple of terms, though, we marched about in old-fashioned cream sweaters and big boots. With no worries about the rigours of uniform or having to take responsibility for cleaning an allocated rifle, even this, for the time being, was tolerable.

I was given the job of collecting the mail for the Overflow from the front hall. Each house sent a representative, usually someone in their first year, and you had to mark the name and number of items down in a book and get them signed for by the recipient. The front hall porter dished out the mail first thing in the morning. He was a strongly opinionated old Naval Chief Petty Officer with whom it was unwise to tangle. He always had shoes you could see your face in and a short haircut, which was so neat that it seemed to have been sprayed onto his head. You sometimes had to hang about to wait for the post, but with luck you could explore the front hall and upstairs gallery, which had assegais, animal heads and much else, including a marvellous butterfly collection in glass cases. I have often wondered whatever happened to these collections, presumably made by old boys and Freemasons, once the school closed may years later.

All in all it was better than I had expected. I settled in, tried my hardest at everything, and quite quickly went up another form, to the top stream in my year – 3A. I had friends there, and also in the Overflow and Headmaster's House. This was the start of four years at Ston. I would be there for about 40 weeks a year until I left. It was a busy place and made many demands. Living there was in extreme contrast to the holidays spent back in the pub and the village. To use the adjective we all used, the following chapters are about Stonic life in all its forms –in the classroom, the house, chapel and of course on the dreaded parade ground.

Chapter 15

LIFE AT STON

―――――○✕○――――――

Taking it and Dishing it out

Behind the strict routine and regulation there was a more general toughness among the boys, which left little room for sensitivity or tolerance of anything out of the ordinary. Bullying in modern times has, through social media, become a great and damaging scourge, with no respite at home, because you can be reached and tormented wherever you are. There is at least some real recognition that there is a problem, and, on the whole, schools try to help.

Ston in the 1960s was a world away from this. The prevailing assumptions seemed to be that boys would be boys; that rough and tumble was inevitable, and that LEADERSHIP was developed through giving older boys significant control and privileges over younger ones. LEADERSHIP, in the final years of old-fashioned boarding education, was regarded not just as a vocation but almost a religious idea. In practice giving very lightly supervised control to boys of 17 or 18 meant that they exercised an overall power and patronage, which meant that bullying was inevitable. If you were a duffer at sports, lacked entertaining qualities of wit or displayed insufficient 'ladmanship' then prefects, who had formal powers, would pick on you. You were also vulnerable to older, rougher types, whose behaviour was often beyond the reach of prefects. Of course that legitimised others to join in informally, including the ones who thought they might be vulnerable if they did not do so. So much for Leadership.

The Beams period in Headmaster's House was particularly bad in this respect as his 'robust' approach set the tone for the house. He was heavy handed, even for Ston. I can remember very well a boy named Bonell, a lumpy and awkward lad of 14 or 15, with big feet and a general air of clumsiness. He was good at neither gamesnor any kind of sport. He was usually in trouble for one kind of minor infraction or another. Corps parade was a complete nightmare for him. The boys in charge set the tone, and most other people joined in, either actively or by collusion. The 'head in the bog' torture for perceived lack of cleanliness was one regular torment, and boys like Bonell were simply expected to put up with this and much more, including the steady drip, drip, drip of ridicule. In one way or another we were all part of it – institutional hierarchies make standing out very difficult. I do not remember anybody ever standing up for Bonell, or any adult form of authority intervening. He would have found it very difficult indeed to complain for himself, as the telling of tales was part of an honour code underpinned by our own insecurities about becoming the focus of attention.

The best protection was to be part of a group of friends, and better still if you were part of the 'in group' of your year, both in the house and the wider school. As ever it was usually a mixture of prowess at work and games which got you into that enviable position. Those who were shy or isolated for one reason or another suffered worst.

I remember a boy called Fairhurst. He became a target to be used by all who wanted to feel secure and superior, and in the end he made an attempt to hang himself in the cloakroom, with bootlaces tied together. He was away from us for a few days but then came back, and I do not think things were much different. While not directly involved in his bullying I know that, secure in the safety and sense of superiority of my own group, I did nothing about it either, and laughed no doubt at some of it as well.

Most public school regimes had a ridiculously complex code of dress and behaviour differentiated by age and progression, including the number of buttons you could leave undone and whether or not you could place hands in pockets. Juniors also went through the experience of fagging. You did a good deal of boot cleaning, tea making and fetching and carrying. The best strategy was to just obey, and the rationale for it all was that as you progressed year by year you would one day have these rights as well.

The group you had to be aware of and keep in with were a gaggle of fifth formers, members of 'The Remove', the old fashioned public school term for those who would not be going into the 6th form and would be leaving at the end of the school year. They had learned best how to warp formal authority to their own needs, a skill frequently found among those who have spent a long time growing up in institutions as they had. They knew that once the authorities had tried and failed to beat things out of you they were often stuck about what to do next. There were five or six of them in Headmaster's House, all quite tough and mainly from the north. They were fine if you did their bidding and did not cross them, but they could be trouble if you answered back. It was a kind of traditional and expected form of bullying, and Beams, to his discredit, just took it for granted and let it go. The honour code of course meant that no one ever said anything – Audi Vide Tace all over again.

Their leader in my early years at Ston was Johnny Strange from Liverpool. Some gave him a wide birth and some, like Mullens the Headmaster, tried to reform him by reason and not a little patronage. I suspect he was attracted by Johnny's wildness and energy, with his quiff, drawl, and rebel without a cause manner. The Head certainly wanted to win him for the establishment. His motives were of course suspected, and he was certainly ridiculed by Strange himself.

At the beginning of my second year at Ston I had some leather gloves, a present from my parents, stolen. I knew that Johnny Strange had done it. It took some agonising for me to accuse him, but I did. It was right at the end of the Christmas term, early in the morning when everyone was preparing to travel off home. Of course he denied it and laughed me off, and I got nowhere. At the start of the next term it was impossible to go back to it. Johnny seemed to get away with everything. He was probably better equipped for leadership than those who went through the formal processes, but I do not know what happened to him after Ston.

Food and feeding

All the meals at Ston took place in the big Refectory with its beamed ceiling and dark panels, though it never seemed to me a gloomy place, and on a sunny day the light would stream through high ecclesiastical windows. All meals at Ston began and ended with the ringing of a big bell and the saying of a grace. At lunchtime this was usually a full-blown Latin blessing.

Each of the eight houses had two long wooden tables with benches either side – one for the junior forms and one for the seniors, with prefects at the top placings of each. While you could choose who regularly to sit next to, everyone moved one clockwise place per day. This meant that you moved steadily towards the small block of prefects and higher levels of decorum, but once you had crossed over and begun to move down the opposite side, conversation and behaviour could become more informal. On either side of matron at the bottom of each table better manners were expected again, though the Headmaster's House matron was fairly deaf, and one of the crueller games for the daring was to make indecent suggestions or risqué remarks in tones quiet enough not to be heard by her, but loud enough to amuse your neighbours.

Each meal had its menu strengths and weaknesses of course. We would trudge into breakfast at 7.30 each day, scratching in our corps khaki on Tuesdays. It was usually two courses, so we were well fed, though my prevailing memory is of a curiously cool porridge, which would lie like pale glue in the white bowl and only become workable with plenty of even colder milk. There was always plenty of tea – we never had the offer of coffee. One of the first things you noticed about the mugs and cutlery was that they usually had the initials RMIB on them – Royal Masonic Institution for Boys.

Lunch was the main meal on every day of the week, after morning school, or chapel on Sundays. While we moaned about the food as a routine response to the institutional offer, I think the diet overall was well ahead of its time for health and nutrition, and I certainly enjoyed most of it. There were exceptions of course. Most weeks we had a neck of mutton stew with thin pearl barley gravy, and on those days the potatoes always seemed lumpier than usual. 'Bone stew' was one of the few Stonic offerings which I loathed.

We always had an early supper, between the end of afternoon school, or games in the winter, and the start of prep. This was the last meal of the day and as with lunch there was a set of dishes, which came rolling around regularly and hardly ever varied. This meal often involved soup and cheese, but occasionally we had a revolting combination of savoury mince served on fried bread, which I could never manage to eat.

The person in charge of catering at Ston was a tall and rather attractive middle-aged woman. She had a ringing and very posh voice and her name was Mrs Venables. I never heard her first name used by anyone, and she seemed to be the monarch of all she surveyed in the refectory and kitchens. She had a small snappy dog which, away from the Refectory, was always with her. She would stride formidably along like a ship in full sail and the wretched dog would run along furiously on its tiny legs to keep up. She married one of the masters in the end, so she cannot really have been as old as we imagined.

Without choice at school we all learned, at least, not to be fussy eaters, but the endlessly rotating menus, and the fact that we never ate out during the holidays because of the pub routine, meant that by the time I had left school I still had very limited knowledge of food and its wider possibilities. Spaghetti always came in tins as far as I was concerned, and fish was always in batter.

We were hardly ever officially exposed to alcohol at Ston, and it was always water or tea with meals. There were very small exceptions once you got older. The Headmaster would offer you a small sherry when it was your turn in the first year 6th to sit with him in the book-lined study of his house and try to respond to his questions about your interest and studies. We were once given a small amount of beer after winning the house Rugby Cup in my last year, but only enough to make you wish there was more, as by then some of us had already found the Swan and its willingness to serve us. We had other ways to experiment with drink – once you had a study, or at least the share of one, both smoking and bottles of wine became possibilities, as we all sought the sophistication we craved. Surrounded by the stuff in the holidays I did not really bother, and the truth is that I had a strange and ambivalent attitude towards booze. I knew perfectly well from an early age what alcohol had done to my father and some of his customers, but I liked the warmth and confidence it seemed to give, especially if you were down.

Sex and mainly thinking about it

Years after leaving Ston I came across a second-hand book entitled 'A young person's guide to sexual behaviour' by that well-known author A. Housemaster. A quick thumb through this work revealed that of 12 chapters, seven at least were about masturbation. The information conveyed about this activity included many of the hoary old myths about the sapping of strength and willpower, and the likelihood of extreme moral degradation, which would certainly follow for the most persistent and committed wankers. All this reminded me very strongly of the line taken by Ston and its masters, where all these ideas were still in circulation as Britain entered the so-called 'swinging sixties'. There was never much sensible information or advice about wanking, or any other aspect of sexual development, at either the Junior or Senior Schools. This perfectly ordinary activity was never talked about by masters in a spirit of education or reassurance, and several times we had the classic line about prolonged activity potentially damaging your eyesight.

Of course we just got on with it anyway, some more than others and some not very secretly either. I can remember there being 'wanking races.' There was also a game involving someone shining a torch against the dormitory wall so that obscene shadow displays could be created. I suppose that we were actually very naïve and unsophisticated, compared with adolescents today. We were protected from pornography, mainly because it was much harder to get hold of then. Occasionally a well -thumbed magazine would appear from someone's older brother, or scavenged from the street, but by modern standards they were very tame indeed. The models all had faraway looks, and usually some wispy covering so that not much was revealed.

The vaginal area was always air brushed both of detail and any suggestion of hair. I have already mentioned the times at J Ston when some of us crouched away in the quiet seclusion of the drying room and looked at pictures like these. Most of us had very limited awareness of what female bodies might look like in detail and the pictures, though exciting, really did not take your anatomical knowledge much further.

We did all manage to read the one well-known and by then widely available piece of literature which dealt graphically with the details of a sexual encounter. Lady Chatterley's Lover, or LCL as we all knew it, was always passed around inside brown paper covers. An alias title was always prominently handwritten on the front. Ours was Bleak House, an interesting choice, but I can also remember Silas Marner being used. There were other sources of quality filth if you knew where to look. In the classics section of the Library there were editions of Ovid and Catullus with some very steamy scenes, and as the English translation was given on the opposite page to the Latin you did not have to be a scholar to get to it. The volumes concerned, otherwise untouched, had bleach-white edges save for a thin grimy line showing you where to look.

Neither at J Ston nor Ston itself did we have anything resembling sex education. Eventually in the Fourth Form there were a few biology lessons about the relevant male and female organs, but absolutely nothing beyond line drawings and learning some of the proper words. Even this very basic guide to the plumbing lacked any reference to the actual dynamics, let alone anything to do with sexuality or the implications for relationships. The result of all this was that in the Senior School, and with older boys around, you picked up the alternative adolescent version of things, quickly learning all the illicit words, as well as the dreadful assumptions and jokes which young men, especially those with no real experience, make about girls and women.

Many of us lusted after the maids who worked in the kitchens and served the food to our tables. These Irish girls, mainly from County Wexford, were admired from a distance in the otherwise single-sex desert of life at Ston. In their blue uniforms and white aprons they had to bend and stretch over tables to collect plates so that all adolescents in the vicinity would hope for glimpses of flesh and pretend rather too obviously not to be looking. There were occasional smiles, but they were forbidden to fraternise, and most just seemed to ignore us, though it cannot have been very pleasant for them. The school quite sensibly changed in later years to using men and later still to self–service.

In my four years at Ston, for about 38 weeks a year, I had no normal sociable company with girls of my own age, and back at home in the pub, I had lost my connections to the children I had grown up with. In the holidays I had no real idea, stuck in the village, about how to break out to meet girls my own age, or better still, older! I do remember trying to bridge myself back into local links by writing to a girl of my own age, Janet, when I was 15. We had gone off to the Aylesbury schools at the same time, having had years together in primary school. I wrote about school and the things I was interested in, and got a reply which was friendly and pleasant but tactfully pointed out that her boyfriend would not like a regular correspondence. I do not know what I had expected, but I suppose I had been desperate to do something.

I wish, looking back, that I had shown more gumption about this, but I was shy, and our relative family poverty meant that we wore school clothes at home, so I certainly did not look the part either. I would never have admitted the thing about clothes back at school, where most people talked about the gear they had at home, and I avoided the subject as best I could. My parents, beset with their own problems, seemed to have no idea that this might be an issue, and I just could not find a way of raising it with them.

An assumption often made about traditional boarding education was that homosexuality was widespread. You would never guess this from the asexual atmosphere of the Frank Richards stories – no queers at Greyfriars – and even A Housemaster was very guarded about the subject. Even allowing for the confusion and uncertainty of adolescent years, Ston must of course have had the normal range of sexuality and early sexual experience you would find in any group of young men. Given the hothouse atmosphere of an all-male institution there was certainly some quiet experimentation going on. There was certainly more opportunity for that than for getting close to girls. There were certainly crushes and some close friendships, which people labelled homosexual, whether they were or not.

For myself, I never had the slightest uncertainty about my own heterosexuality. I was pretty clear about what I lusted after – I just had no realistic idea about how to get it. I remember at the first Army camp I went to in Devon being sized up by a boy a year older who had been allocated the bunk below me. He wanted to be friends and share a bivouac when we were out on the overnight manoeuvre, but his trying both to monopolise my attention and become physically closer than I was comfortable with warned me off, and he got the message quickly enough after that.

I do not remember any particularly bad treatment being handed out to boys who were discovering that they were gay. On the other hand this was not a place or time when coming out would have been a practical proposition, so beyond the usual jokes about 'pretty boys' and a degree of affected campness, there were few signs of what was really going on. It must have been hell if you were gay, but probably no worse and possibly safer than the real world outside Ston, before the Sexual Offences Act in 1967 began the very slow process towards a more civilised society. John Osborne once said that in England in the 50s you only had to wear something like a yellow sweater to be regarded as 'queer', and for all the looking back to a so called swinging 60s it had really not changed much by then.

As to the staff, intimations and assumptions were made about some of them. What we now know about closed institutions like Ston suggests that there must have been paedophilic behaviour, but to be fair I came across none of it, directly or indirectly. The liking of some for the delivery of caning may of course have suggested another strongly-related vice.

At the Senior School, most of us were preoccupied with unfulfilled heterosexual lust, with an unfulfilled longing for direct contact with girls and at least some kind of sexual experience. A minority had some of that, or at least said they did, but we were almost all still virgins by the time we left school. Hoping for better later on, you might say, but not expecting much for the present. Most of us gawped at the Irish maids and our frisson of excitement at a flash of thigh or cleavage was like a drop of water in a drought – reminding you why it mattered but only serving to underline the shortage.

The problem with all old-fashioned single-sex boarding school education was that it claimed to protect adolescents from premature sexual exposure, but in reality it just kept you short of information, and provided no opportunities to test anything out about relationships. Worse, it caused some really unhealthy pre-occupations and misunderstandings about gender and maleness. While it may be true that there are greater sexual pressures on young people now, they at least have access to better information and a far greater understanding of difference. I hope that sublimation of lust through hefty exercise and cold showers has gone forever, along with A. Housemaster and his concern about wanking and its impact on the Empire.

In my last year, Mullens, the Head, was still fighting what he saw as moral decline because of a perceived worsening of discipline. He called a special assembly, in which he preached at us for what seemed hours. There were hints about loose morals and a suggestion that some were involved in sexual activities with women (lucky them). Though no details were given, we knew of several illicit relationships with maids. As we milled about afterwards the atmosphere for a few minutes was almost revolutionary, and I can remember Boghole Marshall getting everyone to sing 'They're all queers together' to the Eton Boating Song. The spark nearly caught, but not quite, and the moment passed, but it was a sign that the 60s spirit was arriving at the gates at last.

Chapter 16

STONIC TEACHING

———∞———

Today's teachers are properly trained to teach, whether they are going to operate in private or state education. Schools and teachers are judged by results, and on the whole education is a much more participative process than it used to be. Teachers have to engage with students as opposed to simply controlling them, and the idea of keeping discipline by inflicting pain must seem barbaric to young people now. Thinking about the Stonic teachers and their methods over 50 years ago takes me back to an age when teachers had much freer rein without any real system of enforceable standards and regular inspection, certainly in private schools. So far as I know the Inspector never called at Ston.

There were some very good men among the teaching staff. Typically for Ston they all were all men, albeit in many shapes, sizes and ages. The good ones could catch your interest, and even inspire. What marked them out as being effective was that they managed to bring with them some feel of the outside world and its promise. They had a currency in language and attitude, so that their lessons shone with activity and optimism. Unfortunately there were very few of them. What you got most of the time was a plodding chalk-and-talk approach, but some of the worst teaching relied on material and method which had developed long ago and had been unaffected by the passing of many years. A fair proportion of these plodders, not surprisingly, were housemasters or assistant housemasters, so that as well as teaching you they would also be involved in house discipline, games and everything else which affected your life outside lessons. They supposedly had responsibility also for pastoral care, though my recollection is that this really amounted to very little beyond a general encouragement to follow the rules, and learn how to take and give the knocks without complaining.

Six mornings a week, including Saturdays, we had four lessons separated by a break. After lunch in the autumn and Easter terms the weekday afternoons until 4pm were always given over to games. We then had three more lessons in the late afternoon. By then it was usually dark outside and warm inside, so that it was often hard to stay awake and concentrate on algebra or Latin verbs. If a neighbour slipped off to sleep the decent thing was at least to nudge them if they were snoring, but sometimes this was too late. The desks certainly didn't encourage sleep. In my time they were sloping wooden surfaces on an old-fashioned metal frame with a big inkwell – more suitable, even then, as an exhibit in a museum about Edwardian life. We all wrote in ink, but usually with a fountain pen, having left J Ston and its handwriting lessons, behind. Biro was absolutely not permitted.

We were certainly worked hard. After supper there were two periods of prep for the third and fourth years and a third period for fifth and sixth formers. One of the advantages of doing the work around long tables in the house day room was that help was usually on hand, and the done thing was to help if asked. This did mean that the brighter and more assiduous types were in great demand from those who were struggling, either through lack of understanding or laziness. Each house had a small number of shared studies, and sixth formers were able to work in these. They were also a pleasant bolt-hole from the crowded tedium of life in the main day room. In a study it was much easier to be idle, or get up to no good, and when the time came I did both. Having fallen behind badly in 'A' level Latin I remember spending evenings lounging about and blowing illegal cigarette smoke up the study chimney before scribbling out translations from Cicero or Virgil which had been borrowed just in time from the exercise book of a compliant and better-prepared friend. As effective cheats will tell you, the secret is not just to copy but to build in some differences. The idea is to escape notice with respectable mediocrity, which is unlikely to be challenged. I was not challenged, but there is of course the inevitable reckoning, and I duly failed the exam badly, having wasted two years.

We were all streamed by ability, the A forms being the most academic and the D forms the least. In my first two years at Ston, in the third and fourth forms, I worked very hard and made it into the top stream, but my weak area was always maths. My teacher was a man called Burgess – 'Squeaky' we called him because of his high-pitched voice. In common with several other staff members, 'Squeaky' was a 'man of the cloth' – in his case a rather grubby cloth with a dog collar and sports jacket. He had thin straggling hair and huge horn-rimmed glasses. His breath always smelled of stale pipe tobacco, and you got a strong burst of this as he leaned over you while you attempted maths problems. As I wrestled with some poorly explained algebraic process he would be working his dusty way around the room from desk to desk, full of praise for some, but usually petulant and impatient with the likes of me. His sighing with exasperation served only to fuel my feelings of dimness.

With hindsight I came to see how poor his teaching was. I had always wondered if I was just no good at maths, and never could be. I was delighted to give the subject up when I started 'A' levels, but years later, when I had to do a statistical course at university, I was helped to good results by decent teaching and a very patient friend. I realised then that I was perfectly OK but had endured some very poor teaching at school. As is clear from this account it may be true that no one forgets a good teacher, but they remember the very bad ones just as well.

The Stonic approach to education was based on a series of compartments into which we were all placed. Your compartment was based not just on 'A' Level of academic prowess but perceived aptitude. This meant that as you went forward to 'A' level you opted for Arts or Maths and Science, but never a combination of the two. Your academic level also governed some of the subjects you took. In the A stream we did no art, or woodwork or metalwork. My own father's inability to do anything practical, without using excessive force and the wrong equipment, meant that I had not received any kind of paternal example, and so the lack of practical subjects in my schooling just compounded matters. I think the assumption must have been that your academic prowess would guarantee you a life in which others would be paid to do these tediously practical things for you. Alas this was never likely to be the case, and I wandered into adult life having gradually to learn how to manage basic tasks by a process of painful trial and error.

It was a great pity not to have had these subjects at school, not least because some of those teachers were among the best we had. A man called Ken Littledyke had achieved some renown beyond the school for pioneering work on helping boys build and sail canoes. The Art teacher was a man with a goatee beard and the exotic name of L.A.L.D. Renoir. We believed that he was actually a descendant of the great man himself, and perhaps he was. I am not sure what Mr Renoir's lengthy set of first-name initials stood for, but he was a great teacher, and ran a Sunday evening class for all comers. I always went to this, initially to escape the general bleakness of the Stonic Sabbath, but I quickly learned to enjoy his friendly encouragement to try things out and use the different materials.

There were other strange streaming assumptions. Commendably everyone took a modern language, but the lower forms learned Spanish and the higher ones French. This was supposedly on the grounds that Spanish was easier, which now seems a curiously insulting assumption to make. Dear old JR Wards, my Overflow housemaster taught the subject, though anyone more English and less Spanish it would be hard to imagine. The story was that the school had been short of a Spanish master in the War and he had learnt it from scratch by book alone.

Another anomaly was that if you opted for German in the first year at Ston, then you never studied geography again, from the age of 13. This was another educationally unwarrantable omission, but it also meant that you missed the entertainment of Geography lessons. The main Geographer was a man called Adey, whose lessons were legendary. They were delivered in a lecture hall with tiered fixed seating. He stood at the front gesticulating at the board or maps with a pointer and seemed to have too tight a collar, delivering his information in long monotone passages and staring at the class over his horn rims.

He relied very heavily on what were known then as 'Filmstrips'. They were the educational precursor of PowerPoint or video – a series of projected images revealing the geography of the Alps, or some such theme. He would talk through each picture elaborately. To show them effectively you had to have the lights off and blinds drawn and in the darkness beyond his reach the class would come to life. A quiet free-form mayhem would develop. Boys would crawl about; small experimental fires might be started, and one or two in the furthest corners would secretly wank – at least as secretly as could be managed in the back seats of a geography lesson. Once this act was interrupted by someone crawling under the desk with a ruler and whacking the part concerned with painful results – pain which had to be endured silently for fear of discovery.

Overall, teaching methods were very dull and traditional with a great deal of working through exercises and much repetition. I do not remember there being much ill discipline, the Geography room excepted. There was kudos in being in the top stream – as is often the case at that age, finding learning easy was matched by physical confidence so that a number of people were good at both work and games and formed a kind of 'glittering' elite in each house. It seems now to have been very unfair – where was the room for the late developer, or the person with a non-academic special skill? However the music regime at Ston was an exception. The head of Music, Graham Gorton, was a very talented and energetic man who somehow managed to put music at the centre of school life, and although I made a very poor show at learning the piano because of my failure to practice seriously, most of us had an opportunity to learn some music and to take part. There was the military band, an orchestra, occasional imported concerts and of course the singing we all did in chapel, whether we were in the choir or not.

A consequence of the fast track streaming was that I took my 'O' levels a year early, along with most members of my form, so as to push us ahead and gain a year. If we wanted to include German in the subjects to be taken we were given extra lessons, enabling us to do the course in two years from scratch. The only word to describe our teacher, E.A. Riches, was 'redoubtable.' He was a tall fat man, bald and with a huge bulldog face. He dressed always in venerable dark double-breasted suits, always with a large knotted tie, and often with a pipe. He would plod every day after lunch back to his rooms in the C and D tower and smoke the two cigarettes he allowed himself. He was a creature of long-established rather obsessive behaviour, every day. His was a highly patterned and Spartan life. In class he performed German rather than spoke it, with precise enunciation, and a swoop between high gentleness and a deeply booming bass. He could become alarmingly angry if he sensed inattention.

Several times a week the small group of us selected for special tuition would go to his rooms at the top of the tower. It was Stonic folklore, handed down from year to year, that it was very, very inadvisable to go to his room in games clothes. We were pretty safe in a group anyway from the implied risk of being groped or worse. We sat around working through a translation very slowly, and although it was a laborious, mechanical process it helped most of us to get reasonable marks in the end. E.A. Riches, for all his sonorous and sometimes fierce manner, could be patient and kind, especially if he felt that you were doing your best. He was the only member of staff I remember being regarded by the boys as a paedophile, though the word was not then in general use. If he was, the evidence of recent times is that he was unlikely to be the only one, but we knew nothing beyond the handed-down warnings.

He had been at the school since long before the war and knew everything about it. His long and little-read history of the school until 1938 is still mentioned on the Amazon website, but there is no post-1938 sequel. This work and his love of the school might have turned him into an obese version of Mr Chips, but his reputation prevented that.

With my ill-digested German and six other subjects I duly got my 'O" levels a year early. It had seemed a good idea at the time, but as I was to realise later, it was too far too fast. Apart from anything else, I went into three Arts subjects exclusively, with no more Maths and no more Science. This was much too early to specialise, and I had little real advice about my choice of subjects. Although I was quite clear about wanting to do English, I just went for Latin and History because that was the normal grouping for Ston. There was no flexibility in this system and none of us seemed able to challenge it. It now seems as arbitrary and silly as the whole idea of pushing us on faster than our level of maturity merited

My sixth form teachers were a curiously assorted bunch in both personality and approach. The two English teachers were the best, though I may have been more responsive to them because this was certainly my best subject. They were both demanding and creative teachers. A.J. Tough (known to us as 'Jack') worked us hard but had some flair, though you had to see beyond the sports jacket, brogues and very carefully driven Morris Minor. Jack had written a book of extracts to illustrate Elizabethan theatre beyond Shakespeare and we looked at that, as well as reading plays. He invited us once to his house to do a play reading. It was *The Admirable Crichton*, by James Barrie, so not exactly kitchen sink style, but to be there in a family home, for an evening with polite little coffee cups, coloured sugar and being taken seriously mattered a great deal then. I had never encountered multi-coloured sugar before!

My other English teacher, a man called Quibell Smith, was younger, probably not long out of Oxford, and took charge of the annual school plays. He would let us argue the toss about things way beyond the syllabus, and it was great to find your voice and make an argument. Even when things began to go wrong in my final year I managed to keep going with English Literature and somehow managed a top grade at the end of it all.

It was sadly not the same with History. Again we had two teachers. Smith was a terse and self-contained character, with a dusty black gown, and large bags under his eyes. He was a heavy smoker as well, and despite this unhealthy appearance was actually a fine cricketer and the coach of the rugby team, so I had even more to do with him when I made the first XV. He taught us, very drily indeed, the Tudors and Stuarts. That he was able to make a period of history so full of intrigue and the dark arts quite as dull as he did says something about the tiredness of his approach and his overreliance on a couple of set books. The facts were rattled out, but with no sense really of the shape or the context of it all. His colleague, Higgins, had an extraordinary and even duller approach. For two years he simply worked through large notebooks. He would sit by the window and dictate these notes, with a marked lisp at a completely regular speed, without discussion. That was how my class was taught 16th and 17th century European history. We recorded word by word his notes about Reformation, Renaissance and war. We crawled through Luther with his 95 'thethes' in Higgins speak. We slowly reached Charles V and the 30 Years War, all of it droned through in hour-by-hour dictation, standardised down to the very adjectives and verbs, as though we were Victorian copy clerks rather than learning to be proper students of history.

I was probably unwise to take Latin – JR Wards took most of the lessons in his gruff voice and shambling manner. He had a traditional approach to the set books and the teaching of Roman history. I got the idea of the poetry and loved the Virgil, at least in translation. We grappled with it line by line and although I made a good start in the first two terms I never really got to grips with the analysis of iambic pentameter, diphthongs and so on. By the second year, when we went on to one of Cicero's Verrine orations with its complex structure and fine orator's tricks, I was losing ground rapidly and losing heart as well. The work between lessons was often unseen translations for practice, so as time went on I relied increasingly on those friends who were willing to let me crib at short notice, often at the last minute in the breaks just before lessons.

When I began to have real problems in my 'A' Level year with anxiety and depression, my ability to cope gradually fell away, so that by the time of the exams I had done very little work, and no real revision. The one thing I hung on to was my love of English, and although there too I had fallen behind and never managed to complete several of the set books I sailed through those two papers, managing huge quotations from *Paradise Lost* and *King Lear* as my mind and pen raced on almost joyously. But the exams for the other two subjects were the only ones in my whole education where I knew that I would fail. I sat through the papers, mainly to avoid the interrogation which would follow walking out early, but I knew how far short my answers had fallen. On my last history paper, having improvised and half invented my brief answers, I spent the final hour drawing an imaginary picture of the execution of Charles 1st – complete with souvenir sellers and fast food stalls – but did not hand it in.

How best to sum it up? Stonic education was extremely traditional, and anything but child centred. It was elitist, without really doing justice to those of us supposedly more 'academic.' We were certainly not given much time to think for ourselves and the emphasis was very strongly on rote learning. There was no evidence of pastoral care so that if your performance dipped, as mine definitely did, there was no enquiry about this and no sense that help might be available. It was a very buttoned-up institutional approach, and it meant that the slightest kindness, or recognition of a personal interest, glitters in the memory.

In some ways the greater success of Ston was to help less 'academic' boys into reasonable work. This was often in the world of finance and insurance, so powerfully represented in the world of Freemasonry. The careers teacher, an old stager called Blake who walked with a stick, had many connections and a reputation for fixing people up, but it was always in those two fields, so that when anyone went to see him they came back to the house to be greeted by a chorus of 'banking and insurance'. He was known as 'Giddy' Blake, for reasons I never knew. There were decent men at Ston and he was the kindest of them all.

A significant number of the staff, I am sure, were themselves Freemasons, but we never had any obvious pushing of Masonry as anything to be applauded, promoted, or even explained. The influence was subtler than that. It lay in a strong emphasis in compliance, conformity, and doing what you were told.

This was true of most aspects of the day to day life at Ston, as already described, and the approach to learning relied on similar assumptions. Behind all of this, though, were the four main pillars of institutional life which underpinned and reinforced the Stonic approach of Audi, Vide, Tace – the Chapel, the Corps, the fear of beating and the endless playing of games.

THE FOUR PILLARS

Chapter 17

CHAPEL DAYS

———⋖⋗✕⋖⋗———

The core values of a Stonic education were represented in the four main pillars of traditional muscular Christianity – chapel, games, the Cadet Corps and corporal punishment. You could summarise this quite tidily as praying, playing, marching and beating. These activities, all compulsory or unavoidable, reflected the Masonic faith in church, state, obedience and order, without discussion or any right to dissent. It all came as a single package, and chapel was at the heart of it.

The Chapel of St Alban had been donated by another ubiquitous Masonic benefactor, Charles Edward Keyser. It was a low flint-faced building with a small tower to one side. Its interior, with black and white tiles and dark wood furnishings, was said to have designs and carvings by Hubert von Herkomer, a German artist who had had his own art school in Bushey before the First World War. Here and there in the dark wood and wall decoration were signs of Masonic identity with squares and compasses. Otherwise the Stonic chapel was utterly C of E. The pews ran most of its length of the chapel on either side with an allotted section for each house. The choir, red gowned for Royal Masonic, faced each other across the middle near the powerful organ. A red strip of carpet ran up to a step near the altar, on which sat a huge brass eagle lectern with a big black bible.

Chapel was a mainstay of the daily institutional timetable at Ston. We went there every morning, Saturdays included, before the day's lessons began. If you were anxiously facing exams, or had not done the work at last night's prep, you had a little time to ask for help through divine intervention. Mind you, all the evidence suggested that God concentrated his help on those who had helped themselves. The morning service was short – a hymn and prayers, with a reading, but it was definitely a service rather than an assembly. Each day's bible reading was done by fifth and sixth formers on a rota, and you had to be very sure of the day when your turn came round. If you forgot there would be an embarrassing silence, entertaining initially until the moment when you realised too late that you were the cause of it. Retribution would always follow.

The requirement to take your turn in reading made no allowances for anxiety or limited reading skills, so that it became a cruel and dreaded experience for some. The wise went early, found the right page and did some practice, by at least reading the passage through in advance. The text was, of course, like everything about Stonic religious observance solidly King James Version, so there were plenty of pitfalls.

A real risk, however well you had prepared, was that anyone who wanted to trip you up, or was generally wanting some entertainment, could shift your carefully marked place and move it to somewhere at the other end of the huge book – probably somewhere in the nether reaches of the Old Testament. It was a fairly risk-free form of vengeance, popularly used against those regarded as religiose or generally over-conforming. If you were in on this you had the vindictive but entertaining pleasure of watching the reader solemnly leave the pew in the final verse of the hymn and mount the step to the lectern, only realising then that the book was turned to Deuteronomy, say, instead of Acts. Even if you had taken the extra precaution of noting the page number, and most had not, a great deal of page turning and stress was involved in getting to your place.

The hymns were sung lustily enough, with treble and alto from the first two rows and deeper voices from the back. We got to know most of the Public School Hymn Book, and some came up regularly for festivals and commemorations. We all looked forward to the one which marked the end of each term – 'God be with you 'til we meet again'.
Inevitably some of them stuck for life. My brother David can still give a lively performance, embellished with actions of that old favourite:

Christian, dost thou see them, on the holy ground,
How the troops of Midian prowl and prowl around?
Christian, up and smite them, counting gain but loss;
Smite them by the merit of the holy cross.

On Saturdays, after the service and before lessons, we always had a whole-school singing practice. It was led by the Head of Music, Graham Garton. Whether or not you had any individual musical education, at Ston everyone had some involvement because of Garton's influence. I was not musical, did not sing in the choir, and only managed two ham-fisted and under-practised terms of piano lessons. Even so, I benefited as we all did from this experience of singing as a large group, with some rehearsal and an effort to try to get us to understand the notes and the content.

We all went to the Morning Service every Sunday, swapping our blazers and flannels for the uniform grey suit. Until quite late in my schooldays this was a hairy and scratchy herringbone, a cut that seemed to have been unchanged since the 1930s and looked utterly institutional. Later on it was replaced by a more up-to-date, though highly conventional, suit that was more comfortable, and at least looked fairly normal outside school.

The Sunday service was always the old Book of Common Prayer Matins. The readings were usually by senior teachers, though one or two of them also fell foul of the shuffled pages trick. The Chaplain usually conducted the service. In my first two years this was a nice old Welshman with a fine accent and quite a dramatic delivery, the Reverend F.A. (A for Aneurin) Pike. He died suddenly in the year after I was confirmed, and we all went to the chapel funeral service. It was the first funeral I had attended, with the coffin carried in and the service taking place around it. After he died the Rev Brian Stowe came back into our lives from the Junior School. He still had a long white face, jutting chin, cowlick haircut and big black-framed glasses. He looked like Buddy Holly's older and uglier religious brother. He was not popular and had a reputation as a kind of closet sadist – smiling to your face, but not to be crossed.

We all sang up on Sundays in the company of most of the live-in masters, the headmaster and his sister, and the Bursar's family. The Bursar's daughter, a little older than most of us, was not especially pretty, but in our all male world she got plenty of attention, especially from our end, near the door where the senior staff pews were. The Bursar himself was a shadowy figure for us, and aside from Sunday mornings he was only ever seen hurrying in his dark suit from one part of the school to the other and never speaking with any of the boys. There was of course Evensong as well, though this was not actually compulsory. In the winter term, certainly, it was reasonably attended because of the sparseness of a Stonic Sunday night with just the radio, no television and nowhere else to go.

Of course religious observance was not confined to chapel services. Every evening you had house prayers as well. Headmaster's House was probably typical of the practice going on in all eught houses at the same time on every weekday evening.

Prayers came after the second period of prep and for all but the sixth form it marked the end of the day and bed at 9pm. As well as the prayers you usually got notices and 'buck up' messages about routine. House prefects had to take the prayers very often and I can remember having to do this for the first time, and how awkward it felt.

Many of us became very sceptical about it all as the 1960s arrived, and we became more aware of what we saw as the hypocrisy and datedness of the Stonic brand of muscular Christianity, with its basis in God, games and the Corps. In the military ceremonials and associated church services there did seem to be a strong message of God On Our Side, which we bridled at, helped by the Dylan songs. It was our fate to catch the later and eventually terminal stages of that 19th Century ethic. This still dominated public school education in Britain and had sent countless thousands out to Empire and war to be unchallenging, to do the right thing and be generally be the right kind of chap. This industry supposedly produced god-fearing men, brought up to regard themselves as 'leaders'.

It endured for longer at Ston than most places. The assumption of the Freemasons funding the school must have been that the formula was still right for the fatherless boys they were trying to help. It appealed to the Masonic love of tradition, discipline and continuity, and they must have been convinced that it would work with us whatever our backgrounds or circumstances. There still seemed to be an unchallenged belief that good and frequent dollops of Anglican ritual were essential ingredients in turning out right thinking, reliable chaps who might make a solid career in banking or insurance. We would emerge as right-thinking, God-fearing fellows, thoroughly fit for purpose and loyal to the system.

Most of us were aware that in the real world things were on the move. Music, films and the television which we saw in the holidays all made that plain. Ston, though, seemed determined to keep things as they were. The tension between those two worlds became stronger and stronger as time went by. Stonic Chapel seemed such an important part of that tension that for many years afterwards I saw the Church of England as a huge and hateful totem for all that dusty conformity and hypocrisy which I loathed, and never mind that God had all the best tunes. It took me a very long time in later life to let go some of my assumptions about organised religion and find a way back.

The compulsion was an important issue, but not the only problem. Ours seemed to have been a religious education based on rituals and attendance rather than any teaching of values, or why it was all supposed to matter so much. Apart from Chapel the Religious Education classes at Ston were particularly poorly taught. Challenge and discussion were certainly not welcomed. I cannot remember any reference in chapel or those lessons to any other religion, let alone other kinds of Christian. No religious context was given, either, to any of the major issues affecting the world and the place of our faith in responding to them. This after all was the world of Sharpeville, the Berlin Wall and a general fear of nuclear disaster. Eventually as sixth formers we received an occasional talk from the outside world about current affairs, but we had nothing of this from the endless hours of religious participation we all went through. It is interesting that for all the chapel bashing of boarding school life, the earlier messages and memories from primary school are still the ones that remain.

It could be said, in defence, that the Masonic Schools did not encourage or provoke sectarianism. They just ignored other denominations and religions. The whole place was so monocultural, white and enclosed that we might be expected to assume anything else was either of lesser worth or just plain wrong. The result was that, intentionally or otherwise, the Stonic Chapel reinforced a good deal of the pervading prejudice and ingrained racism which underpinned all those ideas about the lesser breeds without the law, and the importance of being properly patriotic.

It also added a religious gloss to those assumptions about the primacy of order and obedience.

In the end Keyser's Chapel did not see a full century of use, at least for religious purposes. Before the developers finally moved in there was a final service, and the old place was crowded with old boys. The singing was as lusty as ever, and that was poignant certainly. The building seemed badly neglected, with cracked plaster and an air of damp and decay. Afterwards I was glad to get away as fast as I could, and found that I really did not care what happened to it all. If Ston's old boys have qualities in common, it is a general ability to get on easily with people and be quietly kind. Those qualities owe a great deal to their having to cope with loss at an early age, and the experience of sharing a life in a tough school where you needed to help each other to cope. They owed very little at all to chapel and what went with it.

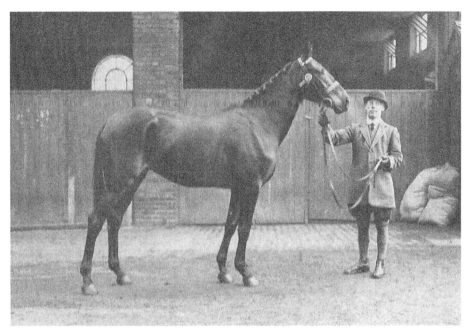

Victor Hedge

Emily Hedge

Granny and Granddad Williams are on the right hand side – he is still clearly suffering from his back injury.

New to the trade - my parents at an early Licensed Victuallers do

1st year at Waddesdon C of E Primary, 1953.
I am sitting on the floor to the right of the picture.

A later picture of the Red Lion - it was all grass at the front in our time

St Mary the Virgin, Haddenham

Mum and Dad in the bright bar

Victor and John Victor outside the pub

David in an early St Mary's school photo

The First Haddenham Cub Pack 1958. I am second from the right in the back row.

The Banbury to Princes Risborough autotrain

Henry outside the back door one afternoon

The front drive and entrance to St John's Hospital Stone

Headmaster's House in my second year at Ston.
I am the tallest one (as ever) in the middle of the back row.

Panoramic view of Ston from the quad

General Festing inspects the Stonic cadets

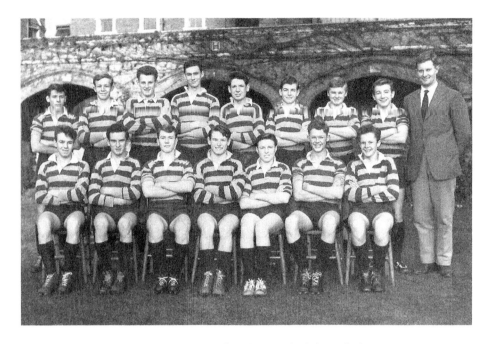

The Ston Colts Team. I am fourth from the left on the back row.
Beams is the master in charge.

Ston, featuring the famous clock tower

Oxford United v Preston

Oxford United 1963-4

Uncle Johnny and Aunty Doreen

With David and Bryan not long after we left the Red Lion

Outside the new place

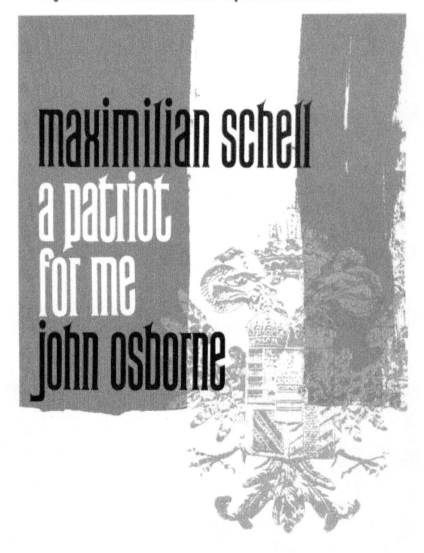

maximilian schell

a patriot

for me

john osborne

Programme for A Patriot For Me

Two old boys

Royal Masonic School badge, in Headmaster's House red

Chapter 18

CRIME AND PUNISHMENT

———❦———

It was about 8pm and second prep had just started. At the long tables around the day room 40 boys worked, or pretended to work, with their heads down. The silence was punctuated only by the occasional shuffling of a neighbour, the creak of a chair, or the clank of one of the sturdy old-fashioned radiators. The room was very warm, and as this was the winter term it was dark outside save for the dim lighting along the cloisters. It seemed to be a routine evening with an air of companionable hush, only disturbed by the occasional quiet sigh of someone who had finished his essay or given up the struggle over a maths problem.

Then the small bell near the door rang, and the duty junior at a nod from the prefect got up to answer the Housemaster's call. He came back several minutes later, reported in and the duty Prefect announced languidly that I was to go to the Housemaster's room. This was hardly ever good news and I had, at that moment, no idea what it would be about. I went slowly up the stone steps and knocked on the door.

I have mentioned Beams a good deal already. He was a hearty type – zealous about sport and the corps, and highly competitive in the various inter-house events. He had normally smiled upon me for my effort and sporting ability, but this was different. Suddenly, it seemed, judging by his heavy frown, I was in big trouble. He described the offence in the usual clipped Beams way, so universally mimicked within the house. The school procedure for replacing full exercise books was to have them signed for replacement on the cover by the Form Master concerned. Having run out of pages and not allowed enough time I had resorted on a few occasions to signing for him by copying his initialled signature. Conveniently enough the initials of J.R. Wards were so basic in his handwriting that this had seemed very easy. The last one, though, had been spotted. Beams waved it at me in evidence. This was now to be taken very seriously and I was to be beaten. This had not happened to me before at Ston, and my heart began to beat faster.

Beams used an unpleasant ritual. He told me to go to the dormitory, put my pyjama trousers on and wait for him. I did this. I was already scared and I knew that he meant me to be scared. The wait, on my own, in thin pyjamas, in the cold dormitory, was awful. He came in with his cane and strode along the polished wooden floor. He told me to bend over the nearest iron bed, with its hospital-cornered blue counterpane. I looked down at the pillow in front of me and there was another long and intended pause.

Beams stood back, then took several steps forward, making the floorboards creak. There was a swish and then the most indescribable pain. Just as it sank in and began to dull a few seconds later came the whole thing over again – steps, swish and sudden biting pain. He did it again, then again and then once more. I shouted out each time with the pain, but part of the code was not to cry, though my eyes certainly watered. I knew that downstairs, as always on these occasions, the whole house would sit silently and listen. They would hear each blow, as they were quite loud. Everyone would count out the number of strokes in their head, only thankful that this was not happening to them. At the end they would hear Beams walk back along to his study. There is no doubt that one aim of this carefully followed ritual was its deterrent impact.

Beams was always given to little homilies as a parting shot. 'In future, Hedge, leave forgery to the Chinese Secret Police' he said. I got my trousers back on and went downstairs. My backside throbbed painfully as I walked. The entry back into the day room was an awkward one to make. It was best done quietly, and without tears or any demonstration of defiance or pain. You were left alone then, presumably to try and concentrate on work but for all the attempted nonchalance I remember seething inside with the humiliation of it all.

Once prep broke up there was some solidarity and commiseration and you were expected then to tell the story. As usual in this kind of institutional setting, the main reaction was relief that this had not happened to them, at least this time. Beatings were not everyday events, but happened often enough, certainly most weeks, for others to think warily about their own vulnerabilities. Friends were supportive and sorry for me, and this was about all that helped.

Inside an hour I was in bed. By now I was aware of some large red welts and even a trace of blood. My backside felt very warm, and there was a vaguely sexual throbbing behind the dull ache, which surprised me. A few years later and out in the wide world I understood very well why some men from the older style of Public School needed to pay to have the experience replicated in later life.

A whiff of notoriety persisted for the next day or so. Unluckily I had a PE class in that time, and we went to the swimming pool. As another of Ston's Spartan rituals was to require naked bathing, I had to bare my stripes to all. Even if someone else was in the same position as you this was a further unpleasant humiliation, however much you made a show of bravado. The feelings inside were harder to deal with. I had generally managed to cope with my lack of confidence and general insecurity by working hard and achieving. This seemed to be the only way of staying afloat and coping in institutional life. Being beaten seemed to negate all that, and for several weeks I felt adrift and glum.

This happened to me four or five times at Ston. I was beaten again by Beams for cutting the elastic out of a pair of games shorts. This minor damage, carried out at short notice to sort my gaiters out for corps, earned four strokes and the requirement that I should repair the shorts with needle and cotton as best I could. The other beatings were from senior House Prefects, as Ston, for a long time, supported the delegation of corporal punishment to senior boys. In my final year the Housemaster who replaced Beams, Richard Dilley, did away with this, to his credit. It now seems extraordinary that 17- or 18-year-old boys were expected to do this, but it had been a central feature of the old regime. We may well have been in the last years of the old imperial legacy. Outside places like Ston the 1960s and new ideas were developing, but inside them the British tradition of expecting young leaders, even in the aftermath of Empire, to know how to keep up discipline lived on at least for a while longer. For the old believers, including our Masonic patrons, hierarchy and discipline mattered and in this creed discipline relied always on the prospect of physical pain as a practical deterrent.

Looking back from 50 years on, the strong reliance on beating at both the Masonic schools in the early 1960s seems not only cruel but also unwholesome. There was absolutely no recognition of its potential either for satisfying kinkiness, or promoting it in others, and no recognition of the wider emotional implications for both the beaten and the beaters.

There were lesser punishments at both schools. Ston especially had an almost Talibanic code of rules and responsibilities across the whole of daily life. To avoid infringement altogether was almost impossible, certainly for someone as untidy and clumsy as my 14- and 15-year-old self. If you were seen to be slow in getting ready for games, then you might have to practise dressing and undressing at speed three, four or five times. You could be in trouble for untidiness, running where you should walk, walking when you should run, and much else besides.

Punishments might involve undertaking menial domestic tasks for prefects, or even the old standby of standing in the corner. A common one was to have to write 'sheets'. If your shoes were not clean, for example, you might be given two or three sheets of paper with a tough title and told to write to that subject. It was often designed to be difficult. You had to avoid over-spacing or writing too big and you had to do both sides of the paper. It played up to the skills of the more verbal, but was tough for many. It was pseudo-educational, as you certainly didn't bother with research and just learned to waffle endlessly – good training for filibustering, but not much else.

In hindsight I do not remember much punishment relating to our actual schoolwork, unless prep was wilfully not done. There was detention but it was not extensively used, and did not amount to much of a sanction. It did mean your missing the limited amount of free time we did have in the school routine. Interestingly, aside from the Grundy and Jenkins scandal at J Ston, I can hardly ever remember suspension or expulsion being used, though the deed was sometimes carried out in the holiday period so that occasionally you were aware of someone who just did not return.

For all this disciplinary vigour we still broke the rules, tested boundaries and had fun, of course. There was also, increasingly in the early 60s, a developing counter-culture, and some people managed to live an almost parallel existence while keeping their cover intact. In our house 'Granny' Graves had survived the various beatings, had no academic aspirations as he was in the lowest stream of his year, and was not much good at sport, which was probably the source of his nickname. By the fifth year he had become a very practised evader of the rules. No one bothered much with him and he was able to spend a good deal of time at the local pub, the Swan. If you were there with him he was clearly regarded as one of the regulars. He smoked and wandered the area, usually with impunity. He had essentially seen through it all – one of a very few who managed this.

Curiously there was never any significant attempt at organised rebellion, but even Ston could not keep the music and the spirit of change at bay. Many of us already knew the early Dylan songs, about Hollis Brown, Hattie Carroll, and the rest. We began to feel strongly about the hypocrisy and conservatism of places like Ston. The severity of our own treatment just reinforced that. It gave people like me a permanently ingrained identification with almost every kind of underdog. For many of us Ston's traditional public school reliance on strong hierarchy, the delegation of power to senior pupils and the principles of succession (so that you knew your turn would come) produced a set of reactions completely opposite to those intended.

Looking back over the years, the Stonic beatings seem to me now to be extraordinarily disproportionate, and so far as I know our parents were never consulted or even informed about these punishments. Much of it would now be regarded as abuse, and not just physical abuse. Many of the Stonites had been continuously in boarding education since the age of eight or nine and had come from a home where a parent had died or, as in my case, where there were major problems. Some children, and I was one, came from families where there had already been domestic violence. At Ston, regardless of all that, and whatever was meted out, you were expected to carry on and cope regardless. At no stage throughout my school life at Ston, with an ongoing home background of debt, mental illness and alcoholism, did anyone talk to me about any of this, offer any advice or take any genuinely pastoral care. You were unlikely to get as much as an arm around your shoulder. You became, on the face of it, resilient and apparently durable, but those were brittle qualities, as I was to find out soon enough.

As to the Freemasons who funded the school but intervened in it so little, I am not sure that they would have seen much to complain about. Those were not child-centred times. Most of them had been through the war in the services and had a rough and ready approach to behaviour and sanctions. They were also a class of men more than usually committed to upholding order and the establishment. They regarded challenge rather suspiciously, wherever it came from. It is a real commentary on that culture that while the likes of me were being beaten for fiddling to replace an exercise book, Sir Denys Lowson, chairman of the Governors, was continuing his predatory and illegal fortune making in the City. He was known around the world for his unscrupulous behaviour. He died at the age of 69, just before criminal proceedings began. Lowson gloried in the pomp and circumstance of the City but quietly amassed a huge and ill-gotten fortune. He was shopped by a former employee, clearly someone who did not believe the Stonic motto Audi, Vice Tace – hear, see and be silent.

One of the other commonly heard things which people used to say about physical punishment was that at least it was over quickly. As will be clear from this account, that did not mean it was forgotten, ever. And so, if anyone who reads this knows whether David Harvey Hector Beams has by now gone to his long home, and where that might be, could they please let me know. I will go to water his grave – and not with tears.

Chapter 19

ARMY DAYS

———◆◆◆———

Tuesday mornings were different from the other days of the week at Ston. It was Army day, when the entire school was given over to the Cadet Force. The day would start not with the usual seven o'clock bells but with a solitary bugler at the base of the tower who had to play reveille. The duty bugler usually took up position there so as to be as far away as possible from the four houses on that side of the quadrangle. If he got it wrong and came too close, he was likely to be hit by a missile from one of the dormitories. His bugling was the signal for us to struggle into either the battle dress or denim uniforms, which we had alongside our normal clothes. The choice depended on the dress orders given out the previous evening. Whichever season we were in, neither option was pleasant. The khaki shirts seldom got laundered, and managed somehow to keep you cold in winter and overheated in summer. They were worn with a rough khaki tie.

The heavy boots were supposed to have been cleaned to a military gloss. If you were 'keen' this would have involved the disgusting process of spit and polish, slowly working the boots into a gleaming guardsman's mirror. You anchored everything together at your waist with a webbing belt. Trousers and boots were kept together with webbing gaiters, which had to be strapped round each ankle. This arrangement was enhanced, again for the keener cadet, if you had chains of weights to keep the gaiters and trousers neat. The less keen, like me, made do with elastic, but this never kept things together for very long.

All the webbing was supposed to be 'blancoed' – not in white but khaki. To make this work you had to use a tin of paste, wettened so that it could be applied evenly with a brush and rag. If you were lucky this gave a fine smooth surface, ready to be dried slowly. If you got the mix too thin the surface would look grainy and rough, but if you made it too thick it would develop a pattern of cracks, like a dried-up river bed. Those, like me, who felt they had better things to do would rush the process at the last minute and then try to dry it all out fast on radiators, which were festooned on cold Monday nights with badly done Blanco. The brass buckles at the front and back of the belt had to be polished as well, and then you gingerly tried to fit it all together. Finally you had a dark green beret and Staybrite cap badge, so that as we went off to breakfast we resembled a small army which had invaded mysteriously in the night.

We were the Army Cadet Force, not the Combined version which many schools opted for. Our formal title was that we were the First Cadet Battalion, London Rifle Brigade. A good deal of folklore was attached to the LRB, as it was known. Next to the Durham Light Infantry it had the fastest marching pace in the whole Army, and we had a variety of old boy heroes, including a VC, whose deeds in North Africa were marked in a picture just outside the Library. The Army Cadet Force began as the Officer Training Corps, set up in 1908 in public schools to ensure a steady supply of pre-packaged young leaders for the Army. Within six or seven years, of course, it had become a conveyor belt for the subaltern slaughter of the trenches.

A specific training regime was established for the ACF after the Second World War – Certificate 'A' – which we all did in two parts. Certificate A training involved a variety of 'fieldcraft' activities – tracking and walking or crawling silently – the so-called 'ghost walk' and 'leopard crawl'. More obviously useful skills were included, for example map reading with a compass, but the syllabus was otherwise almost entirely military. This included having your own rifle and learning various drills with it, so that each Tuesday you had to collect your rifle from the Armoury before parades. This small brick building on the far side of the school had enough rifles in it to start a small war. It was supposedly secure enough to ward off any chance of theft, but it would have raised the hairs on the neck of any modern security adviser. It was opened at lunchtime on some other days of the week, so that you could dismantle and clean your allocated Lee Enfield .303 by way of a lanyard and a small piece of oiled pull-through cloth. When it had been done properly you could look down the breech and see the gleaming spiral of the rifling.

From time to time I would do this in desultory fashion, but I was often in trouble at inspections for having a grubby rifle. You would be told that it had enough dirt to grow potatoes in and sent off to the kind of specific punishments the Corps could impose. This was yet another variety of Stonic sanction. It usually involved having to run about, or doubling as they called it, often with the offending rifle held above your head.

Although the ACF was supposed to be a youth organization, and a voluntary one at that, membership of the Ston militia was compulsory. While the Scouts may also have done fieldcraft, our version of it mainly involved learning how to creep up on people and kill them. You were certainly expected to 'make an effort'. As we were all involved we amounted to a sizeable force, strongly associated with our regiment, which was engulfed later by a series of amalgamations.

As we got older some of us began to be more rebellious

about being required to take part, and we were outraged when an advertisement for the ACF appeared in the *Daily Telegraph* (where else?) with a picture of one of ours. He was a very bright classics scholar and a good athlete, but very unhappy at this unsought fame. We wrote a letter of protest, but were not very surprised when it was neither acknowledged nor published.

The First Cadet Battalion had eight platoons, one for each house, and you joined up with the adjacent house to make the next size up, which was a company. Everyone had a rank in the Corps. Most had the basic one, which was Rifleman, but once you passed Certificate A you might be promoted to Corporal, Sergeant or in one or two cases the dizzy heights of Under Officer with a Sam Browne belt, no Blanco and a swagger stick. Not surprisingly the Platoon hierarchy more or less mirrored the regular one in the house – but there were entertaining anomalies with an occasional senior determined not to progress in the military.

Each Tuesday had specifically planned activities, but there was always a great deal of drilling with rifles. To stand on a freezing January day with your finger sticking to the trigger guard of a Lee Enfield as you stand to attention is not pleasant. It was less numbing, at least, when marching. We became quite good at drill, though it was a much harder business if you eventually got to the stage of having to give the orders yourself.

It is probably clear already that I did not enjoy life in the Corps very much. It has to be said, though, that however disaffected you were it was hard to resist the siren call of marching to a band. There did seem to be something fine and exhilarating about swinging along in step and responding to commands, especially at parades. We were about 350 strong together and had a fine band, so that people did come to watch at the school gates for events like Remembrance Day. And whether or not you liked the military activities, and I did not, there was a seductive pleasure in marching behind a band playing *Sussex by the Sea* or the regimental march itself – 'the 95' as it was known. The band was, of course a good thing to belong to. Organised by Graham Garton, the Head of Music, it had better uniforms, less marching and much more indoor activity. It included all the brass instruments as well as drums and bugles.

Alternatively you could try to join the Signals Detachment, a small group who wandered around the school and grounds with wireless packs to not much apparent purpose, but with relative freedom. The Signals offered fine skiving options, but you had to be careful. On one occasion a boy named Turnbull found a seat outside the Swan, in Bushey. This pub was always generously willing to serve Stonites, with no proof. Turnbull, in his last year, was definitely a leader of the counterculture. He sat there in his sergeant's uniform with his pint and broadcast his progress to control, making up sights and sounds along the way. This was fine until the controller told him he should be able to see him now, so where was he really? Some retribution followed, but nothing very serious.

Turnbull, like Granny Graves, was one of those consistently subversive characters who occasionally turn up in institutions. Having exhausted all the disciplinary options short of expulsion, the authorities seemed in the end either to pretend not to notice or to play the offence down. To achieve that distinction requires both an insight into the limits of authority, and a courage which I did not have at that age. I have no idea what happened in later life to Turnbull, but I do hope he did well.

Progress in the Corps accompanied your progress through the school. You started in the first term or two with a sweater and boots and learnt the basics before getting your uniform and being allocated a rifle. As time went by you took certificate A in stages. This involved being tested on the content of an ancient Ministry of Defence manual, using well-tried and handed-down mnemonic answers to absolutely standard questions. As is often the case with that learning method, I can remember the mnemonic DEPLAPCW perfectly well. It had something to do with a platoon in attack, but I now have absolutely no idea what the initials stood for.

To get promotion after Part 2 of Certificate A you had to go through a term as a member of the 'cadre' – a group which was being intensively prepared. If your number came up for this, then you had to put up with a much more rigorous regime each Tuesday. You were marched around at blistering pace and taught 'leadership' – mainly about the briefing and tuition of others in a range of military activities. This might be explaining map reading, how to strip a machine gun, or, indeed telling them what DEPLAPCW was all about. You were marked at the end on turnout, knowledge and all-round general keenness. I hated Corps generally and hated that term like no other, but without the courage to rebel about it and lacking any useful precedent, I just conformed in a half-hearted way. I did not want to do well; I certainly did not want to be seen to be 'keen', but I did not want to come in last either – I think I finished third from bottom, so that was fine. As a result I got a single stripe – an Acting Corporal, which was the lowest rung on the leadership ladder. Even at this level, however, I was required to contribute to the training of others, but it did at least offer the chance for some quiet subversion. Again, though, you had to be careful. While most of the boys for whom you were responsible enjoyed the avoidance of activities and lapped up the entertaining disinformation, which we provided, you had to be careful to spot emergent 'keens' who might find ways of stitching you up. I made no progress beyond my single stripe.

There were three big Corps events each year. First, the Remembrance Day parade, at the front of the school, facing the Ston war memorial. It was a moving event even if you were not generally keen on the Corps, and to this day, whether I like it or not, the sound of bugles and a military band makes my spine tingle. It was a very serious business, but enlivened at rehearsal one year when, just as we reached the pinnacle of the parade –

the last post and all standing to attention – an elderly gardener came through on his way home, pedalling very slowly past the massed ranks and down the drive, with his shopping bag draped over the handlebars and his roll-up at the side of his mouth. It was a wonderful moment of barely suppressed hysteria.

The annual Inspection Day in the summer usually involved a visiting military dignitary. One year it was an Indian General and we woke to the bugle and the flag of India flying over the tower. Sadly the Indian theme was not reflected in the day's food. At these ceremonial inspections best turnout was required, and we all paraded across the main school pitch to the rear of the school. The band played for all it was worth, and you spent a long time at attention. The usual advice on a hot day was to avoid fainting by gently rocking forward and back on the balls of your feet and back. As Sergeant Majors have always said, you didn't know you had balls on your feet, did you? Each year, despite the warning, you were usually aware of people dropping here and there, to be attended by a scurrying stretcher party. As long as you could carry it off, of course, it was an effective way out, providing the numbers were not so great as to suggest conspiracy.

The third and biggest event was the annual Corps camp. This came at the end of the summer term, so going off home was delayed by a further week. It involved all but the youngest, and those teachers who were Corps officers went with us by train to some Army camp in a far-flung part of rural England. It usually involved a special train and marching down to the station, with the band playing. It must have been a big planning challenge, and may originally have been intended to serve as some kind of holiday for those who might not otherwise get one. I did not expect our family to get away, but this did not stop me from sharing the general view that camp blighted the end of the summer term, and was an unwelcome delay in getting school over with for the year.

In fact, of course, however much you resented having to go, some interesting and even exciting things happened at camp. Some standard elements were always included. One of these was going to the firing range. I remember the sensation of first firing proper rounds from my .303. It had not been cleaned for a time and I was rather worried that it would somehow, as suggested in horror films and westerns, explode in my face, but it didn't. You were told to hold it tight to your shoulder and it did indeed buck very strongly. I scored pretty lowly. At the end the shell cases were counted in. There was major consternation once when the resident psychopath from our house, a boy called West – not bright but with a fierce interest in violence, arms and motor bikes – was found trying to retain some live rounds.

By the final occasion I went to camp, in deepest Norfolk, I was already well into subversion and avoidance. On the range I managed to be get the job of 'marking.' This involves sitting in a deep trench, just below the targets, and watching the bullets thumping into the large caricature of a Eurasian charging enemy with a fierce face. You had various pointer signs for the impact of each round – inner, outer, etc – and you marked each shot so that the person firing could adjust their aim. This provided plenty of opportunities for subversive disinformation, including liberal use of the red and white strawberries-and-cream flag for a miss.

There was always a night exercise. I remember one on Dartmoor, with plenty of noise – thunderflashes and blanks. Once was enough and thereafter I always contrived to have blisters or other minor handicaps. Another standard component was a day's route march. This could be quite tough going, but at least you saw the scenery. You had your kit including your water bottle to carry, and I remember the joy of gulping icy water in midsummer from a Dartmoor stream.

On an equivalent march in the flat lands of Norfolk the following year a plan was made to go poaching. Four of us managed next day to get hold of a pheasant, kill it, break into a disused railway hut and cook it up on the stove we found there. Trampling through a barley field on the way back we were chased by the farmer, who caught up with us and summoned the Colonel. We spent a time in the guardhouse expecting the worst, but essentially we were let off in a display of leniency, probably based in the assumption that the only offence had been running in the barley.

There were other easy ways to have fun and be subversive at the same time. I remember one exercise when our platoon was being led by one of the 'keens'. We fanned out behind him as we traipsed through the undergrowth in search of the 'enemy'. We had great merriment from taking turns to throw clods of earth into the undergrowth. Each thump would cause him to panic and bark commands to take cover, flinging himself to the ground as he did so. The trick, as with all subversion of this kind, was not to overdo it, so that he never cottoned on.

Sometimes you got to talk with real soldiers informally. This was in the years when soldiering was unfashionable, and the ones we met certainly felt no need to dress things up for us. I remember two pieces of advice, which certainly made sense in the Army context, and were more generally sensible as well. First, never volunteer for anything, and secondly if you don't have to stand, sit down, and if you don't have to sit down, lie down.

I think there were four basic attitudes to Corps life and you saw this most clearly at camp. First you had the keen lot. There were not many of them but they liked the military, participated enthusiastically, worked very hard at their kit and just occasionally went on to Sandhurst. The second and largest group we might call the 'conformers'. Corps was a fact of life and whether you liked it or not it had to be coped with, so that you tried reasonably hard, and did what you could not to get noticed too obviously. The two smaller groups were the subversives (hostile to the basic premise of the corps and trying to throw spanners into the works without being spotted and punished if at all possible) and the challenged. This group was the most unfortunate, and included those who could never manage to get their drill or kit right, lacked physical confidence and were generally regarded as either as dim or weedy. Corps for them meant only a series of opportunities for public failure and humiliation. It must have been awful for them.

I would have placed myself in the conforming group for my first two years and then I moved steadily into full membership of the subversives as political awareness began to dawn on me. There are limits to this basic typology, of course. For example, you would have regarded West as a 'keen' – he was an excellent marksman on the .22 range, to the great pleasure of Beams, our housemaster, who was a big Corps supporter. He was also, always, immaculately turned out. Of course his other psychopathic qualities would have made him just the kind of man the real Army should never take on, but sometimes does.

I do not remember out-and-out refuseniks at all – opposition yes, but complete refusal was simply not tolerated if you were to remain at the school – Audi Vide Tace again. Corps was seen as an important part of the obligatory muscular Christianity which Ston specialised in, and that was that. My four years' obligatory membership of the Corps covered about 15% of my time at school. At no stage was there ever any explanation of the reasons for this military training or its relevance to our country and its place in the world. We could be shown training films which bluntly were about the most effective ways of killing an enemy, but no one ever engaged us in discussion about who that enemy might be, or why at our age we should be learning these things. The film I most remember was shown at camp one rainy afternoon. It was called 'I'm a sniper' and was to do with hiding away at the top of a building or tree and how best to pump lead into people a long way off without being spotted.

The whole Corps operation went on unchallenged for many years. Many of the staff and most Freemasons came from the World War II generation, and saw this as being just the right stuff for boys. Conscription had only recently ended and over the years that followed many of that generation held on to the view that having it back would be the antidote to just about every one of society's ills. As I grew older, and the more challenging atmosphere of the 60s began to seep through even into Ston some of us certainly began to argue back. I remember Rodney Hills and I, both of us then beginning to be keen on Labour politics, trying to have a go at the Head of the Stonic Army. He was Colonel Kaye, an immense, corpulent man who looked like a cross between the old comedian Fred Emney and the cartoon Colonel Blimp. He had a strong taste for sherry and a strangely high-pitched and cut-glass voice. We ranted on, but he just soaked it up with the sherry and that was that. Rodney Hills went on to an impressive academic and political career in the York Labour Party. I made it as far as Parliamentary candidate but took it no further, and we did not stay in touch, which I now regret. Like most of my generation at Ston, he never seems to have mentioned the place in later life if he could avoid it.

As I became more unhappy in my final year and things went wrong both at home and at school, the Corps began to represent everything I had come to hate about Ston. I remember a moment when I came very close to losing control during a parade. Though depressed and angry I fell in with the others on time, and was marching along in the house platoon to some activity elsewhere in the school. Whether I was marching in an odd way or just looking fed up I do not know, but one of the junior Music masters bawled me out. He was an effete-looking younger man named Bell (inevitably 'Tinkerbell') and normally a wearer of yellow pullovers and tweed jacket. Dolled up now in his new uniform, he no doubt felt that he needed to play the part. He offered me some strong advice to buck up and try, or words to that effect. He will never know how near he came to being charged at and assaulted by a rifle-bearing adolescent who had

had enough. The moment passed, but it all came back to me the moment I saw the film 'If' and the rebels who bombed the corps.

The ACF at Ston was the organising body behind the Duke of Edinburgh's award and I did value those activities, but they were very different, and participation was obviously voluntary. The Corps was one of the harder edges to Ston, and I would have learned so much more in the Scouts without all the nonsense of scratchy uniforms, rifles and films about snipers. It must have cost large amounts of public money, and I have resented my compulsory involvement ever since.

Chapter 20

GAMES

The fourth great pillar of the Stonic regime was a daily dose of required sport. This approach drew, as most things at Ston did, on the enduring Victorian tradition of muscular Christianity – sport as the great preventative against unwholesomeness, and the true path to a healthy mind. Mens sana in corpore sano, we were told, and a mens sana definitely meant one not preoccupied with 'beastliness'. Both schools had huge grounds surrounding them with enough pitches for each house as well as several show place areas for school teams to play on. We took all this for granted at the time, of course, and only understood much later how privileged we had been to have all this carefully tended space available. In fact these wide acres, when not in use for wholesome sporting endeavour, also provided safe and distant cover for smoking, drinking, and some of that beastliness which the school was so keen to suppress.

Most afternoons were spent on some games activity or other. It was always 'games' rather than 'sports' and your personal prowess or otherwise was a major part of everybody's reputation and self-image. This was wonderful if you were good at games but grim if you weren't. The predominant sport followed a seasonal pattern – you played rugby in the autumn term, hockey in the Easter term and cricket plus athletics in the summer, so that however much you may have preferred one sport over the others that was the only slot you had for it. Everybody had to take part, and sick notes were not easy to come by. The main focus for games was your house, so that most of the time you were involved in pick-up games within your house group. There was, though, a hard-fought inter-house competition each term. The best players made it to the school teams, and until quite late on in my time everyone had to turn out to watch the school team and cheer. There was a prevailing and long-drawn-out chant – 'Ohhhn Stohhn' – which always sounded rather mournful, whether we were winning or not. For those playing in the school teams away fixtures, of course, offered a welcome albeit brief break from school.

The pitches for the main school teams were magnificent. The cricket pitch at Ston was known as 'The Table' and had as its backdrop the clock tower and cloisters, so that the whole scene on a late summer afternoon conjured up an Edwardian idyll, as if Henry Newbolt's Close, desperate hush and all, had travelled forward in time. The main rugby pitch and a running track were at the back of the school in a kind of natural arena known as 'The Dell'. At Ston the most successful school team was always the Hockey XI, but the rugby and cricket sides also had good fixture lists, and we did well for a school with only 300 pupils.

Before going away to school I had very little experience of playing in organised sport. St Mary's, the C of E Primary School, had stretched to rounders on the village green but not much else, and my brief time at Aylesbury Grammar School had given me only a brief and unhappy exposure to rugby plus one wheezy cross-country run, when I finished almost last, and was left hoping that I would never have to do this again. Most of my sport up to the age of 13 had been those intense and endless games of tennis ball football and cricket on the pub car park with my brother, with chalked wickets and goals, and a wychert wall at one end which we regularly knocked lumps out of.

My father, a great one for the toughening-up approach when the mood took him, would occasionally bowl to us. He could still be quite fast and to see him coming at you from the gents' lavatory end could be quite scary. In a similar way he bought me boxing gloves one Christmas, against my mother's wishes, and managed to make my nose bleed with a demonstration jab which I was supposed to have been able to parry, apparently. The car park games were always fun, and gave plenty of scope for fantasy but no experience of what playing in teams might actually be like. The result was that I thought I was better at football and cricket than I really was, and when I went to J Ston that was obvious; it took time to find my level, and become fitter and slimmer on the school diet. When I got to the Senior School and had a fresh start with rugby I was not only fit but very tall for my age. I discovered that this was sport to enjoy and that I was good at it. Rugby was a game to enjoy, and I found that I was good at it. Headmaster's House was very strong at Rugby, with its reputation for toughness. Beams as Housemaster gloried in this and the house regularly contributed players to school teams. Beams would often refer to players from previous years, notably a character called 'Peach' Ridgeway, supposedly so large in all directions that he had simply risen from the bottom of a loose scrum and carried it and the ball over the line. The tale had grown in the telling and we all had images of a giant shaking players off to left and right like a juggernaut. I played against him in due course when he turned out for the Old Boys, and sadly, but not surprisingly, he could not possibly live up to his billing.

Beams was intensely enthusiastic and competitive, though his approach would horrify any modern coach. In our day-to-day pick-up matches in the house he made no allowance for age or size difference. This would now be regarded as both ridiculous and dangerous. It meant that if you were put into the front row of a scrum you could be pushed about painfully, and there could be thumping tackles from much older and heavier boys. Amazingly, and fortunately, there were few serious injuries. This approach clearly disadvantaged two distinct groups. First, and obviously, those who were small for their age or not very confident physically. Usually stuck out on the wing, they would spend the game praying that the ball never reached them. The second group were those who had excelled at soccer and played for an excellent J Ston team. Having only been allowed to play rugby after they moved to Ston, they were left only with informal pick-up games in the limited spare time we had. It seemed such a waste.

I had a fair share of injuries in my Stonic rugby career. I had become a second row forward, and so was usually in the thick of things. Once in a house match I had my shoulder crushed beneath a very heavy and normally amiable boy called Otterson. 'Otto', as he was predictably known, didn't know much about it, and although it hurt a good deal I played on, though unable to raise my left arm very much. As it still hurt at full time I asked for help and was told to go off to the Peace Memorial Hospital in Watford, about two miles away, to have myself checked at Casualty. This was the normal Stonic approach to the walking wounded. I trudged off to the hospital and it turned out that I had chipped a collarbone. I was bound up and sent trudging back to report to the Infirmary. For the next six weeks I was off games, and missed the rest of the season.

In my other significant injury I could not claim to be an innocent victim. In a school match, hunting for revenge with my fist ready, I crouched over a loose scrum and a head came up, hitting me full in the face. This time I left the field and was sent to walk down again to the Peace Memorial, to learn that I had a broken nose. This time I was back playing soon afterwards.

Others had worse to contend with. I remember my friend Paul Griffin having his face sliced open by a stud nail, leaving a long duelling style scar, which lasted for a very long time.

Beams was less keen on hockey, though this was the game that Ston's teams did best in. Too tall and clumsy to find hockey an easy game, I never had much success with it, and was quite happy when the extended and endless snows of 1962/63 wiped out the entire hockey season. Throughout that term each House had to arrange alternative activities and the Beams solution was to invent a game of indoor rugby played in Big School. With the stage at one end, the chairs stacked away, and a sizeable open space, the aim was for your team to get the ball to the opposite end and ground it. With 20 or so players on either side this activity was a cross between the Eton Wall Game, British Bulldog, and Pamplona without the bulls. We called it Bastard Ball. It was fun, supposedly 'toughening', quite dangerous and typically Beams. Again, somehow, there were no serious injuries, and if, like me, you were a confident rugby player and used to taking a fall it was enjoyable. It must have been thoroughly miserable for those who were less keen. They would hover on the edge of the action, either trying to create the impression of being involved or actually hovering near the side, like wallflowers at a dance being run by Hell's Angels.

Although exams dominated summer terms, I loved the cricket at Ston. I was never the greatest player but I enjoyed the whole business of it. In those days cricket was much more of a national interest than it is now, and we all had our favourite players and heroes. I had played for the J Ston first XI and was just about good enough, but cricket can be a very anxious game if you want to do well, and this is especially the case if you have just made it into a team and you know that the standard is just beyond the edge of your ability, so that however hard you try you are unlikely to be a regular choice.

As with all school games, you tend to remember the highs and lows best. While I can remember occasional and unexpectedly agile catches, or shots when the ball clicked easily away for 4, I also remember one long afternoon at the Royal Grammar School in High Wycombe. As a generally clumsy fielder, I had dropped a catch and wanted to redeem myself by making some runs. I waited, the moment came and I was out almost straight away for nothing. It was more fun in the house team, and then the Stonic Second XI. In both those teams I opened the batting with David Davies, later to become a distinguished sports journalist and head of the FA. We batted together a great deal and had become very good indeed at short runs, so that with plenty of backing up and a strong shared understanding we could steal a run from the slightest misfield.

It is extraordinary how most sportsmen at whatever level can remember their youthful golden moments. They are the more memorable because as a fair but unexceptional performer you have far fewer of them than the effortless star whose stunning deeds are a regular event. I remember a dazzling catch in the slips when I Instinctively threw myself to the right and held on as I hit the ground, and two really long kicks at goal. In one I helped win the Cock House match in my final year – by kicking a penalty from the touchline 30 yards out and seeing it glide through the posts, knowing that it would from the moment I hit it. The second kick was to convert my own try from a similar place in a game for the school against the Old Masonians, Peach Ridgeway and all. My father was there and it was almost the only time he ever saw me play. Although our relationship was a complicated and often troubled one, I was pleased and proud that he had been there to see it.

Though dominated by the three main sports, Ston did offer some other options. The most regular and grimmest, especially when the weather was foul, were the set runs to prescribed routes – usually about five or six miles but occasionally longer. They had all had different descriptive names – Short Way, Long

Way, and so on. One variety was called the 'Melly Way.' It was long and convoluted and had been invented by one of the Housemasters, a Biology teacher named Clarke. He was an odd-looking character, always with a very short haircut and in clothes which never seemed quite to fit. He was a rumbustious man with a rather uncoordinated way of walking and several strange chin-jutting and neck-twitching mannerisms. He was a fairly strong disciplinarian but reasonably good-natured. His nickname was 'Melly' – a mimicking of his rather stilted manner of speech. He asked one of his senior boys one day why the run had this name and in a brilliant improvised response was told that it was because everyone ran it together in a crowd – a melée, in fact!

I did my best to avoid the runs, which always seemed to be tiring to no good purpose. They were not races and we were already fit. Often there was no escape, but in the summer, at least, there was the option of athletics. Ston as a school was not great at track and field, and apart from a small number of enthusiasts who stood out we were not terribly good. Even I, as a rather limited high jumper, made the team. I used my height and an outdated scissors technique, but never got beyond five feet. We would sometimes go to matches at other schools, sometimes quite posh establishments. If only involved in one event you would go off to it, wait around to do your bit and then hang around some more. The high jump usually took place in some far-flung corner with little supervision, so it was all very relaxed. With two jumpers from each school, I would inevitably come last in a field of four, but nobody complained and I was not, it must be said, very highly motivated. I remember one such day, lounging around at Marlborough School and watching one of their prefects, a floppy-haired and upper-class looking character sauntering from place to place with a clipboard, with several smaller blond boys following him around like cherubs behind a recording angel. It did look rather fishy.

We had swimming and water polo, neither of which was much to my liking, not least because of that strange requirement to swim naked. There was basketball, available now and then in PE periods, but with no great inter-house tournament. I was forever being told that I should be good at this because of my height, but there is more to basketball than that, and I never was.

There were fives courts at Ston – the game you play in a walled court, like squash, but the ball is served and hit back with a glove. Some were keen on this, but again it never appealed to me. Later on those of us in the counter culture realised that the fives courts were good as smoking dens.

While this all suggests considerable choice, most of the effort and emphasis was on the main team games. If you succeeded and represented the school consistently and well you might be given your colours – at Ston this meant having a red blazer and tie, which you had in addition to your regular gear, and you could choose to wear them when you wanted to. These were sparingly given, with considerable fuss made at lunchtime in front of the whole school. The most I managed was a blue tie for colts colours for rugby, but I kept it for years.

Ston was a very physical place, with little personal privacy and an emphasis on discipline and conformity. The ideal Stonite was someone talented enough to represent the school well at sport but scholastically successful as well. Such a person would follow the rules, play a straight bat and demonstrate the manly resilience which lay at the heart of Stun's muscular Christianity. The encouragement of rule-following all-rounders with straight bats and a manly resilience lay at the heart of the late Victorian approach that persisted at Ston. Other activities, music, crafts and so on, might be admirable too, but the successful sporting scholar was the thing to be. We had a small number of counter-cultural rebels, of course and they certainly grew in numbers as the energy and challenge of the 1960s began to reach even Ston's Edwardian nooks and crannies. A smaller number still managed to juggle conventional conforming success with crafty misdemeanour, but this was hard to sustain.

This hearty hierarchy was massively underpinned by the four pillars I have been describing, and the required sporting life was a key component. It did not suit late developers, and those with other quieter or individual skills and interests. They had little encouragement and less recognition. Games at Ston did not in reality offer much choice, and I think were intended to spot and encourage leaders, with everyone else learning how to conform as a follower. The same held good for the Corps and the House hierarchical system, with everything held together by that fourth pillar of discipline and punishment. How stultifying and wasteful it now seems looking back – an entire educational establishment, well-resourced but resistant to challenge or any kind of independent thinking, with a closed mind to the existence of unconventional talent or the creative possibilities of unorthodoxy. This may have been the case at many traditional schools of the period, but it had a special resonance at Ston and our Masonic motto of Audi Vide Tace, Hear See and Be Silent.

Pleasingly, many of the predictions about what would happen to some of us turned out to be a long way short of the mark once we had left and discovered a wider and freer world of options outside. A very good example is Anthony Andrews, the actor. He joined Ston, without having gone to the Juniors, as a mousy-haired, undistinguished 14-year-old. He was not sportingly or academically successful, but clearly had a potential which Ston's limited dramatic options failed to spot, and not long after leaving he was one of the leading boys in the original production of Alan Bennett's *Forty Years On*. He never looked back, it seems, and certainly never, so far as I know, in Ston's direction.

HOME AND AWAY

Chapter 21

FOOTBALL, FOOTBALL, FOOTBALL

———⟨✕⟩———

Football always mattered within our family. My father, by all accounts, had been a formidable, traditional centre forward, in the days before the pub and drinking. He had been, I think, the kind of player often described in those days as 'burly,' well able to use his elbows as well as his head and feet. As with many in his generation it was cricket in the summer and football in the winter, and he was strong and confident at both – fast bowler and front man. As a result my brother and I both grew up mad on football, though our primary school didn't offer any organised opportunities. Our playing was entirely those endless games on the pub car park with a small rubber ball.

My brother's bad leg, sadly, meant that he could not play when we went away to the Junior School. For my part I learned quickly that for all my sense of skill and imagined glory in the car park, it was a harder game to play on real grass with mud and a proper ball, which got wet and gave you a good thump when you headed it. I made the house team at J Ston as a large and rather galumphing fullback, but got no further. The school team, as explained earlier, was made up largely of young Geordies and Mancunians. They were extremely good, and regularly saw off by large scores teams from posh prep schools in Hertfordshire and North London. Of course when we all went on to Ston it was rugby only, and no option. This was of course based on the traditional dreary stereotype about it being he gentleman's game, but it has always seemed to me a dreadful waste and shame that those fantastic young footballers just could not play in organised competition at a time when they should have been making progress in the game they best liked.

I did like rugby and was good at it, but I loved watching football, and all that went with it – the crowd, the history and the connection with all the different places around the country. The customers at the pub always talked about it. They brought us programmes every week. In the 50s and early 60s football programmes varied from club to club much more than they do now. Spurs, legendary double winners in 1961, had a single folded sheet with no pictures, whereas Luton Town, our nearest league club then, had a programme with quite a few pages, and plenty of advertising – often for beer and local businesses. I remember 'Ivor Thirst, the football fan, a most discriminating man' who stuck up for the local brew.

Sometimes games would be on TV and we always had plenty of people in the back room each May to watch the FA Cup Final and sing 'Abide with Me' in a mist of beer and nostalgia. When Manchester City won against Birmingham in 1955 my father put blue ribbons round an old darts cup in honour of my mother's team. In the days when players lived a good deal closer to the supporters, the story in the Williams family was that at one time they had been given a pram by Frank Swift, the legendary City goalkeeper. She was one of 10, so they must have needed it. They lived in Chorlton and so did he. This must have been just before the war. Big Frank went on to become a football writer and was killed in the Munich air crash less than three years after the 1955 cup win, when the hero of the hour had been Bert Trautmann, another City goalkeeper who had played to the end, having broken his neck, in those days before substitutes.

In the days before my father's drinking became overwhelming, when there was still plenty of money, he bought a Luton Town season ticket, just after the club had made it into the First Division for the first time ever. He did not go for very long, but when things became more difficult some friends of his from the office took us to a few of the games. They were the first top division matches we ever saw, with Luton's once in a lifetime team of Gordon Turner and Billy Bingham in the attack, Sid Owen in defence and Ron Baynham in goal. We had never been inside a proper ground before, and it was really exciting to go through the turnstile, join the big crowd and climb the steps to get a first view of the bright grass, the goals and the big stands. There it all was, in front of you, for real at last.

Our first game was against Manchester United and must have been a year or so after Munich. Like many boys of that time we had followed the Munich disaster and its aftermath and with our Manchester connections we felt a loyalty which my brother has followed ever since. As often happened then, we were put over the retaining wall at the front of the stand and sat on the cinder track next to the touchline so that we were incredibly close to the speed, the collisions and the skill. It was a great thrill to see men who had actually been through the air crash playing in front of us – Billy Foulkes, and of course Harry Gregg, the goalkeeper who had been such a hero in the disaster. It was actually a pretty poor 0-0 draw, but that took nothing away from the excitement of actually being there.

Football remained through the 1950s and 60s a working-class game, strong on tradition, cheap to watch and relatively trouble free, but once we went away to school we did not see much of it. We had no access to television, and the best you could hope for were radio commentaries, often listened to in transistors under the covers after lights out. If we did go to games at all it was in the holidays, with my father, and often on the train. Like many people in those days he would always wear a shirt and tie to games and usually a raincoat, whether or not rain seemed likely. My father particularly never understood our need for non-school clothes, and there was very little money by then, so that we went in our school uniforms. Since the Stonic uniform looked as it if had come from the era of Jeeves and Wooster this could occasionally attract comment, and we had little option but to look straight ahead and front it out.

I remember him taking us to the Hawthorns once to see West Brom play Manchester United, when I was about 15. I was sent off to get tea and Bovril and had to endure some real mockery in the queue of the 'look at that queer fucker' variety – more shaming than threatening, but upsetting. Thinking back it is surprising that we did not make more of a fuss, as it was very upsetting, and tough for a teenager. It did make you feel weird. I suppose we knew that things were very tough and making a fuss ran the risk of making everything rockier still at home.

Our local team, actually, was Oxford United. Until recently they had been Headington United. The name change was part of a push under the manager, Arthur Turner, to get into the Football League. This was very far from an automatic process in those days, and involved a great deal of reputation building and lobbying. In January 1961, just before we went back to school for the start of the Easter term, my father took us, on a supporters' special from Aylesbury, to watch Oxford play Leicester in the third round of the FA Cup. That day still conjures up for me the spirit of cup games and excursions, when the underdog team's supporters go to the big famous ground with all to play for. You spent the whole day surrounded by crowds of people who all want the same thing, hoping against hope. We had floppy rosettes of gold and black stuck onto bits of cardboard and sold outside Filbert Street, which was the biggest stadium I had ever seen.

You can never really shake off the first commitments you make to the team you follow, and you always remember as long as you live the special days, the special teams and the sense of continuity and history. For the record Leicester went on to win 3-1 that day, and reached the final, only to lose to that double winning Spurs team. I did manage to see the final on TV at school, but in a classroom with just a few other enthusiasts, so it seemed a rather subdued and cold experience.

Oxford, partly on the back of that cup run, did make it into the League, at the expense of Accrington Stanley, who had gone out of business. Towards the end of the summer holidays in 1962 we went to their early home games at the Manor, still a very basic ground with one end just a barely terraced bank of red shale. The first home game against Lincoln was on a golden evening. Albert Scanlon, anther Munich air crash survivor, was on the wing for Lincoln. Though they took the lead Oxford managed to win 2-1 in the end and so the night ended well under the floodlights. It was great.

The warmth from going to football, and those shared experiences of joy and disappointment, still explain why people have gone on loving to go to matches despite the years of poor conditions and being treated like animals which were to come later, and last for so long. For David and me, going through the years of yo-yoing between the Spartan life at Ston and the chaos of the pub in the holidays football was an escape into normality. Football was a safe area with our father, so that talk about players, the game and his stories from the past blocked out for a time all those worries about money, the pub and the anxiety about another crash into mental illness.

When we were away there were normally no real opportunities to go to matches, but this made it all the more important to have a team to follow, and in the autumn and winter of 1963/4

Oxford had a big cup run which made national news. They had, exceptionally for a Fourth Division team, made it into the fifth round to play Blackburn Rovers, then top of the First Division, and with famous stars like Ronnie Clayton, the England captain. It was the commentary game on Saturday afternoon. I managed to avoid the usual Stonic games requirement and stayed in the changing room listening on someone's transistor radio, proud of my allegiance, and letting everyone know about it. Astonishingly Oxford won 3-1 and I can remember the commentator's shout and the crowd's roar as the final goal went in and the giant-killers had done it. I waited on to hear the draw, as all the games were then played on the same day, and Oxford were drawn against Preston North End. The draw for the quarter-final gave Oxford a home game against Preston, a Second Division team. No team from the lowest division had ever got this far before, and that draw now seemed to offer a real chance of getting to an unthinkable semi-final.

I decided straight away that my brother and I must go. I wrote home. As usual this was to my mother. That was how it always had been, and it was almost always she who replied. I asked if my father could get tickets for the game. Her reply seemed positive and so I got all the permissions required for us to go home on the bus. I heard nothing more from home about it and just assumed that all would be OK. Given the state of things at home, it would with hindsight have been very sensible to check. However, we arrived back at the pub at lunchtime on the Saturday of the match. It was obvious immediately before either my mother or father said anything that we were completely unexpected. There were of course no tickets. I remember still the mix of disbelief, tearfulness and thwarted teenage rage. It was not so much the match but the big build-up I had made about it to everyone at school, so I dreaded the thought of having to go back and admit that we had not even gone to the match. My brother, as ever, was more stoical, but I went upstairs, on my own, and paced up and own in my anxiety between the bathroom and the underused upstairs sitting room. Any slight hopes I had left receded minute by minute as the clock reached 2pm – an hour before the game, nearly 20 miles away, with no bus due, and no tickets.

There were moments throughout my childhood and adolescence when my father, always unpredictable and emotionally volatile, was able to understand what really mattered and follow his feelings. He may have struggled to explain or talk about those feelings, but there were moments when he just understood the need to do something. This was one of those times, and he virtually commandeered Nobby Clarke to drive us to Headington in his van. Nobby was a local odd job man to whom my father often turned. He had rough ways and a reputation for being heavy handed, but he was one of our regulars and on this occasion willing and able. The van was very basic and we charged off towards Oxford with the two of us in our school uniforms rattling around in the back with the tools and bags of cement as my father gave directions from the front. We got to the London Road outside the ground just after kick-off time and my father bought tickets from a tout to get us in, narrowly missing the first goal – to Preston, by their centre forward Alex Dawson.

The Manor had temporary stands on the far side, and the gate remains the biggest the club has ever had - 22,750. We squeezed along towards the pitch near the dressing rooms and just managed to get a view of the game, played on an old -fashioned worn and muddy pitch with the crowd almost on top of the players. We were very close as they came out for the second half and I remember still the broken nose and tough, broad physique of Alex Dawson. Though Oxford went down 2-1 eventually, you felt to the end that they might bring off an equaliser, and it was just great to have been there. I can still feel it, and the newsreel of the match, still on You Tube, brings it all back, with the heaving stands, the cup fever, the feeling that you were part of the adventure, and the whole sense of so near and yet so far which followers of smaller clubs all know so well. We went back to the pub on the bus, stopped off at home briefly and then travelled back to school. On the bus I felt rather rueful about my earlier outbursts, but I think I knew that if I had not made a fuss we would not have gone. I was just grateful in the end to be able to get back to school and have the story to tell without losing face.

What I remember most of all is that my father was able, for all the problems he had, to put things right that day for my brother and the moody resentful me. I am not sure that I ever really told him what that day had meant to me. I was able to talk about feelings with my mother and often did, but for all his struggles with his own emotions my father only managed to talk about his feelings when he was angry or ill and nothing you could say got through to him. Those rare moments when he 'got it' and acted on his feelings were powerful and surprising, but for most of the time, and for the rest of his life, it was always much easier to keep to things he would share willingly. Of these, football was always the easiest and most obvious. Football went on being that safe meeting place for him and his three sons over the years – a setting where we had plenty to talk about and memories to share without other deeper emotions having to be aired directly. It is a familiar story among men and, right or wrong, it's the reason why all that reminiscing about great games, old players and famous goals matters so much.

My father eventually found himself a berth within the game he had always loved, Many years later, after he and my mother had moved to Manchester on the back of a legacy from Aunt Win, he became a gateman and then supervisor at Manchester City. So, at long last, he had an official stake in the game, and it was at Maine Road that we had the final games together on high days and holidays, with him enjoying the company of his grandsons and regaling everyone with names and dates of teams and players he had seen. This is what football meant to him, and is the reason why – though it concerns cricket and not football – my brother read Francis Thompson's poem 'At Lords' about my Hornby and my Barlow long ago. It was just right.

Chapter 22

PLAYS

‒‒‒‒⊷✕⊶‒‒‒‒

If football offered one escape route from life at Ston, the other important one for me was theatre. For most of my last two years there I developed a passion for plays, and particularly new ones which seemed to offer tantalising prospects of wider horizons beyond the yo-yo world of Ston, the bright bar and the village. From the dressing-up box days of primary school nativities and the fun of getting our own play together at J Ston, I had always loved the bustle, the excitement and the achievement of conquered nerves. I had also gained some early sense that plays could be powerful and deal with serious matters.

At home in the back room of the pub we spent a great deal of time watching TV and the two channels available from 1955. Pretty much left to see what we chose, I especially remember an Armchair Theatre play about the Craig Bentley case. It was broadcast in 1958, when I was eleven. Watching it, I was haunted by the whole business of the vulnerable Bentley being prepared for execution. I tried to imagine the frightfulness of knowing throughout a last night that you were going to die at a set time in the morning, with nothing you could do about it. The play was hard to watch, but you could not turn away.

I suppose that many more conventional or attentive parents would have regarded this kind of thing as 'not suitable for children', but I can date my awareness of capital punishment and its horrors from that play, and I have never forgotten it. There were many more plays. In the spirit of the time they were often to do with issues of the day, and they really did have a big impact on the way I was beginning to see the world, with much more impact than reading or radio. At Ston we were cut off from it all, as the Canute-like regime did its best to isolate us from modern times. In the holidays, though, I went on watching in the back room. These were the days of the new theatre and new writing, but like many young people I got my access to it all through TV drama.

As to direct involvement in theatre, Ston did not offer many opportunities for performance. I was cast as the first witch in Macbeth when we did that in 1964. The other two witches were a boy called Dean Whitehouse and my friend from the same house, David Davies. We had a minor success and enjoyed a short-term celebrity as we emerged from a dry-ice fog with our glittery make up to stir our cauldron and give Macbeth a fright. For anyone interested in the history of real celebrities. the future star Anthony Andrews who I mentioned earlier played the part of a scullion, or messenger in tights. The play was directed by our English teacher, John Quibell-Smith, who made a good job of it, given the limited time available and the pressures of the school routine. I was in some awe of Armitage, two years older than me with his ability to learn all the lines and carry the production as Macbeth. In classic boarding school fashion, a boy with a high voice played Lady Macbeth.

The following winter term, I was given a part in Ston's production of the rather creaky John Drinkwater play *Abraham Lincoln*. This was done soon after the death of Kennedy and was intended to support the memorial proposed by the Runnymede Trust. It was again directed by John Quibell-Smith, who was one of a very few younger staff members, and quite liberal, to the point, occasionally, of being mildly permissive. The stage directions called for my character, William Seward, to light a cigar in the second act. This could perfectly well have been cut with no impact on the action, but was kept in. I was allowed at the later rehearsals and on each night of the performance to smoke and actually finish a sizeable cigar. As I was already an early smoker I enjoyed this, and in the darkness backstage was expected to share it with a number of other enthusiasts. It was a long and episodic play and as I featured only briefly there was plenty of time to wait for and then enjoy the cigar. That, apart from our all fancying ourselves in the snappy Edwardian costumes, is really my only memory of the performances. It was my last winter term at Ston and the final months before things began to go badly wrong for me as the problems at home began to infect everything, and separation from them only served to heighten my fears and anxiety.

As I have mentioned earlier the school was stronger for music, and once or twice drama and music came together with more impressive results. In the Easter term that year we did a mimed accompaniment to Handel's oratorio *Samson*, and acted out the action as the soloists sang. The big thing about this production was that for the first time ever known, it was done jointly with the fabled girls' school. I was to be Samson's father Manoah, a role which gave plenty of opportunity for mournful praying to heaven as woe descended, and I certainly made the most of it. At the first shared rehearsal in the Girl's School one sight of Delilah, as she danced enticingly down the aisle after a grand entrance, and I was smitten. She had dark hair and a pretty face and she moved sinuously towards the ill-fated Samson.

By good fortune I was on the same small table at tea. I was certainly shy. The alternation between school and my sequestered village holiday life had not provided much prior experience of this kind of chatting. However, I did my best and was really pleased to find that she responded well, or so it seemed to me. I relied on an older and more obviously confident friend, Macbeth/ Armitage again, for support. He was getting on well and easily with her friend, and I arranged to write before the home fixture the following week. I did write and made an arrangement to meet. On the night I played Manoah for all he was worth and then went, all nerves and anticipation, for my assignation afterwards, but she did not turn up. She was sufficiently popular, the star of the show really, that I was easily bumped out of place, as the lucky one concerned was very keen to point out to me later. I brazened it out, but by now I was struggling with work, and losing ground. I had a very low opinion of myself and not much confidence that I could do anything about it, so the hurt was real enough. I longed to break out of my shy beanpole adolescence, but there was no one to confide in, least of all my parents, or so it seemed then.

The final school show that I can remember, in my last term, was a grand staging in the school quadrangle of *Agamemnon* by Sophocles. Again it had all kinds of music, with use made of the corner towers with trumpeters perched on each. I was by then out of sorts, angry and outside the ranks of people likely to be selected for this piece. Beset with my own worries and now part of the school's outlaw culture, I did not give it a thought until I saw the production, when, for all my hostility, I felt sad and left out, despite myself.

Drama in those days could not be taken as a subject. It was neither part of the curriculum nor seen as a serious activity, which could be challenging or creative. It was my interest in modern plays, fired by television, which kept me going during my final terms at Ston. Though, by then, I had become lethargic about much of my formal school work, I could always find energy for reading plays and thinking about them This was not really because I wanted to be a performer, or because I had even seen very much, but because the writing and the spirit of change it represented really excited me. It was as far away from the stuffy über-conformity of Ston as I could get.

I was too young to understand or now remember the fuss about *Look Back in Anger*, which is usually reckoned to have marked the arrival of the new theatre in 1956, but I read all about it and as many of the plays which followed as I could find. My guide to it all was John Russell Taylor's book 'Anger and After', which came out in 1962 and gave me an idea of the personalities, their work and some of the theatre history. In the holidays I would spend hours in Wethered's bookshop in Aylesbury, where all the second-hand bargains, including plenty of plays, were in boxes on the floor. Mr Wethered himself was a charming old-fashioned bookseller with grey hair to match his grey suit and a gentle manner. Later on, after I had left school, I tried to sell him some of the Stonic books I had kept, and politely but properly, he turned down the ones with school stamps in.

As well as plays from the second-hand boxes I always bought new anything from the Penguin Plays series, which came out regularly and were cheap. They usually had three plays in them, sometimes with no obvious connecting theme, so you might get Arden with Pirandello and Sartre, for example, or J.P. Donleavy, Bernard Kops, and Henry Livings. I loved Wesker, and you got the famous trilogy all in one paperback. Wesker became a real hero, and I felt that I really 'got' what he was about, especially in Roots. I enjoyed most of the others too, and loved the language and humour of the Behan plays, though I liked the Quare Fellow better than the Hostage. I liked best plays about real life, as I saw it, and didn't really get stuff less obviously connected with the kitchen sink or the working-class life I now so wanted to identify with. I sometimes did not really make much sense of plays, like John Arden's, which less obviously dealt with those themes, and I really struggled with the Sartre plays, then very much in fashion, which had complex philosophical themes and rather alienated characters who were harder to warm to.

I read *Plays and Players* in the school library every time it came out and tried to keep up with what was going on, but I could never manage to see very much. I managed to get to the Palace Theatre in Watford a few times, on my own and usually for matinees. It was a pleasant, slightly seedy old place. I remember a terrific production of *A Taste of Honey* – exactly my kind of thing. Coming back from that and straight into life at Ston was by then very hard to take. In the holidays, though constrained by lack of money and the bus timetable, I did try to get to plays in Oxford, and managed a few productions at the Playhouse and the New Theatre Oxford. I remember sneaking into the back seats of the Playhouse to watch rehearsals of *The Hostage* and being fascinated by the nuts and bolts of the play being put together.

Early in 1965, I saw an afternoon performance at the New Theatre, Oxford, of a new play by Joe Orton. It was the trial run of *Loot,* which later became a huge and substantially re-written success, but was at that point being tried out, as things were then, in 'the provinces'. Orton was famous already, for his dark comedy *Entertaining Mr Sloane,* and this, his second play, was a completely crazy farce about two thieves who rob the bank next to the funeral parlour where one of them, Dennis, works. His colleague Hal's mother has just died and they hide the money in her coffin. The coffin and her body turn up in different places around the house as they try to throw the police off the scent. As a play, it satirises not only all the conventions and sacred cows of death and bereavement but the behaviour and corruptibility of the police. It got absolutely panned on this first tour. This was partly reaction to the radical blackness of the humour, partly to the need for tightening of the script and to a fair extent also the miscasting of an unnecessarily glittering cast, the worst example being Kenneth Williams as the Police Inspector. I enjoyed it, though. I could see that it was strong stuff and beautifully likely to offend. The most surreal thing of all was to watch from the New Theatre cheap seats with about 30 people in that huge space, and to have the customary string quartet tinkling along in the interval as if we had just been watching Noel Coward or Terence Rattigan.

In the weeks just after I finally left Ston I celebrated my new freedom and uncertain future by going to see one of the first performances of the latest John Osborne play, *A Patriot for Me*. I had read all his earlier plays, but this one had been refused a license by the Lord Chamberlain. Tony Richardson at the Royal Court was staging it privately for members of the English Stage Society Club, so I joined and got a ticket. The play concerns an Austro-Hungarian Army Office, Alfred Redl, whose homosexuality is used against him to blackmail him into espionage. It is a play on the grand scale with a huge cast. The best-known, and then notorious, scene was a full-scale drag ball involving senior Army Officers. This was intended to show up the hypocrisy of a decaying society and the treatment, as was usually the case in Osborne plays, of the outsider. The fuss over it now seems extraordinary and it certainly helped to do away with the Lord Chamberlain's Office. I am not sure that I found any of it very shocking at the time, for that matter. The 'generals' in the famous scene included the famous English Stage Company founder George Devine, who sadly died during the play's run.

A Patriot for Me had plenty of Osborne tricks, some of which I didn't get, and Schopenhauer hurtling onto stage through a trap door at one point was one of them. But I did get the guts of it right, and understood much more several years later, as an undergraduate, when I heard Humphrey Berkeley speak about the Homosexual Law Reform Bill at Manchester University. But more than anything else, that night at the Royal Court showed me what theatre could do, and it was very exciting. Afterwards, I remember getting back to Aylesbury by the last train, and starting the long six-mile walk back to the pub, which was the only option, as I had no money left. I got down to the turn at Hartwell by about 12.30 and felt really good. It was a night full of stars and silence apart from the occasional car. I kept walking, and a mile or so on a bloke with a van just stopped and offered me a lift, so it all ended very well and I had plenty to think about.

In my last year at school, and in the period after I had left, I was an odd, imbalanced mixture of real and often painful experience from the problems at home alongside a naiveté and gaucheness left by years of boarding school isolation. I knew a lot more about mental illness, booze and football than I knew about how to approach girls or have a normal social life. Through that whole period it was plays and theatre that gave me something to believe in and the prospect of a more open-minded world full of ideas and wide horizons. I liked films and TV drama as well, and they too could reflect things I cared about, but there was something special with being able to read plays and have the words in front of you to relish and repeat. When I did manage to see modern plays performed, a sense that real life, with its pain and joy, had been captured and shared was able to excite me more than anything I had ever experienced before. This was my enthusiasm and investment in a richer and more liberated world than life at Ston or at home could ever offer, and when everything else seemed to be heavy going or depressingly stuck and hopeless, it got me through.

My love of theatre has always stayed with me and over the years I have seen many wonderful plays and performances, but then it was actually a lifeline.

Chapter 23

VIOLENCE AND STICKING PLASTER

Just before Christmas in 1964 my brother and I came home from school via Marylebone on a cold bright morning, changing to the local train at Princes Risborough. As we lugged our cases down the hill towards the pub I was certainly pleased that term was over and, as ever, I hoped that Christmas would turn out better than expected. I was more anxious than usual, though. Recent reports from home, however played down and camouflaged in my mother's letters, had been worrying.

It was clear as soon as we came through the back door that things were not good. Behind the warmth of my mother's greeting and hug was an atmosphere as taut as piano wire. My father was around, but they were plainly not speaking to each other. It was just a question of how long it would take, regardless of our being there, before one of those long hateful, running, looping arguments began. We knew these very well. They had a life of their own and it had no effect if we tried to intervene.

They would be punctuated only by a call to the bar during which there would be a brief interlude of put-on bonhomie as one or the other of them attended to a customer. After that you silently prayed that it would not resume, but it always did, with endless improvisations on the same themes and recriminations. Our arrival provided an interval, but that was all.

This was the way it had usually been. Coming home for Christmas from Ston always managed to start with high expectations, but in the back room of the pub things quickly became glum and lonely. Out front in the bright bar there was a seasoning of public bar merriment, with dollops of festive sentimentality. In pub life the difference between front and back is never starker than at Christmas. In the bars it was generally all bonhomie and cheer, with plenty of spirits, seasonal cigar smoke, garlands and fairy lights. In our back living room, for all the presents and the efforts made, it was always more subdued, as if family life had to be squeezed into the left-over times.

This meant that Christmas dinner was often quite late, and the atmosphere then depended on my father's condition at the time and my mother's level of exhaustion. In the drinking days he easily became embarrassingly sentimental. Later it would depend on the impact his ever-present medication was having. She had always juggled cooking and serving in the bar, and kept going on Guinness and cigarettes, so that you might try to help but merely got in the way. The ritual of crackers and paper hats would carry on at the same time as the grinding on of argument and recrimination, and I remember very well the point at which you got a lump in your throat and tried to hold back tears of misery and desperation.

The rows always seemed to spoil the time we had together. Though it was always more painful and poignant at Christmas, arguments followed a similar pattern the whole year round. They always involved the delivery of separate litanies of accumulated grievance. From the age of 14 or so I would sometimes try to get them to 'see reason', since I was still young enough to think that this was what was needed. It took me a few more years to understand that this kind of row is never ever about reason, but always a ventilation of the dissatisfaction and frustration of two people who feel that they are chained together with no way out. Reason does not come into it, and the subject matter is just the familiar available weaponry.

The temperature would fluctuate within a long row and there was sometimes real fury from my father, but the most typical pattern was a punctuated, running call and response of grievance and counter-grievance. They never really swore beyond the usual bloodies and things usually petered out eventually rather than anything ever being resolved or any apology being made on either side. We knew that they both loved us, and that life was hard for them, but knowing those things did not stop it all being sad and upsetting. You felt completely powerless, and always lived with a background feeling of anxiety, however acclimatised you thought you were to it all.

For all this, there were lighter moments. In those days the licensee had the option of closing only on Christmas night, when the village was silent and people would have stayed by the fire anyway. We usually closed at the Red Lion and those evenings meant that we could all be together for once. This must have been a considerable relief to them, and for us it was usually the most trouble-free time of the season. For all that money was often tight, my parents always did their best with presents. That year they bought us a small table tennis table, which we set up in the landing. This produced some interesting bounces off the walls and stairs but enabled us to play an endless tournament. My brother, who was much better than me at the game, always managed to be at least two or three games in front, and I never got closer than that however long we played for.

After Christmas there was not much to do. For one thing we were stuck in the back living room. We could not use our old hideaway in the pub's upstairs sitting room as Dave, a building worker from Luton, was living there. Although he was away until the New Year it was now his place and we were not allowed to go in. This stopped several activities. I used to go to the box room attached to it, so that I could secretly try out smoking, and despite the early dizziness had quickly learnt to enjoy it, and there was nowhere else that was suitably close and secret. We went for walks, visited Aylesbury once or twice and carried on with the endless table tennis tournament, as there did not seem to be much else to do. By now we had no real contact with anyone of our own age in the village. This was a consequence of being away at school certainly, but the fact that we did not really try to make contact was also to do with the way we felt about things at home, and indeed what others might think about us. It was all very isolating.

Dave was still away several days after New Year when it happened. It was late on Saturday night. I had gone to bed in the room at the front of the pub, facing the church across the Green. My brother was asleep in the room at the other end of the landing, which had once been my grandfather's. My baby brother was in a cot in my parents' room between the two. The wind was gusting, and in the moonlight the clouds flew quickly. I half dozed as I heard the final tunes on the jukebox, the distant shouted partings and the chink of glasses being collected. Silence finally came, but then I was shocked awake by my father, slamming the back door hard and shouting angrily and hoarsely up the stairs.

'Your mother's in the back of Stan Birch's car with her clothes up!'

It was sudden and shocking. I knew what he meant but could not believe that this was happening to my mother, less still that she wanted it to, and least of all that it should be Stan Birch. He was a local farmer, a long-time regular, and king of the cow shit boots in the public bar, with a bumpy red face, dusty old hat and rumbling low voice.

Moments later the shouting and screaming started from the car park, first of all seeming far away and then horribly close and brutal. Inside the house I heard slaps, and a crashing as my mother fell against furniture. My father went on hitting and abusing her as a cow and a whore. I was scared, and paralysed. I wanted somehow to do something, but dared not.

Soon there was a devastating silence. My baby brother had begun to grizzle and my mother came to see to him. My father must have stayed downstairs that night. I could not sleep. Once the first shock passed there came the endless replaying in my head of my father's shouted words and I tried to fight away appalling images of my mother in the back of a car with her skirt over her head under a grunting farmer.

The next day was strained and unreal. My mother had bruised eyes and a cut mouth. I remembered from childhood the black eyes of Buckle Ing's wife in the butcher's over the road, and the tutting of local people. Now this was here, and in our family. Through the day her bitterness and denials smouldered and occasionally ignited. My father brooded and did not respond. My brother must have been awake, but I did not talk to him about it. We were close, but neither of us had the words to dare speak about this. I know that I felt guilty about being so terrified that I could do nothing to help. This is what violence at home does to children, and in our case the separated life at school and the Stonic training in stoic denial did not help either, especially since going back after all this might feel like an abandonment rather than any kind of personal escape.

We went back to school soon afterwards, very anxious, certainly, about what would happen. My father's need to have faith in the redemptive benefits of boarding school must have helped him believe that we would be safe and secure. My mother was, though, more tearful than usual. As the Green Line coach took us back to Bushey my feelings were split between real fear about what might happen at home while we were away and a guilty relief that at least we would not have to be there. I told no one at school. There was no real pastoral care available and I would not, in any event, have trusted anyone enough to share things which seemed so private.

My parents never discussed these events again, so far as I know, beyond oblique references to trust and anger. It certainly added height to the mountain of accumulated grievance between them, but they seemed unable to escape from each other. I came to see much later that my mother, only 40 years old at the time, was so lonely and so frustrated with her life that the invitation may have been an exciting one, especially after a few drinks at the end of a long evening. I never managed to raise the subject over the years that followed, doubting that it would do any good, but I now wish that I had at least tried. I never told anyone else either. It seemed too shocking and too intimate. Keeping that kind of secret was a bad habit to acquire, and although I learnt to confide and trust later on it took a long time and a strong marriage, within which we could share some very similar experiences, as it turned out.

Children and adolescents who grow up in troubled backgrounds where there is physical or verbal violence tend to feel and take responsibility too soon, and are burdened with a sense of responsibility for things they really can do nothing much about. I still remember that night for the paralysis and fear I felt. At school I could play the part of a confident achieving and clever all-rounder, whatever was going on inside. At home, already 17 years old, I felt lonely, scared and powerless with no clear idea of what I could do. I never tried to leave. I thought of it, but had no idea where to go or who to turn to. I also felt that I should try to stay for my mother's sake – what would she do if I went? Actually the experience forced me back to more basic child-like emotions – solitary sobbing, a basic wish to be comforted and for things to be 'normal', whatever that might be like.

I am not sure if this event, so big to me, was really a turning point for my parents, and I realise, too, that there probably had been other violence when we were not there. My brother and I never knew really knew what else went on in our absence, as through all those years we were only at home for school holidays. In reality the New Year crisis was probably one more unpleasant waymark on a gradual slide into the dysfunction and disaster which was going on at home. Like most slides there were occasional upward bumps of hope, with apparently fresh starts, and then, like most people, my parents opted for hope over experience, almost to the end.

For me, though, it did mark a turning point on two counts. First I sensed that from then on I could try as hard as I might to reason and talk my parents round but that there was always going to be something broken and unfixable which I could not change. I also knew that the more public violence meant that the protective barrier between the bright bar and our own private lives had been breached open, with liberties taken and nothing really secret any more.

In that spring term of 1965, though by now disaffected and holding on to unshared and stressful secrets, I managed to keep up appearances, and must have done enough work to make a showing at the 'mock' 'A' level exams. I did well in English and scraped through both Latin and History, by luck and judicious choice of questions. The range of questions which I could not have begun to answer, especially on the less well assimilated recent material, should have highlighted the work I needed to do, but all life then seemed to be an obstacle race and just getting by was enough to think about before the next hurdle.

There was worryingly little news from home, and what there was seemed bland enough, as if they had decided that the big bust up had never happened. My father came up on his own at half-term and took us out. He was reassuring but said little about things at home. It came as a big surprise several weeks later when my brother and I were called to the Housemaster's study during the evening. On our way to his room several dreadful possibilities crossed my mind – had one of them died? Had he killed her? Had she killed him, for that matter? Had we just become orphans and the news was to be broken to us in a kindly way as had happened to several people in our time at school?

It was none of those things. He told us that because things were difficult at the moment (well we did know that!) it had been decided (of course without any kind of discussion with us!) that we would spend the Easter holidays at our Aunt Doreen's (which one was she?) in Manchester. We were not to worry. That was it. He said no more – I doubt if he knew much more, and I still have no idea whose idea this really was or who arranged it all. I suspect that my father had given a socially acceptable and charmingly edited explanation of the 'difficulties' and that this explained the Housemaster's approach. Our response in hindsight was extraordinarily passive. I am not sure if he was surprised how accepting we seemed to be. Perhaps he had expected a more obvious reaction. Mr Dilley was a kind man and may well have tried to give us the time to ask more questions or talk about it, but we didn't. You tended not to let feelings show much to people like Housemasters at Ston, unless you were very trusting, and we were not. We took an unspoken cue from each other, stayed silent and went back downstairs.

And that is how, at the end of the term, instead of going back to the pub, David went straight off to Manchester, and I left with the Duke of Edinburgh's Award expedition to Yorkshire, to go on to Auntie Doreen's a week or so later.

Chapter 24

Outward Bound

———✕———

As it turned out, the expedition and being away doing new things really did help at a time when I felt lonely and preoccupied. For all my concerns, and although I was hostile to much about life at Ston by this stage, I still took part in most school activities. One of these was the Duke of Edinburgh's Award Scheme, or D of E as we called it. Although participation was voluntary the opportunity was offered rather selectively to those seen as possible 'leaders'. I suppose I went along with it because my friends were doing it, and I went along rather passively. Looking back, although I wandered through the scheme without very much commitment, I have always been glad that I did it. By the standards of the time we were certainly very privileged to be given easy access to the opportunities and activities involved.

The D of E was Prince Philip's first big personal initiative and began in 1956, so that Ston had been an early adopter. Though the scheme has evolved mightily in style and reach since then and has broadened out from its early public school territory, it remains largely true to the central ideas of Philip's mentor

210

Kurt Hahn. This Jewish teacher had opposed Hitler and left Germany in 1933, later to found Gordonstoun. In his memoir, *Flannelled Fool – A Slice of a Life in the Thirties*, TC Worsley records his impressions of Hahn's energy and commitment to educational development, but he later became more critical of Hahn's 'despotic, overpowering personality'. Worsley says of Hahn: 'He revealed himself as having a fierce temper, a strong hand with the cane, and a temperament which hated being crossed. Especially damaging to my very English view was his dislike of being defeated at any game.' He was a fervent moralist, according to Worsley: 'We were going through the classrooms when, in one, he suddenly stopped, gripped my arm, raised his nostrils in the air, and then, in his marked German accent, he solemnly pronounced: "Somevon has been talking dirt in this room. I can smell it."'

The D of E drew heavily on Hahn's notion of the 'six declines of modern youth' – all to do with a perceived loss of fitness, initiative, skill and perseverance. This was all supposed to be happening because of the corrupting nature of modern life. In many respects Hahn's educational ideas could be summarised as Thomas Arnold's last hurrah – muscular Christianity meets Moral Rearmament. It is easy to see how attractive it must have been to the Stonic establishment and its Masonic Governors.

The D of E regime prescribed four areas of activity to address the dreaded 'declines' – some fitness work; a project of some kind to reflect an interest or hobby; an expedition, and some training in rescue or public service. At Ston it was all organised under the auspices of the Cadet Corps. The activities were carefully programmed, so that compared with the choice and effort you would have to make in a day school we did not have to do much more than turn up.

I still have my battered green record book from the D of E, which confirms the dates and activities of my Silver Award year in 1963-4 and the Gold Award a year later. I see that in

March 1964 I passed a preliminary First Aid Certificate for the silver award and then the Adult Certificate the following year. I have thought ever since that everyone ought to do basic first aid, though you need to keep up to date and a great deal has changed since 1964! We spent a great deal of time on learning various slings and bandages, including the dreaded tourniquet to stop serious bleeding. We were told that at the scene of a disaster you might well need to apply these. They were bandages tied in a loop, and then applied around a limb ever more tightly by cranking the pressure with a stick. You were told that you should write the time it was applied on the victim's forehead (presumably with some commandeered lipstick) as permanent damage would occur if they were left on too long. Nowadays, thank goodness, the motto for first aiders is to interfere as little as necessary and at least do no harm. We were reasonably proficient by the time we took the exam, which mainly involved practical tests to see if you could actually do particular dressings or suggest the right remedy in a situation you were given. Fortunately most of the 'victims' we practised on were reasonably compliant.

Like most young first aiders we both wanted and feared the chance to apply our skills in real life. The best bet often seemed to be the rugby pitch, but few got the chance to apply a ring pad to the head or find a pressure point, not least because, as my own experience of mild concussions, a broken collar bone and broken nose confirmed, the usual assumption was that you would bash on regardless and walk on down to the hospital at the end if it still hurt.

As to the fitness training, I see from my Record Book that for the Gold Award on 15th January 1964 I managed 12.2 seconds for the 100 yards, and completed the other physical jerks a few days later. They were all signed off, but with very little supervision. A stopwatch was certainly used for the running, but otherwise we were trusted a good deal not to cheat, and on the whole we didn't. Of course we spent six days of every week engaged in physical sports anyway, so the tests were not evidence of our having had to do much to address Herr Hahn's concern about the 'decline of physical fitness due to modern methods of locomotion'.

The 'pursuits and projects' activities, which were much more intended to allow personal choice, were also supervised in a rather casual way, and you could if you wanted choose a different interest for each stage of the Award. If truth be told my real-life pursuits between 1964 and 1965 would have been collecting football programmes and trying to sound cool and arty. In practice you had to pick something worthy.

My choice for the silver award was 'Archaeology'. What this really meant, when I had done very little and the deadline loomed, was a trip out on the bus to Verulamium, as St Albans was not very far away. My friend Paul Griffin and I found the site on a pleasant spring Saturday, walked around for a while making some notes, and then found Ye Olde Fighting Cocks, a small and attractive pub which claimed, and still does, to be the oldest in England. We had several pints and watched some of the Cup Final – West Ham beating Preston, whom I had seen a few months before ending Oxford's dreams in the quarterfinal at the Manor Ground. We had enough information, and the guidebook, so that my project report passed muster, though my history master, who signed it off, did not, I think, pay it much detailed attention. There is nonetheless a fulsome and totally undeserved write up in my record book:

'Hedge went to considerable trouble, and no small personal expense, to make a thorough survey of historical data at Verulamium. He produced a well-documented and well-illustrated survey of his studies and observations.'

I love the reference to 'no small expense' – the beer cost more than the bus fare.

For the gold award, of course, I did Drama. At least theatre was a real interest for me and something I cared about, although I had read more than I had actually seen or done. Apart from having quite a small part in the school play, I had not done much beyond go to a handful of productions. By this time I was beginning to struggle with my work and increasing worries about home, so that I had little energy to organise anything more challenging. Fortunately my English teacher, Quibbell-Smith, with little actual involvement, waved me through with generous overstatement – my acting was supposed to have 'matured considerably' and my visits to West End plays had been 'observed with enthusiasm and attention to detail'.

The two remaining D of E elements were the expeditions for both silver and gold, and the public service contribution at gold level. If some of the other D of E requirements had not stretched me very far, both of these had a real impact on my experience and attitudes. The expeditions were both real 'Outward Bound' events. For the silver trip we went to the Penwith peninsula in Cornwall. We spent most of a warm spring day getting to St Erth on the train, to be picked up with our kit bags by a three-ton Army lorry. The camp was already set up, and we were organised into groups for rota duties – cooking (basic stuff, of course), cleaning, and latrines (unpleasant in the extreme). We were also detailed as teams to take a series of temperature and other readings about the weather conditions, though to what purpose I never really understood.

But each day we also did something I had never done before – kayaking what seemed to be a long, long way along the Hayle estuary, and three days actually out in a small group trudging around the Penwith peninsula, camping in small tents and having to fend for ourselves. It seemed to drizzle most of the time, so that everything steamed gently in the damp Cornish air. West Cornwall, then, was less given over to tourism, and seemed quietly neglected as we trudged between archaeological sites and disused tin mines. It was quite hard going and certainly challenging, especially finding your way around for the first time with a map and compass. You argued the toss about which way to go in the absence, usually, of any obvious clues, so that you did see the necessity of concentrating on the OS map.

On one of the base camp evenings before we went back, we bumped our way to Penzance in the back of the three-tonner to watch a rugby match between Penzance and Saracens. In the days before leagues Penzance were a significant national club and there was a good crowd. I forget who won, but I remember very well the frantic post-match pub crawl. By the time I made it back to our transport I had gulped down many bottles of cider, and I lay on the floor of the lorry listening to the rustles and groans coming from the dark far side of the lorry where two of my more experienced and sexually confident fellows were in intense clinches with local girls they had picked up.

Having the odd illicit drink was all part of our defiance of the Stonic regime, but this was different. Off the leash for the first time, in a place I did not know and with no one counting, I got into previously unknown territory. However much I had seen my father and everyone at the pub drink I had no sense or warning about what it would feel like to be very pissed indeed. I went from elation and merriment to the staggers and then that point when your tongue seems to fill your entire mouth so that sentences may be formed in your head but cannot be delivered. You can shake yourself into a brief rallying of your sensibilities, but this is a huge effort and you then subside again into incoherence.

Once back in the tent, having somehow by trial and many errors made it into a sleeping bag, I hoped just to sleep, but then of course everything got worse. The horizon, sickeningly, would not stay still and more than once I needed to blunder out to the latrines to be sick and pee. Being drunk in a sleeping bag in a tent is never advisable – just staying warm is impossible, apart from anything else. When the dawn came, I woke with the worst kind of sick hangover. No one else seemed to be quite as badly affected. The staff either did not notice, or more likely, had decided to just let me go through it without too much interference. If so I can see with hindsight that this was very decent of them, and not at all Stonic.

We were going rock climbing that day. In ropes and harnesses we climbed, in turn, the steep and windy Porthcurno cliffs. Having made it to the top, I stood up straight on the edge, as we were told to do, quite fearlessly, though most of the others found this scary and could not manage it. This was not actually fearlessness on my part. At that moment I was just past caring and the very thought of cider made me want to retch. I felt better later and eventually at the end of the week we all dispersed around the country for the Easter holiday. My record book only has one comment about my performance – 'satisfactory', which was quite generous in the circumstances!

The gold expedition in North Yorkshire involved five days out on the moors in small groups in very wild country. I remember our group being taken to Rievaulx Abbey and being left at those soaring ruins anxiously thinking about the long days ahead of us, with the wind roaring over the moors and grouse squeaking across the sky. One morning start involved clambering up a very steep hill, and by then I was certainly struggling to keep up. For all my rugby playing and trying to look confident I was actually rather underpowered for my height and not at all used to slowly grinding out the miles with a pack on my back. I was helped through it by the encouragement and support of the others. This was impressively kind and mature of them, as I certainly could not have managed otherwise. We had some laughs along the way, as well, but I always struggled in to the checkpoint at the end of each day miles behind at the back. I did make it through, though, and remember some beautiful places. We camped one evening near a river, which you could hear rushing through its stony bed. I remember being desperate for a drink and clambering down the boulders to get to what seemed to be the coldest and sweetest water ever.

At the end, on a fine night, I remember there being a major

heather fire on the horizon with huge flames running across the hills as far as you could see in either direction. We knew we were safe enough with the river between us and this awe-inspiring blaze, but above all I remember being glad that it was all over, and that I had managed to do it. I travelled on to Manchester the next day as planned to spend the holidays with my Aunty Doreen. Although I knew most of my mother's family and had lots of other Manchester aunts and uncles I could not remember Doreen, so I went off towards the unknown with no recent news from home, unsure about what to expect and carrying everything, including a pile of dirty washing, inside a huge canvas kit bag.

I found my way to Uncle Johnnie and Aunt Doreen in Wythenshawe and they were really welcoming and kind. One of the pressing things I had to do in the month we were there was to find some kind of 'public service' to do for three days as the final requirement for my gold award. In fact it was not difficult. I went to see the Secretary at the Withington Hospital in south Manchester, a bus ride from Wythenshawe. In those times before the growth of the Health and Safety industry, when hospital bureaucracy was small, visible and easy to navigate, I just had a short interview and did the three required days as a hospital porter, mainly in the A and E department. Those three days, and the paid work which I was able to get after that, were interesting, slightly scary and fun. The staff were friendly and I had my first really close up experience of crisis, injury and indeed death. I asked to stay on and be paid after that and learned even more, but it would not have happened without the prod of the D of E requirement.

Back at school for my final term I eventually got my D of E report book back. It gave me a lot of credit for having had the courage to keep going during the expedition. I had not expected this to be recognised or understood. It was the only statement I can remember from that time which suggested that the staff concerned had some understanding and appreciation of my position physically and emotionally. It made a good deal of difference to the way I saw myself, and was at least one light shining in the increasing uncertainty of a year when everything else seemed to be getting out of control.

So, somewhat to my surprise, I had finished the whole thing. Did it matter and was it worth doing? In hindsight I think it was, and getting through it while much else was going wrong was much better than sitting out on the sidelines. Despite the link to the hated Cadet Corps, it enabled me to try things which would never have happened otherwise. I still have real doubts about some of the founding ideas and assumptions, but it did provide some valuably testing experiences at a difficult time, and some sense of achievement when other things were chaotic and depressing. The main members of staff involved clearly put a great deal of work in.

The Stonic scheme was led by a man called Hudson, a craggy looking PE teacher who was a fine cricketer. He was helped by a short bespectacled Geordie called Metcalfe who had a nervous habit of hunching his shoulders. He went on to paint astonishingly detailed watercolours of the vistas and rooftops of Ston long after the school itself had closed, and it was clear that the old place must have represented a golden age for him.

I find myself feeling more positive about the D of E than anything else at Ston. The activities generally looked outwards from our institutional life and in practice it was not significantly connected to the Cadet Corps. These were the early years of the D of E and I think it is all much better managed now – less selective, more widely available, and with more girls involved. It operates in a wider range of school and community settings, and is more fairly available than it was in the old days. I have always been glad I did it. I may have doubts about the wilder claims made for 'outward bound' generally, but getting some experience of having to work within a small group coping with tough conditions was a really valuable experience which stayed with me.

While things were to get much more difficult in the coming year for me and my family, one of the few really positive things to happen was the eventual presentation of the gold award, which also involved a picture and write up in the local paper. By then I had left Ston and the family had left the pub. In those days the presentation itself was at Buckingham Palace and my mother came along to see me meet the Duke, however briefly, as we all filed through and the band played. She was so proud, and having, as she saw it, lost her boys to school for so long, it was some kind of small compensation, though it makes me sad to think of it now.

FINAL TIMES

Chapter 25

AT AUNTY DOREEN'S

———◇———

Going to Manchester may have been intended to relieve David and me of the pressures of life at the pub, but it opened life up for me in so many ways that I could see beyond the yo-yo life between Ston and home for the first time.

Manchester had always been important to us, growing up. We had been to see my mother's family at rare intervals throughout my childhood, so that those trips always stood out as very special events in a life that seldom got beyond the limits of the pub and village. My first memory had been of being trailed around hot streets by my mother in a search for black material, so this must have been just after the death of my Williams grandfather in 1951. On another visit a few years later we stayed in the rented house in Chorlton where my grandmother and my younger aunts and uncles lived. My brother and I shared a bed, and were given copies of the Beano and Dandy to read – the Beano pictures of urban streets, lamp posts and uniformed park keepers fitted Manchester much better than the village, which was all I knew beforehand.

My Granny Williams was a tiny woman who had lost fingers from her left hand during a munitions accident in the first war, and brought up a large family of 10 through the depression and the second war, before losing my grandfather in his 50s, following a building site accident and then cancer. She had survived all this with great resilience, supported by Woodbines and an uncrushable sense of humour. She never knew what to make of my father, who could be very charming, no doubt, but always seemed to her rather exotic and very southern, so he tended to be treated almost as if he was a foreigner who could not quite be expected to 'get' normal life.

The last visit had been a few years earlier, soon after my youngest brother Bryan had been born, the year after David and I first went away to school. We stayed with Aunt Jessie, her husband Vic, and their 3 children. It had been a long journey, and on the final leg to Manchester Piccadilly my mother had to breast feed Bryan in the train toilet, so strange and unhelpful were the standards of decorum as late as the early 1960s. I had been detailed to stand guard.

I loved that visit; for once we did things as a family. We were taken round Manchester to see different aunts and uncles and my father took us to out first floodlit football match – United against West Ham. United won against Bobby Moore and Co 6-1 with Bobby Charlton getting two of the goals. We eventually got home puffing into Haddenham station to be met by 'Topper' Hopkins' in his usual slippers and 'Ow be on, John?' to my father, who was in a foul mood coming back to the pub and village life. Back from the big city to life with the 'swedes', as he regarded them.

Since then there had been very little contact with our Manchester relations, so the visit to Aunty Doreen, without our parents, was something completely new. David had already been there a week. Arriving with my kitbag at Manchester I had no idea what to expect or where I was going, though I did have the address in Wythenshawe. Having hiked around the dales for a week I just assumed they would expect me to find my own way, so I got there in the end by bus to find that no one was at home. A very kind neighbour invited me in to wait – I remember it being a Saturday afternoon and the Beatles *Ticket to Ride* was on the TV. It turned out Uncle Johnny and Aunty Doreen had been waiting at Victoria, with much concern and loudspeaker announcements, when they thought I had not showed up.

The time in Wythenshawe was great – probably better for me than David as it gave me opportunities for the first time to knock around in a city with plenty to do and much to try out. The Gallaghers were lovely people, with their own two boys, younger than us. They showed us a warmth and generosity, which made us feel very comfortable. Johnny was a bricklayer, short and stout with large hands and a round red face. He had his chair and ashtray by the fire and would tell us about his work and the sites he was on. He said he always hated starting a new job. He would get there in his car, which we rode in as well. Johnny had never passed a test and always said that he had learned his driving on a tank in the Army! He had plenty of traditional working-class fatalism. Why worry about smoking? Something is going to get you in the end anyway, so it might as well be that.

Doreen was one of my mother's younger sisters with the dark hair and high cheekbones of all the Williams. She shared my mother's tendency to anxiety and was a great worrier, relying on endless brews and not eating enough. Like several of the sisters she was beginning to suffer with the arthritis that had already crippled my Aunt Jessie. To us she was really kind. Neither of them asked us to talk about home, and we did not hear much from there in the month we were away, apart from one or two letters.

Wythenshawe was in South Manchester and was best known for the large council estates built there before the war. To us the Gallaghers' house seemed pleasant, homely and well organised. We had been used to yo-yoing between the institutional hardness of Ston and the relative chaos of life at the back of the pub, so this seemed absolutely calm and secure by comparison.

One of the first things I did was to follow Uncle Johnny's advice and go to Withington Hospital, a bus ride away, to ask the Hospital Secretary if I could do my three days of service there for the D of E Gold Award. I managed this and was then able to work on for a further fortnight as a hospital porter. This was a really good time, particularly once I was teamed up with Billy, a serving member of the Parachute Regiment, home on leave and doing some extra work. Billy was in his mid-20s and a very cool operator, and he guided me through some of the niceties of work avoidance – for one thing always appear to be 'going somewhere', and for another always being clear and realistic about who is really in charge when you are at work. In those days, in hospitals, it was never doctors or administrative people. It was always nursing sisters, and they ruled their wards as fiefdoms. Billy's nickname for me was Lurch – this was the name of the butler in the Adams family on TV, so if you were very tall that would do for you.

Billy was kind to me but not above setting me up occasionally. We were sent once to collect a body from the ward. At 17 I had never seen a dead body, let alone handled one. We got the required long metal box on wheels with a hinged lid, rather like a giant food warmer. It had a pillow and rug on top to create the impression that this was just another trolley. Needless to say no one was fooled by this, with the result that either full or empty you could part crowds of people by just pushing the box in their direction.

I was anxious, as may be imagined, but determined to keep that under control. We entered a side room on a men's medical ward and there the body was – completely covered in white bandaging from head to toe. Billy, who clearly knew the ropes, directed me to the head and I gingerly put my hands round the bandaged shoulders. We both lifted together and as I placed my end down on the trolley the head fell backwards and made a loud clang. The sister was very cross and Billy was vastly entertained. We pushed the trolley over to the mortuary – another first for me – and the attendant opened the door, a tall man with a roll-up in his mouth. He actually did look something like Lurch the butler. I was very relieved that we did not have to go in. He took over and we went on our way for a break and a cigarette.

One evening soon after the body episode on the evening shift, Billy set us both up with two of the nurses, and to my great delight we quickly got into an extremely intense clinch with our respective partners – for hours, or so it seemed. This really was my first experience of sexual intimacy, and the unbuttoning and wandering of hands was the more wonderful because it came so unexpectedly. I went back to Wythenshawe in great elation, convinced at last that I was pretty much normal and not such a shy and lanky freak after all. It was pretty much a one-night stand – operating on my own and away from Billy I was inexperienced and gauche. But it was a start, even if, as was clearly the case, I was only Billy's wingman!

The short time at the hospital gave me some other experiences to think about. I remember the shifts on the Accident and Emergency Unit, and all the front-line camaraderie that you get in those places. I remember especially stroking the hair of an old lady on a trolley. She had no one else and seemed to me to be incredibly frail. By the time I came on shift next day she had died, and I was very upset by this. I also spent time on the maternity ward, and even as a porter you could see clearly not only the incredible joy and celebration of most people there, but once or twice as well the misery of a red-eyed couple departing in obvious grief into the taxi with no child. It was a powerfully emotional place for a 17-year-old to work, given what had been going on at home and school for the past year, but I learnt a lot very quickly.

I remember a great deal about Withington – the long wards,

the clanking lifts and the general bustle. We had to do many jobs, from calming down patients to moving dead ones, and always clearing up. We had to do the bin collection and I remember learning the hard way not to press the waste down with your boot. I got a used syringe in my leg and had to go for a tetanus jab, but nothing bad happened. I remember, too, that there were always flowers around the hospital, many of them delivered there after funerals. We were told to take them round to the wards. There was one Irish sister who always refused the funeral flowers on principle, as if they represented an evil omen or the tempting of providence.

Apart from working I had plenty of time free, and as my brother mainly played with our cousins I went out to the cinema, sometimes the pub, and saw something of the city. Manchester was the first city I got to know in any serious way and I loved it

Our holiday at the Gallaghers ended and we went back to Ston directly, with no stop off at home in the pub on the way. Within the space of about five weeks I had walked half way round the North Yorkshire Moors and learned to navigate some equally big challenges in a big city, so it felt very strange to be re-entering the cloisters and closed-off life of Ston. I was pretty sure that I did not really want to go back. I faced the long summer term with those dreaded 'A' Level exams at the end of it. I now knew that I would really struggle; I had fallen behind and seemed unable to summon up very much enthusiasm for the grind required to have any chance of turning things round. I remained very anxious about how things were at home. Overall there was a good deal to be concerned about as I went through the big gates to start my final term, and so the clouds came down again as I trudged towards the clock tower and the house.

Chapter 26

DESPERATE

———◇———

While I knew that I no longer wished to be at Ston I had no sense of what else I wanted to do or where I wanted to go. Having had a taste of what the outside world might offer I just knew that I was effectively finished with school.

For a week or two, though disaffected and restless, I went through the motions of the daily routine. I found it increasingly hard to settle to work and concentrate, however, and preferred to hang around with my friend Rodney Hills in his study next door in Keyser House. We drank illicit red wine, put the world to rights and endlessly listened to his small collection of records. I can never to this day hear *Rhapsody in Blue* without thinking of that time. There were, though, beginning to be moments when I felt adrift, lonely and out of control, but without enough energy to actually do anything about it. It never occurred to me to talk to anyone about those feelings or what might be troubling me, and as ever, I hid it all away.

There were things to be upset about, certainly. I knew perfectly well that my work was now in great disarray, from weeks of disenchanted avoidance and a developing struggle to concentrate. It had reached a point where teachers had, it seemed to me, begun to bypass me in lessons. I was also still very anxious about what was happening at home. There had been limited news since our stay in Manchester, but I knew that my father had been in hospital again and that my parents had major money problems.

I was also living a kind of double life. As a house prefect I knew, in my heart, that giving out orders and tasks was not likely to work out well if you were disorganised, inconsistent and breaking most of the rules that you were supposed to be upholding. My evident hypocrisy meant more than I had realised to several of the more challenging upcoming fifth formers. After several weeks of the term this led to my being punched in the face by one of them, a real counter culture merchant called Pizzey. In the closed community of a boarding school house this was quite a scandalous moment. The shock and shame were worse than the bruise on my cheek, and it had taken me completely by surprise, so that the jolt to my pride and confidence was sudden. My closer friends were supportive and appalled on my behalf. What made matters worse in the hours which followed was that the housemaster had not seemed to me to have taken this 'outrage' seriously enough, nor had there been any effort to talk the matter through with me, or with my attacker, who was now plainly smug and triumphant.

The next morning I made it through breakfast but felt odd and disengaged. Soon afterwards I found myself in utter desperation and standing alone in the bright dormitory, sunlight streaming through the windows. Everyone else was in the second period of morning lessons, and all I knew was that I could not face them. It was more than not having done the work set. I simply could not face anybody. Just not turning up was something I had never done before, and I had no idea where it would lead. There was no plan.

Surprisingly, no one came. There were distant voices, but they came no closer. I had no idea what I would say if someone did come. I could not name or understand these feelings myself, let alone say anything about them to anyone else. I can only remember a strange detachment – could this be happening, and was it real? I walked slowly up and down the long room, along the shiny wooden floor between the rows of beds, as just sitting down did not seem to be possible either.

I walked on up and down, again and again. I was very tired and very lonely. I knew that something was going to happen – if nothing else the school machine would grind on and people would come back. I felt that I had to do something. I took some aspirin from a bottle I had. There were not many but I took them all and knew that this was much more than the usual dose. They seemed after a few minutes to have no real effect, so I went on a search around the house, and next door in Keyser, roaming around the studies to look for more tablets as my commitment to doing something drastic took hold. I found a handful, took them, and waited. I did not know what they were.

The house came back from lessons and I had to brave things out, with a sense of being on 'automatic'. Nothing happened beyond feeling very drowsy and even further blocked off from real life. Lunch came and went and I managed to hang on, helped by the fact that this was a Wednesday half-day, so there were no house activities to get through. I stayed in a quiet corner and slept for a time, but was probably saved from real loss of consciousness by the innocence of the unknown last handful of pills I had taken.

I still felt unable to say anything about how I felt, and much later, reflecting on the experience, I realised very well that harming myself had been less important than just making something happen, so that my hopelessness had to be noticed somehow. That it did not work and that I came to no harm was good fortune, though it did not feel like that at the time. What still seems to me to be extraordinary is that nobody did seem to notice, and not a word was said. I must have seemed at the least sad and preoccupied, and in the hot house of the Ston regime there should have been plenty of other clues that all might not be well. As the day came to an end I was left with feelings that I could not manage and a desperation somehow to escape from this place and the way I felt inside.

A central feature of institutional life is its ability to carry you along in a tide of routine, however dead you may feel inside, but once you have moved out of that rolling current, as I had that day, everything was changed. I had never felt so alone. I went to bed that night and did not sleep. Hearing in the summer night the quarters and hours from the clock tower, I knew by 2am that I would have to go. I suppose I thought I would go home but not much beyond that, and I certainly did not know what to expect when I got there

I was out of bed at 4.00 and moved about the dark house silently. I took money from my study mate, David Davies' desk, leaving a note to explain that I could not cope any more but would pay it back when I could. It was the first time I had told anyone that I had a problem. It seemed to me to be the final decider, and the crossing of an important line. I left the house just as the sky was beginning to lighten, and walked down the wide driveway towards the gates. I felt very exposed and feared that at any moment someone would come, but I went on to a bus stop on the main London Road. I stopped to buy a packet of 10 Woodbines on the way, and pulled my raincoat round me to try to look less like a schoolboy on the run.

The Aylesbury bus soon came and I went to the warm and smoky upper deck. Men off to work got off at stop after stop and I felt calmer the further we went through Hertfordshire and towards Aylesbury. It began to get light and as far as I was concerned the journey could have continued forever in a kind of limbo where decisions were unnecessary and next steps would not have to be decided. The journey was so slow that in the event we did not get to the final stop in Aylesbury until mid-morning.

Anybody who has ever run away, at whatever age, knows the awareness, hard to shut out, that as time passes things will be happening in the place you have left. There will be discovery, alarm, reaction and in due course, consequences. It cannot be undone. You begin to think about all of this. I knew that my parents would be contacted – but not how, as we had no phone at the pub. I stayed in Aylesbury, doing things to hide away from all this. I went to sit in the library and then the small museum. I bought tea and a sandwich. Eventually by early afternoon I went to the cinema and hid away there. The film was *Carry on Cleo* – still regularly repeated even now on television. I sat through it twice in the dark comfort of the Granada stalls, putting off the next step, which I knew perfectly well would have to be my return to the pub. At one point a policeman walked through, and although he was probably on his regular beat I sank lower into my seat as I thought he might be looking for me.

In the end, and with nowhere else to go, I took the familiar bus ride back to the village and the Red Lion, walking anxiously round to the back door and knocking rather than just going in. I do remember my heart thumping as I wondered what would happen and how they would be. Both came to the door, my mother in tears and my father angry and full of 'where the hell have you been?' Someone must have come over from school to find out if I was there, but I of course knew nothing of this.

I could not face this and had somehow hoped for better, though I could not have explained why. I walked away fast and kept walking – down the lane and on through the village, soon aware of my father coming after me, not gaining but not stopping either. Eventually I just stopped. He came up and I burst into tears on his shoulder. At that point I knew that he understood. It must have been hard for him, I knew. His own life had been damaged and thrown off course over so many years because of mental illness. He had invested so much in the vision of school glory and a different future for us, made possible by his Freemasonry and the support of the brotherhood. Yet his following me through the village and his arm around me were so savingly important to me on that evening that I have never forgotten them.

I still felt strange, and very low. It was awkward to be at home in the next day or so, and my mother, once over the early tears, was very happy to have me back, though anxious that I might do something else. I never told either of them about the tablets. I said plenty about school and not wanting to go back. My mother did not want me to, I knew.

Not much was said about it all in the next few weeks. The pub went on as usual, and I forget how my presence was explained. David was still at school, and I had given very little thought to what my running away may have meant to him. At home I spent time with my four-year-old brother Bryan in the back room. I tried whenever possible to say that I did not want to go back to school. In fact I found a job for a few weeks, packing magazines in the local printing firm, and although it was monotonous compared with the lively porter's life of my first work at the hospital in Manchester it was something 'real' to do and perhaps the start of proper living as I saw it.

I continued to feel low and subdued. My father, concerned about my depression, arranged for me to see a psychiatrist – as it turned out the man who had been supervising his own case rather than any child or adolescent specialist. I was relieved that this meant some recognition of a problem, but since I knew that this doctor must have been responsible for my father's long exposure to the scary business of ECT, this was also a daunting prospect. It began with a walk through the entrance of the hospital where I had visited my father so often. The psychiatrist, as it turned out, treated me with some care and respect. I had no idea what to expect or what would happen. He wanted to be reassuring, and acknowledged my depression, but felt that it would pass.

He prescribed some small red tablets – Tofranil, a common anti-depressant. I was to take them regularly, and that was pretty much it. I had certainly expected more talk, and more effort to 'understand' me, but there was none of that.

He was right, I suppose, at least about it passing, as I began to feel better. I have forgotten whether I went back to him to be checked over again. It may have happened, but I can only recall that I did not take the pills any longer. I was also reassured by just being at home and seeing that, although there were problems, life went on. I remained very unsure about the future, and had no one to talk to about this short and very unpleasant illness beyond my mother and father, both of whom had their own problems. My father, for all his understanding when I arrived home, had a huge vested interest in not seeing this as early evidence that I had inherited his illness.

Looking back years later, I knew that much worse might have happened. I know very well, too, that we still have huge problems with adolescent mental illness, much of which goes untreated and unrecognised. Does this mean that my crisis at the age of 17 was of no great consequence? I only have to think back to my standing alone on that morning to know otherwise, and know also that the same is true for every young person who finds themselves beyond caring and battling with feelings beyond their control.

I too was scared about the possibility of getting my father's illness, and there was enormous general fear of mental illness then. It was not a time when there was much opportunity to talk about it, let alone among young people. As a very tall rugby playing youth assumptions were made about my ability to cope and my apparent resilience. My outward appearance belied an insecurity, inexperience and lack of confidence which ran very deep. Keeping up with my friends and playing the successful schoolboy meant that I simply would not have been able to speak of these things to friends – not for lack of trust in them, but because that was not the world we inhabited. I could talk, and did, about anything and everything. I had enthusiasms and ideas, but I could not have told anyone how depressed and desperate I was.

After three or four weeks one of my house teachers came to visit. It was extremely strange, even after so short a period, to be brought back to think about the world of Ston. It also felt very odd to have a member of staff on my own home territory, as I had never wanted or expected those two worlds to meet. Though always aware of my parents' problems I was fiercely loyal to them at school, and the best way to be loyal, usually, was just not to talk about home.

I remember very little about his visit, except that it felt very awkward. The young master concerned, a Mr Leonard, in his apparently standard issue sports jacket and cavalry twill, was not one I had warmed to very much – he did not teach me directly and had only come to Ston the year before. He had a rather willowy frame and the beginning of baldness, so that he combed his hair defensively Tintin fashion at the front. He was clearly there to talk my parents and me into a return to school. As might be expected, given his abiding admiration for Ston, my father was now extremely keen for me to see the term out and complete my exams.

Fairly briskly I was cajoled into coming back and finishing off my 'A' Levels during the rest of the Summer Term. If I had in mind some kind of alternative plan, or the gumption to insist, I probably would not have gone back. Looking back down the years I still do not fully understand why I was such an easy pushover. I had after all enjoyed some independence and was earning money. Though there were arguments at home, and trouble was never far away from the surface my being there, and in touch with it all, felt easier to cope with than being kept away in a state of protective banishment. Now, though, the official story was that I had recovered and needed to get back to work.

At no stage had I been encouraged to talk about what had been so difficult and what exactly had I been struggling with. Even now this strikes me as extraordinary and wrong. I was to go back, though, patched up and best foot forward, to a world I had never wanted to be part of, and had hoped never to see again.

Chapter 27

GOING BACK
AND FINAL DAYS

—◦⋈◦—

I went back a week later, on my own and taking the usual slow route by Green Line coach from Aylesbury. My mother had been calmer than usual and my father urged me to make the best of the time left at Ston, especially in the exams, which were now very near. In the time at home I had hardly given schoolwork a thought, since I had, so I thought, finished with school and everything to do with it. I may not have known what I wanted to do, but I had not expected to be going back to Ston and now had no idea what to expect when I got there. As I walked up the Avenue towards the school I smoked what was intended to be a last cigarette, and in a petulant gesture, intended to be seen by any friends in the library, I kicked the stub rather violently into the road before I walked through the gates.

Joining the school routine again was clearly intended to be a low-key affair. I had a short interview with the housemaster, who asked if I was feeling better and told me that I should raise any further problems with him, but that was it. In the house itself I was aware that beyond my group of friends, opinions were divided, but the priggish head of house, Turner, and his coterie, in one way or another managed to convey their view that I was weak, a bit scruffy and generally rather strange. David Davies, whose money I had borrowed on the morning I left, and Tom Long, were especially loyal and from them I picked up what had been said about my absence. Not very much, it seemed, but they at least had some understanding of how unhappy I had been, though I still found it very hard to explain anything to them about my fears, my family or my depression. I was glad to see my brother David, to whom, in all of this, I had given barely a thought. I think he was pleased to see me, but he could have been forgiven for thinking that my return was a mixed blessing. Always loyal, he never said anything about it.

In the remaining weeks of term I was expected to do my best to catch up and indeed take all the exams. As with everything else about my reinsertion to Ston, no special allowances were made. I had no extra tuition or even advice, and before many days had passed it was clear to me that the whole thing was hopeless. I attended most lessons and lurked about pretending to be involved, but was increasingly resentful. Latin and History were beyond retrieval, I knew. As others revised volumes of notes I tried my best with those I had and a desultory reading of the text books – but there was to be no great catching up on Cicero's Vth Verrine oration, and my knowledge of the circumstances leading up to the English Civil War remained vague and impressionistic. English Literature was different. I had missed less, been taught better, and had both talent and a passion for it. I cut my losses and did not bother much with *Vanity Fair*, or indeed *Mansfield Park*, hoping that I would get by with a careful choosing of questions and an ability to quote Romantic poetry, *Paradise Lost, King Lear* and *The Franklin's Tale* more or less at will and in considerable chunks.

When the exams came I managed to be two different people. In the two hopeless subjects I scratched out thin, estimated, and in some cases imagined answers, but in the two English papers I wrote furiously, quoting with a focus and energy I had lost elsewhere. After the exams had finished, in the few remaining weeks of my school life I became a full member of Ston's dissident underground sub-culture. This had no basis in organisation or shared action but included all those who had put themselves in one way or another, and for a wide range of reasons, outside the Stonic norms and assumptions. There were a few who teetered on the edge, managing to juggle the main requirements of conformity with some elements of 'illegal' behaviour. Several of those who had covert sexual relationships with Ston's Irish maids fell into this category. The activities of the more completely 'lost souls' usually had to do more with smoking, visits to the Swan, illicit bottles of wine, and a vague commitment to 'changing things' A key part of this was the subversion wherever possible of anything to do with the Cadet Corps. I still, somehow, had my one stripe, so I was able, for example, to take part with others in anti-military briefings to younger cadets. This all seemed important at the time. As rebellion goes it all now seems very tame and I am surprised that we did not attempt more serious acts of resistance, given our shared hatred of the place, and those staff members and prefects who most seemed to represent the Stonic establishment.

I had fallen very quickly from levels of high attainment and expectation to becoming a 'disappointment'. I was still living with the aftermath of my depression. I had fears that I might lose control again, and my confidence remained very low. I was still very lost and resentful. In one way the last thing I wanted was to fit into a system I now hated and despised, but living outside it was lonely and hard. It was painful and I desperately hoped that the future might be better than this.

These feelings were strong when my parents came up to the school speech day, which was their last visit during my time at Ston. I had normally won prizes, but that was definitely not the case this year, and I had squirmed as the ceremony ground on with its usual rituals and Worshipful Grand Master speeches.

My brother and I went for tea with my parents in Bushey. It was a hot day, and I remember the itchiness of the school clothes. The summer light made my parents' shabbiness and tiredness very clear. They were plainly still having big problems, however much it had seemed calmer when I was last at home. My mother described her struggles to keep the pub going during my father's latest spell in hospital, but he still wanted, incurably, to talk about school, despite my obvious self-preoccupation and irritability. As usual my brother had to put up with all this, and I was really not very much use to him. I remember insisting on smoking as we were outside school, and I can still almost touch that sense of seediness and desperation – my mother's red hands and baggy eyes, my father rattling with pills and not having the faintest clue about what best to do. The bright sun just seemed to mock us all.

With a week or so to go before the end of term and my final exit I went drinking on a Saturday evening with several others. We went to the Swan and then had wine and cider in the school grounds, far away, as we thought, from trouble. By the time I was reaching the staggering stage, however, we were caught by Turner and several other prefects and sent back to the house, and bed, in disgrace. I did not have much sense of things beyond a strong feeling that this time it was all over. It had been a real binge and one of those when you wish to sleep but everything seems to move nauseatingly up and down. You would shake yourself and try to focus on something to keep the horizon straight. I tried to keep the dormitory windows still, but each time after a few seconds they began to roll and then everything else also revolved sickeningly and endlessly. In the hush of the dormitory I tried to keep my inevitable spewing as quiet as I could, creeping back to bed each time feeling very sorry for myself.

I slept in the end, and woke with a bad headache and terse instructions from the Housemaster to get dressed and go straight to the infirmary. This was, it became clear very quickly, not for my health but as a segregation. He made that, and his disgust at my behaviour, very clear. There were no questions, and no attempt to understand. It seemed that I had now been written off and that my departure was imminent. I was at least spared any obvious recrimination or sermon.

The infirmary was quite a pleasant holding cell before I was to leave in disgrace. The nurse was very kind and sympathetic. On a sunny day it was strange to see the rest of the school pass by on the way to games and lessons, but I had no contact with any of them, not even my brother. I was told that my things would be sent on and the next morning I went off to catch the bus home to the pub and whatever was now going to happen.

It seems to me, looking back now, that I was at that point an odd mixture of child and almost man, struggling to make sense of what seemed to be mountainous and uncontrollable feelings. My brother and I were coping with the gradual disintegration of a family which had been dysfunctional for years, though nobody ever talked to us about it. This meant that at 17 I had seen a good deal – violence, alcoholism, mental illness and the side effects of hypnotic drugs. I had fired machine guns and done outward bound. I had a little experience of day-to-day working and earning. In many other respects I was very naive and immature, having alternated for years between an utterly male institution where attitudes to sexual development remained in the 1930s and a home life at the village pub, where I shyly had lost all contact with the kids I grew up with. In many of the ways that mattered to me then, I was very inexperienced indeed, for all my passions about plays and politics.

Being pushed along a year ahead academically had certainly left me vulnerable, especially in a school where pastoral care did not exist, and where there was very little sensitivity to individual fears and personal circumstances. As a result, and never feeling that I had any real choice or control of what was happening, I fell off all the pedestals of boarding school achievement very quickly. It seemed that there was no possible way back, and although very conforming until then, I quickly became a willing enough outlaw.

The Stonic assumption seemed to be that the regime and compliance with it would smooth out any problems and train us into a safe adulthood, regardless of where we had come from and why. On a spectrum of care, if a child-centred approach was at one end, everything to do with Ston was a polar, institutional opposite. It was a hard school where you buttoned up your feelings and played the game. This was less damaging for the well-adjusted from a good home, but a poor regime for those who did not have those advantages. I had now left without much sense of what I was going to do, or how I might respond, but my brother remained for a further two years.

AFTERWARDS

Chapter 28

WHAT TO DO NEXT?

—∞—

Back at the pub I never knew if the school said anything about my early departure, and nothing was mentioned at home. I felt an anti-climax about it being all over with school, and complete uncertainty about what to do next. There was no guide book for this, and my early departure under a very black cloud meant that I was not going to get any cosy Masonic job fixed up for me through Mr Blake's Masonic links. In any event I wanted none of that, and nothing more of school and its connections. I knew the exam results would arrive sooner or later, but they really did not bother me. I was 17 and had been issued with a leaving suit and some basic clothes. I was very tall and thin with black plastic NHS glasses and a few spots. In the residual school clothes I resembled a rather conservatively dressed beanpole – the original long streak of piss. I was fit, though, healthy and glad to be free. If the 60s were by now swinging I would have liked to be involved, but could not yet find a way in.

Soon afterwards those exam results did come by way of the usual postcard. I had achieved the top grade in English and utterly predictable failures in the other two subjects. The one good grade had been achieved with some luck and almost effortlessly, but it was something at least to hold on to. It represented my ability to do things well when circumstances were right.

I was happy to have left Ston, but things were clearly bad at home. My father was back in hospital, undergoing yet more ECT, and he came home at weekends with a bagful of pill bottles. During the week my mother juggled running the pub and looking after my small brother, who was now just five, and had started school. Like all small children he picked up and reacted to the atmosphere around him. In the back living room at the pub there was a weariness and grimy disorder. He had also become used to later nights than was good for him. My mother was more tired than I had ever known. She was drinking more heavily, and smoked endlessly. Those heavy bags under her eyes seemed to have set in, and her face had swollen and coarsened so that she seemed much older than her 40 years.

There was one evening soon after I got back when she felt ill and did not open up in the evening. She must have felt desperate, as it had never ever happened before in all the 12 years of our time at the pub. Not being open during the scheduled hours was one of the brewery's ultimate sins – probably more important to them than watering the beer. It may have been partly to do with having little stock, and trying to limp along until the next delivery, but it was, I knew, about more than that, and she must have been at the end of her tether. There was not much I could do to help other than keep an eye out and look after my brother, but it was a strange evening with the bar dark and the big front door being rattled occasionally as customers came and went.

Later someone put a scrawled note through the letterbox complaining, and addressing it to 'the most beautiful woman in the village'. I tore it up and destroyed it before she saw it, but it was a cruel, anonymous gesture, and another of those moments when the pub life seemed to mean that you had forfeited any chance of a private life. My mother cried bitterly enough that evening anyway without knowing about the message, and I felt fiercely protective as I held her tight and tried to comfort her. Then, and in the days that followed, I did my best to support her and share the work. I tried very hard to get her to go to the doctor, but stuck in the old fatalism she would have none of it. I put on a capable and responsible front, but wobbled a great deal inside and did not really know what to do for the best. In the days that followed routine just about re-established itself.

Perhaps because of the problems, my father came home on discharge from the hospital. It was not easy. I could sense at times his resentment towards me. It may have had a lot to do with my finishing school in the way I had, but I also sensed that he felt somehow I was taking his place. He must have been frustrated at the state of things in the pub and how few options there now seemed to be. He could now go rapidly into outbursts of scornful rage, which I had not often seen before, and I was sometimes the target. Once I had been reading at the table in the back sitting room, and expressed some opinion or other. He waved his fist at me and bellowed into my face that I knew nothing and had never even been out of the country yet. It was sudden – from calm to boiling rage in a moment – and I was scared and humiliated.

I went on trying to help in a practical way as much as I could, cleaning the bars and mopping the floors and toilets. The atmosphere lightened when my brother came back from school a few weeks later, his bridges remaining in place and unburned. I knew by now though that I had to get a job, help out and just do something, or become sucked into the general glumness of life at the Red Lion.

I had enjoyed working at the hospital in Manchester, so I decided that trying to get something similar was a good place to start from. I went for an interview with the Matron at Stoke Mandeville Hospital on the edge of Aylesbury and was taken on as a Ward Orderly. It was going to involve much more direct contact with patients, and that sounded interesting. There were no tests to take or forms to fill in; it seemed enough that I was fit and willing. Offered the chance to live in, I jumped at the opportunity to get away, but not without a degree of guilt about what I was leaving behind at home. I moved in as soon as I could. It was basically a room with a hospital cornered bed, a basic wardrobe, table and chair – essentially an institutional bedroom, but at least not a dormitory. We had a common room with a TV and meals were provided in the staff canteen.

Stoke Mandeville had started as a wartime hospital, but by then it had become the main hospital for the whole area. I had visited my father there in the days of his drinking when he was admitted with alcohol-induced jaundice, so I remembered the single-storey brick-built wards linked to a long corridor. My job was to work on the wards of the National Spinal Injuries Unit, established by the great Doctor Guttman, who had pioneered radically new ways to nurse and rehabilitate spinal injury patients. Part of his approach was to involve patients in rehabilitation through sports, and Stoke Mandeville was where the whole Paralympic movement originally began. At this stage Jimmy Savile had not yet decided to grace Stoke Mandeville with his presence, though this was to begin not long afterwards.

Guttman's approach to day-to-day care included the recognition that it was long-term skin damage and infection from bedsores which debilitated and eventually killed many paraplegic patients. His solution was that all patients would be turned systematically through the day and night into three different positions. That was essentially what Ward Orderlies were for. There was no lifting equipment. Three Orderlies would raise the patient and hold them perfectly straight and still, suspended above the bed, while the nurse who was doing the round sorted the bed out and checked everything else out, including the catheterisation which all the patients had. We then had to lower the patient gently back onto the bed and into their next position.

You worked systematically round a ward of 40 beds in the same way – screens, lift, adjust, replace and away with the screens again. It was hard work.

On my men's ward the patients had been there for widely varying periods. Some, and I found this shocking at the time, had been there since the place opened in 1953, living the endless routine. If you were fully paraplegic this meant that you had to be helped with every function – eating, drinking, smoking, peeing, nose blowing, shaving and shitting. When we were not involved in the lifting we would usually be helping on one or more of these other functions, so the shifts were very busy.

Inevitably you got to know them very well and very quickly. They were of all ages – men injured later in life in a car crash through to young servicemen who had got themselves injured badly while drunk. More than one seemed to have dived unawares into an empty swimming pool. The more institutionalised old stagers often had little to say, but many really wanted to talk, and have a joke, which not only broke the monotony, but was also an essential way of taking attention away from all this enforced and unavoidable intimacy. I saw a great deal of courage and much desperate hoping for the future. The great goal was to leave and go home, but that was an impossible dream for many, at a time when rehabilitation options were more limited than now. It is very hard for an alert, intelligent man to have to submit day after day to detailed bodily care while maintaining both dignity and a sense of humour, but many did, and that made our work much easier than it otherwise would have been. You just got used to washing false teeth, sharing a cigarette with someone, and having to help them smoke through a plastic holder. Many of the nurses were very friendly and you could work well with them as a team, but several were rather fierce. The most difficult was a staff nurse who was very critical and demanding – I learnt later that she worked without pay as part of some kind of Christian calling, but her behaviour to us 'operatives' did not seem very Christian to me.

One of the prevailing problems, given the endless toileting process, was literally to avoid shit being spread around un hygienically, and if you were a little clumsy, as I was, this could present problems. We had a shift system. One week in three you would be on nights, and would have to do the dreaded suppository round. This involved every patient, and none of them had any feeling below the waist, so they needed artificial help with evacuation. Each had to have a bullet-shaped jelly projectile inserted with a rubber glove. They could not feel the sensation, but you certainly could. Later, as dawn came, your last job on the shift was to go round each bed as fast as you could to collect the proceeds in metal bowls and swab down the patient. By the time you finished, though this was not supposed to happen, your forearms could be caked with shit. Each bowl had to be kept separate and labelled for examination in the sluice room. And then you went off to breakfast!

Having read this account you may not be surprised to know that these jobs were quite hard to recruit to, and we were a motley crew, by age and prior experience. One or two of the older men seemed to be there as a result of other failures in life. There were some temporary workers, mainly students. Of the permanent staff a good number were from Spain. They were often quite short in stature, so that sometimes, being six foot six, I would be holding one end of a patient as I thought quite normally and then when I looked across the other two would be desperately braced with their arms above their heads in a weightlifting pose.

Sometimes you would be sent to the women's wards just to assist with lifting. There was a good deal of implied trust about this – although clothed above the waist, they were naked beneath the sheet. They were not offered any choice about this, and again had to find different ways of coping with this indignity. All this unaccustomed contact with bare bottoms and pubic hair took some getting used to. The clinical setting and the dependence these women had on you meant that there was not the slightest frisson of sexual excitement. Like the men, many were lonely and really wanted to talk, and I especially remember a highly intelligent woman from Northern Ireland wanting to know what I was doing and what my plans were. It certainly made me think. On both male and female wards we had a number of overseas patients, mainly from Arab countries. Some were very anxious about the pain they still suffered when they were moved. Having to cope with that and all the rest of the daily routine without any ability to communicate in English must have been incredibly isolating and tough for them.

There was the usual hospital dark humour, of course, and some things were just unavoidably funny. The nurse's first job on each turn was to remove the catheter and the kipper bag into which urine had passed through the day. It sometimes kept flowing after the bag had been removed. One man had a very long and permanently erect penis, rock hard and pointing at a 45-degree angle. You had to have a glass flask available and then leap goalkeeper-like into position to catch the arcing stream of piss as the catheter came off, sometimes to cheers and boos from your colleagues as you succeeded or failed.

This may all sound challenging, but I was working, and however messy the work might be, it was still unbelievably better than being at Ston. Living in was reasonably pleasant, if a bit isolated, as most of the younger staff lived at home, but there were occasional parties, and you could have a good time as well. I had not experienced much in the way of parties before, and found that I coped quite well and enjoyed myself. Some of the nurses were quite suggestively smoochy after a drink or two, and although nothing very amorous happened it was all very promising.

I went home to the pub to visit once a week and saw my parents and brothers. Things seemed quieter, but this was perhaps my wanting it to be so. I certainly gave them money from my wages, so I felt I was doing something to help.

I did not work at Stoke Mandeville for very long, as it turned out. My conversation with the woman from Northern Ireland had really made me think, and this, together with the fact that some of the younger temporary staff at Stoke were talking about the newly opening Aylesbury College of Further Education, made my mind up. I knew that I had to try again, and see what an extra year would achieve. I signed up at the college and sent in my resignation at the hospital. The Matron who had interviewed me summoned me and asked tersely about my reasons for wanting to leave so quickly. I told her that I thought I had to do this and of course there was not much more that she could say.

I decided that I would have to go home to the pub. I suppose I could have found a room and part-time work, but this never occurred to me at the time. The fact that my parents were willing to have this happen, and for me to change my mind so quickly, said a good deal about the way they valued education despite all the huge pressures and problems they faced, and I have never forgotten that commitment, or the woman from Northern Ireland whose sense of loss about her own education had made me think differently about my own opportunities.

I had signed up at the College to do History and French at 'A' level in one year. I knew this would be challenging – I had a good 'O' level in French, but knew that 'A' level would involve set books and a much higher standard of vocabulary and grammar. I was more confident about the history and was glad that I could forget the little I had retained about the Tudors and Stuarts. I could now get stuck into the 19th Century, which seemed much more interesting. One year was not long to catch up, put things right and make a fresh application to university. It was no longer to be English, I already knew, but sociology. I was as yet not very clear what that would be all about, but I hoped that it would mean learning about people, problems and doing something about them. It was as vague as that, but a powerful motivation nonetheless. The College was as far removed from Ston as I could have hoped. It was bright, brand new and full of people my own age, boys and girls. I felt free and hopeful there, determined to make the most of the year ahead.

The impact of working with people at Stoke Mandeville even for that short period also fuelled my commitment. Sadly it was soon after this that the hospital began its long and destructive relationship with Jimmy Savile. Certainly the place was pretty easy to get involved with and was probably too trusting about both volunteers and employment. In my brief time there I met many volunteers and family members and the place had a very open feel – we would sometimes take the patients who were in wheelchairs to the nearby pub after shifts, so there was plenty of willingness to care. Unfortunately Savile for many years exploited this openness and the hospital's infatuation with publicity and celebrity.

Chapter 29

The Red Lion
Goes Wrong

———◆———

Life back at the pub was chaotic, but life went on despite the mess and confusion. My brother went back to school and I began my course at Aylesbury College. There was hardly any money, but I was enjoying the freedom and brightness of a new start a million miles away from Ston.

One weekday evening in late September I was in the back living room, in its usual state of clutter, looking after my brother Bryan, who was still up and watching television with me. It was not long before closing time. My mother was in the bar, and my father, still hanging on at home but overusing his medication, had gone to bed already. He had started to do this again, and I had learned to see this as an early sign of his next crisis and hospital admission. For now he was hanging on and managing at least earlier in the day to continue somehow as Mine Host.

I knew every inch of that back room with the grubby red and black sofa and utility table and chairs. Although it was next to the bar, it had always been a private place for the family. Occasionally people had been invited in to see TV – usually football highlights on Saturday night, but you always knew who they were. It startled me when a pale young man with a crew cut, a black T-shirt and jeans came through from the bar unannounced. It felt like an invasion. It got worse. He sneered at me and spoke in a loud voice directed back towards my mother in the bar:

'That fuckin' kid should be in bed, shouldn't he?"

He went back into the bar, spoke quietly to my mother and then left the pub by the back door, slamming it shut. I was not so much scared as shocked, upset, and offended. I had felt powerless to do anything and a burning feeling of shame at being bullied. I just wished I could have responded better somehow. Naïve as it may have been, I always wanted to believe that the back room behind the bar was in a separate world from the pub, and that it gave us some sense of a private life. I did not know what this had all been about, but it had never happened before, and seemed to mark some kind of real and very unpleasant change. My mother said nothing, and she was so tired that it seemed impossible to ask any questions. I went off to bed and next morning life seemed to have gone back to normal.

Nothing else happened for some days. I was still preoccupied with getting used to my course in a new place, and taking the bus there and back every day, so I may not have noticed much in any event. Then, on a Saturday morning some days later, I was woken early to be told by my parents that the pub's big front door had been forced in the night and that the police were coming. I did not know what had gone on – something about money from the till, but my parents did not say very much. There came again that sense of anxiety and invasion, and a feeling also that something bigger and out of control was going on.

The police arrived. The pub stayed closed. I spent most of the time with Bryan in the back room. Time seemed to slow down, and no one explained what was happening. The police eventually left and the pub opened so that some kind of normal routine began again, though still my parents said very little.

I remember very clearly the police coming back the following day – quite early on a Sunday morning, well before the church bells across the green started. There were two detectives, and the one in charge was an Inspector named Hankins, middle-aged, heavy and stern. He did not smile, and made no introductory small talk. The local constable was also there. For years he had been an occasional friendly visitor, usually accepting a rum and black from my father if the lounge was empty. The fact that he now said nothing, and was clearly very much the junior in uniform, made the atmosphere heavier than ever. In a practised, smooth procedure I found myself taken on my own into the empty bar 'to answer a few questions'. Only then did I see that they thought I had done it – whatever it was. My heart pounded.

They made it clear that they did not believe I could know nothing about what had happened. At that point, trying to explain that you knew nothing suddenly seemed the hardest thing in the world, and dangerously, I almost began to disbelieve myself, so great was the silent pressure and the relentless sceptical gaze of the Inspector. They were sure enough of my guilt that I was placed in their car, without a word from my parents, and taken off to the police station in Aylesbury.

It was a strange and silent journey. I knew the way so well, but had never travelled it in a police car. The experience had a strange dreamlike quality. Outside in the Sunday morning villages, life was going on normally while my world inside the car seemed to be turning upside down. The journey did help me though. I was still scared, but now angry, too. Angry because I knew I had done nothing, and angry also with my parents. Why did they say nothing? Did they think I had done it? At that point even then, somehow, it did not dawn on me that it might have been one or both of them.

All these years later I can still remember the interview at the police station in a cool, quiet room at the back of the building. To reach it we had gone through a series of passages and offices, all empty on a Sunday morning, so that you did feel both lonely and at the centre of very unwelcome attention. The Inspector spoke to me about what he thought this crime and my involvement in it was doing to my parents. He understood that I might need money. In his experience, he said, these things were often an 'inside job', and they had in fact found my fingerprints all over the door. By then I was enough in control of myself to say that this could not be true as they had not taken my fingerprints, so this lame old tactic failed, and I felt stronger and calmer from then on. I made a short statement, they did take my fingerprints, and then they took me home.

There were no explanations when I got home. Almost immediately my mother was taken to the police station and stayed there, through the afternoon and late into the evening. My father remained at home, tight lipped, very anxious, and seeming to know nothing. He seemed to me barely to be coping and at that moment I wondered desperately what on earth would happen to us all.

My mother came home at last, white as a sheet, and her hands still shaking. She never forgot the interview with the Inspector, his coldness and his staring eyes. To the end of her life she could relive it, including the point at which he counted up her Players cigarette stubs in the ashtray and told her that she must be very anxious if she needed to smoke as much as that. There had been no solicitor – she did not, I think, ask for one, and I am sure that in those days, when police officers followed procedures to suit their own priorities, the Inspector did not mention this possibility.

She was charged, not only with theft of money from the Pub's Christmas Club, but for receiving stolen beer. That was what the pale-faced drayman had been visiting to arrange, and it must have been all too clear from the state of the pub why he had thought we were a likely target. The day had been a dreadful emotional marathon for all of us, but especially for my mother. She was exhausted. I tried to comfort her. There seemed nothing else to do, whatever my own muddled feelings. My father seemed lost, struggling with his own demons, and indeed, within a day or two, he was back in hospital.

In the days that followed I did go to college, feeling the first day or so that everyone would somehow know and that I might be a target for anger or shaming insult, but I realised later that everything always works much more slowly than that. I said nothing to anyone, and tried to go on as normal. It became clear that we would be leaving the pub quite soon, and it did not reopen.

I tried to help. As my mother seemed unable to do anything about getting a solicitor, I decided to go and do something about it. I went to Aylesbury on the bus. I walked around and saw the signs of various firms of solicitors, but did not know what to do next. I walked around the town again and eventually plucked up the courage to go to the largest looking office I could find. I went in and asked to see someone. I talked to a young solicitor who sat, listened and made notes as I just churned everything out as best I knew. He made no comments, was friendly and professionally unfazed. I remember feeling the relief as I got everything out and he made it clear that he would be able to help. It made me feel better that his reaction was neither shock not horror but calmness and practicality. He made several phone calls, one of them being to the dreaded Inspector. The Inspector must have begun to say unpleasant things about my mother, because the solicitor at that point made it clear that he had me in the office with him. I went home eventually, feeling that, in all the mess, I had at least done something practical. A few days later my mother went in to see him herself.

The pub may not have been opening any longer, but while we were still there my mother had to face, in the village, some of the regulars who had saved with the Christmas Club. These included Ethel Bridges, her old friend, who was Bryan's Godmother, and had known us as children all the time we were growing up. One of the enduring qualities of village life then and even now is that you cannot hide away for very long, nor will very much remain secret, even before the local paper gets to work, and in those days court reporting was extremely comprehensive.

Some were loyal and kind, and some were very angry. It was hard to predict which camp people would be in. Some of the angriest included very long-standing regulars. Perhaps not surprisingly, Ethel was one of them. She must have felt that she had been betrayed very badly, since she was the secretary of the Christmas Club. Part of the public show of pub life is that when things collapse you cannot hide away and become a kind of open target for pity, sneering and fury. It was very hard for my mother to bear, and whatever she might have done I knew how hard life had been for her and how hard she had worked. I hated what I saw as the hypocrisy all around us. At 17 and struggling to deal with it all, I felt a kind of helpless and painful rage.

I never really did find out much more about what had happened – the taking of money and what must have been an attempt to disguise it all as a break-in. I do not know how either of my parents would have reacted if I had given into the pressure and confessed to something I had had nothing to do with. I think that faced with the possibility of my being blamed they would have caved in, and one or both would have confessed. Money was desperately short, and I knew that. They had taken out at least one expensive loan, and a year or so before I had been sent off in my school suit, looking as respectable as possible, to pay money directly into one of those big lending firms in London. I am not sure why they sent me on this errand. It was either more convenient to send me, or because neither of them could face it, but it was clearly a significant debt, and they must have been behind with payments. For a long time before the end came life generally had been chaotic at the pub, and the business must have been run on a week-to-week knife-edge basis, with very few of the old packed-out public bar days I had remembered from years before.

My mother took all the blame. I do not know if my father was involved in the theft and receiving. Years later I almost found a way to ask him, but could not, in the end, bring myself to do it. Once that moment had gone I never found another opportunity, and as time passed I came to see that there was no real point anyway. I suspect he knew something, but he had not had to deal with the details of the weekly takings and bill juggling as he was so often in hospital. My mother must have drifted slowly inch by inch into the swamp, borrowing and intending to pay back from the Club, and then unable in desperation to resist the offer of cheap stolen barrels stolen from a brewery which always drove very hard bargains on beer and rent.

In all this, by modern standards, I was perhaps naïve and unquestioning. Alternating for years between the almost Victorian enclosure of boarding school and the loneliness of life in a dysfunctional pub with dysfunctional parents goes some way to explaining why. I felt the emotion of it, in primary colours, but had little faith in being able actually to alter anything – a kind of dogged resignation. In this sense, confronting the Inspector and doing something to get my mother defended did at least mark the start of taking action in my own right.

We have all become accustomed to crime and its detection as a form of entertainment in fiction or fact. We are shown brutality and violence without apparent lasting harm as another type of picture show. This means that we can easily forget or become insensitive about how powerful, long-lasting and life-changing participation in a real life slide into crime can be, let alone the fallout from it for everyone involved. People may pretend that this is not so, but they are usually whistling in the dark.

The experience changed my mother's life even before the

whole business of the Quarter Sessions Court the following spring, and she was never really the same again. Before then though, we had to leave the pub and the bright bar. I did not know where we would be going to or what would happen once we got there.

Chapter 30

LEAVING THE PUB

—————⋈—————

Despite the chaos and confusion at home and the uncertainty about what was to come, I made a reasonable start at Aylesbury College in that autumn term of 1965. It was utterly different from Ston, and good to go there each day, to this new building, full of windows and fresh paint without a uniform in sight and a general air of liberation and fun. *Get Off of My Cloud* by the Stones was number 1 in the charts, and you heard it everywhere. Ken Dodd was having a big hit with *Tears for Souvenirs*, and unfortunately you heard plenty of that as well.

I now knew very clearly that I wanted to go to university, though to get there seemed a mountain of work away. While I had no real sense of what it would involve in any detail, I knew that it was the escape route to independence I yearned for. I had already filled in the UCCA forms and had applied to do Social Science – the sexiest and seemingly newest subject of the 60s. Again I did not have much sense of what the subject would be about, beyond it seeming to connect to my developing but still vague left wing ideas, and a general idealism about social problems and trying to something about them. Those feelings were definitely rooted in my first-hand experiences from home. At a much more fundamental level I wanted to get as far away as I possibly could from Audi, Vide Tace, the clock tower, cloisters and grey-suit conformity of Ston, and all it seemed to stand for. Just as much I wanted to escape as soon as I could from the village and its bubble, where so much had gone so publicly wrong for us. For all those reasons I had applied to far away northern university cities of grit and industry on my forms – including Hull, Sheffield, and Manchester, which was my first choice, since it was the only place I knew and had any connection to.

But all that lay ahead, and the next big thing was our move from the pub. It came quite quickly – early in November. With nowhere else to go we were to be rehoused by the local council. The new place was at the far end of the village, about a mile away, in one of those ribbon-like pre-war developments which most rural councils had built. I had been going in and back daily in the bus. My father was still in hospital and my mother was struggling on through the remaining days at the pub. My brother David was still at school.

My mother had been preparing for the move, and I had tried to help by looking after my brother Bryan outside school hours. There did seem a daunting amount to do as I looked through the clutter upstairs and downstairs, and it all seemed overwhelming. There was really very little money and my mother had arranged with the local coal merchant that he would move our stuff up to the new place on his lorry. This was being done without charge and as a favour to my mother, so it was a very kind and loyal gesture, but I did not see how all our stuff could possibly fit.

In my eagerness to do something, I decided to help make this a completely fresh start by clearing out and burning what we would not need. This process was not really supervised by my mother, so I had an almost free hand. I started in a small way, but in my wish to do away with anything representing our life at the pub a kind of avenging zeal took over. Soon I was burning not only the obvious rubbish, but also books, old toys and, to my later and long-lasting regret, most of the huge collection of football programmes which David and I had built up. This is probably the only thing which my ever-understanding and generous brother has never quite forgiven me for, but then, of course I had no misgivings as I watched everything go through my big cleansing bonfire in the pub garden.

With a few days to go before the move, a dilemma came up. For the last few weeks I had been travelling home on the bus with a student from the course. She was the tall and very pretty daughter of a clergyman from a village a few miles further down the bus route. Madeleine had long dark hair and a lovely open enthusiasm about her life and interests. We had begun by chatting about the course, but she loved to talk. She had been on holiday to Greece in the summer and we smoked many of the Greek cigarettes she had brought back.

I could not bring myself to believe that she might be interested in me, but it gradually dawned upon me that she was. With a limited choice of clothes, no travel experience beyond Manchester and the D of E expeditions, and the kind of family life I did not feel able yet to talk about, I fell back on a performance of intellectual moodiness and cool, as I thought, silences – a beanpole rebel with a turned-up collar. To my surprise this seemed to work. She made the first move, and this was the cause of my dilemma. She invited me to a village event her father was organising. We would not actually have to go to it, she said, just help beforehand, and then I could see where she lived. It all sounded very encouraging and I wanted to go, but it was on the evening of our moving day. My mother had already said that I should go to college that day and not to worry, but this offer of a date would mean not getting back until much later at night. It may have been a dilemma, but

I was so thrilled to have been asked that I just told Madeleine straightaway that I would go and said nothing about the move.

For a day or two I said nothing to my mother. When I eventually managed to say something she reacted with the mixture of reassuring encouragement and guilt-making resignation that I knew very well. I tried to make up for it over the next couple of days by sorting, clearing and packing all that I could – this was a little easier now because of the garden conflagration. I also said, in an effort to make up for my absence, that on the night itself I would not go to the new place but stay in the pub overnight and act as watchman.

On the day itself, I got the bus into college and tried not to think about what was going on at the pub. At the end of the day we boarded the bus as usual. The journey took us past the pub. I had been very vague about where I lived in the village and desperately hoped from the stop before to the stop after that no one I knew would get on and say anything. Worse still, given the recent problems and police involvement I dreaded the prospect of someone getting on that I didn't know, but who would talk about the dreadful people at the Lion who had gone at last, and good riddance. However, no one did get on and nothing happened. As we went past the pub with the sign and the big front door I tried not to look, for fear of seeing chaos or furniture left on the street. There was nothing there. The pub would not open until the following day when the new people arrived to take over.

For all my guilty secrets and concealed anxiety, Madeleine did not seem to notice. I felt bad later about those feelings, which seemed disloyal, but I feared rejection very badly. My anxieties retreated as the bus rolled up the hill and past the old railway station out of the village. The darkness fell, and as we bumped along in the bus our hands touched. I took my chance and held on. I can remember the happiness and warmth as she returned my gentle squeeze.

I might have wished for a longer journey, but very soon we were at her village and a short walk later at the vicarage, a large rambling place where I met Daddy, the Archdeacon, and Mummy – they seemed both much older and very much more respectable than my parents, grey and companionably warm. They were extremely kind to me, though the Archdeacon was preoccupied with his event, a kind of Brains Trust event in the village hall. They radiated a comfort with each other, and their daughter. For all my apprentice radicalism, I found all this reassuring and admirable. It contrasted strongly with the emotional cliff edges and sense of impending disaster which made home for me such heavy going.

We helped as required at the hall, and this did not take long. We walked back to the vicarage in the cold evening air, my heart beginning to thump. We walked through the large house, through the rooms of shining furniture, the cut flowers, and the pictures, into a small sitting room with a large sofa. We sat closer together than before. I gazed at her. She gazed back with big brown eyes beneath long mascara lashes. We kissed and went on kissing. We went further than that, but not very much further. I remember the intimacy, the sharing and the comfort of it. It was enough for me then. The sexual revolution may have begun in 1963 and been a little late for Philip Larkin, but it was a little early for me even by 1965. Actually, for all the talk, and the misty recall you hear from people about those years, this inexperience was not uncommon then. I felt great, though, and as a slow enough starter, awkward and insecure, I now knew that I was probably OK and normal enough after all.

As her parents returned through the planned early warning system of three shut doors, I found it tricky to switch back to polite discussion about their evening. We secretly held hands in the back of the car as I was driven back to my village. I asked her father to drop me off five minutes' walk away from the pub, still unable to come clean about any of that. I was still happy as

I walked to the back door. It was only 11 o'clock, but the village was silent. I let myself in with the only key we now had.

I had known the place, every step of it, since I was five years old, but the night was dark and there are really no places colder or emptier than a closed pub, with all those pitch black corners, and the lingering fruity smell of the years of beer. Buoyed up by the evening and the sense that I was keeping my promise, I turned the back room light on – our downstairs living room. It was empty and you could see the marks on the walls where furniture had been for years on end. It seemed very small and dirty, with scraps of paper on the floor and rubbish in the grate.

I followed through the passage and into the bars, switching on every light as fast as I could at the panel by the bar door. It was the same as ever, but the silence was profound. The bottles were in place on the shelves, the bench seats lay round the walls, and the Queen still smiled above the brick-built grate which still had a hole in it, gouged by my brother and me with darts. A set of those darts, with green plastic flights, lay on the shelf next to the board and I had a final throw, missing the double top as usual.

I walked through the dark porch and into the lounge bar. The furniture here was staying, and the juke box too, still against the wall. I thought about a final go, and switched on the neon display, but it was late and I did not know if anyone would come. It was so quiet that I wondered what would happen if I broke the silence. I played a banana-fingered C major scale on my father's old upright piano, and then I felt really lonely in that place for the first time. I walked back behind the bar, lit a cigarette and opened a light ale, but it was too cold for beer.

I knew that I was putting off going upstairs, but that I needed to do that if I was going to see the night through. I shut the downstairs lights off and turned on the ones upstairs. I went up each bare step, clumping my way on to the landing. I knew straightaway as soon as I was there, with childhood fears flaring up, that I could not possibly look into my grandfather's old room – the one which had given me those recurring nightmares. The other rooms were easier. They were all clear of furniture, apart from the 'best' but seldom used upstairs living room. This still had the table and chairs, which were staying for the new people. There was a platform bench by the window, which faced the church and the green. I decided to try and sleep there, leaning against the wall and pulling my coat around me. I left the landing light on for comfort's sake, but not surprisingly, with the cold and emotion of being there alone, sleep would not come.

I heard several quarters ring from the church clock and then midnight. I thought of all that had happened here. I was sad, but felt that we had managed to leave at last, and that away from here things might improve. As another quarter struck I did not sense any ghosts, but the silence had become so enormous that I felt something must come soon. And as that feeling came to me I knew that I could not stay, for all that I had promised to. I hurried through the house, fear mounting, and switched off lights as I went. Finishing with the downstairs living room, I locked the back door and ran off over the car park and down the lane, neither stopping nor looking back until I knew that I was well away. I have never had those feelings alone in any place since that night, but I learned from it that you do not have to see ghosts for them to be there. I walked through the dark village for a mile or so, up to the top end, and at the new place I tapped gently on the door until my mother let me in.

Chapter 31

AT THE NEW PLACE

The new place was a small semi-detached council house. It had a living room, a small kitchen, a downstairs bathroom and two upstairs bedrooms. There was a brick-built outside toilet, which was not much fun in the early mornings. The fact is that we would have been homeless without it, and my mother had managed to sort everything out to get the tenancy with great determination. By modern standards we would have been regarded as very lucky to have the place at all. Although we had got rid of a good deal of clutter, some of the furniture from the pub had come with us and it looked strange in its new setting. It meant that from the beginning the house seemed crowded.

My father came home from hospital just before Christmas, with his medication lining the mantelpiece on either side of the clock. Christmas, for all the uncertainty still around over my mother's coming court appearance, was calmer than in recent years, and had none of the high emotion and misery of many Christmases in the pub. My brother was home from school so we were really crowded, but already things seemed better at least for now.

Soon after we moved my mother started a job in the canteen at the Lucas factory just outside the village. Given the state she had been in during the last weeks at the Red Lion this was a real testament to her courage in facing the future, and the job also gave her new friends and more confidence. There was always plenty left over from the canteen, and we got used to her bringing home jars and wrappers of left overs for evening meals. I knew that she continued to drink, usually the home drinker's sherry, which you used to be able to buy in your own bottles from a barrel in the grocers. She completely denied having a problem, and would not discuss it. She was secretive about her drinking, but managed to keep going, and she was much happier with her new calmer routine.

In the New Year my father also went to work, after so many years of illness and pub landlording. The job was as an assistant with the Ordnance Survey, and he was required to go off all over the county, to wherever the survey was working. Initially he did this on the bus, but after a time he bought an old moped – the only vehicle he had owned since the elderly and illegally driven pre-war Triumph Gloria which my brother and I had played in during the early years at the pub. It had smelt deliciously of leather and petrol, but Gloria had died on a family trip and was never seen again. Now my father would get up early in the mornings and put on a long belted raincoat and black beret before puttering up the road. He resembled a very slow despatch rider from a Heath Robinson cartoon. He came off a few times as the winter went on but survived it all, despite the ice and the lack of a helmet.

With hindsight I see much more clearly how much courage both of them had needed to start working again after all that had happened and all that they still faced. I had started back at the college in the New Year, and my brother went back to school.

For all the difficulties, turmoil and dysfunction at home neither of my parents ever suggested to me that as the going was tough I should perhaps leave education and get a job myself. I think that my mother in particular had by now invested much of her hope for the future in my making good and training to be something professional. Her assumption, I suppose, was that I would then help and things would get better. That this did not happen, and I married young and had my own life, was something she found very hard to cope with later on, especially after the drink had taken much firmer control of her life and health.

At Aylesbury College it dawned on me that my wish to go to university really did depend now on my working very hard indeed. I had several more dates with Madeleine but knew that she felt guilty about two -timing an absent longer-term boyfriend, and anyway, nothing had been quite as magical as our first evening.

In any event I knew that if I was to have any chance of getting to university I had to put everything else aside and work. Between January and the exams in June 1966 I worked grindingly, and obsessively hard. I set myself the task of working at least 8 hours a day every day. I went in and back on the bus each day, but nowhere else, and stuck to my history and French texts for seven days a week. I shut out everything and everyone who got in the way. I did not feel that I could trust flair or imagination, and in the absence of any independent advice I was sure in my heart that this would be my only chance.

I worked through the evenings on the kitchen table, as the television in the next room burbled on. I worked through my father's occasional relapse into misuse of his medication, when he would sit staring at the television in a drugged state. I worked through my parents' arguments, which could still at times be very fierce, though when he became too abusive and unfair to my mother I would try to reason with him. Trying to reason with a bipolar parent, angry and self-righteous from a cocktail of pre-lithium drugs could never work, but he only really frightened me on one occasion when he stood over me, shouting and waving his fist, dismissing me as a boy who had done nothing and been nowhere. It was incredibly upsetting, but I still worked on.

I went to all the available lessons at college. This helped to keep me on track and check out my progress. Both my teachers were kind and encouraging, and though I tended to shut out most distractions the other students were friendly too. I had in the first term, before my declaration of monastic commitment, played in the rugby team and appeared in a play, but now everything was focused on studying. I had never worked as hard before and never have since. I have always been stuck, though, with a residual, and powerful commitment to the idea of perspiration over inspiration and that grinding it out will usually work. This has often been the case, but not always, and, rightly, my sons and grandsons have had great fun with my two over-repeated nostrums – 'treat it like a job' and 'you can only do your best'.

In early spring all this work was punctuated by visits to three universities for interview – the county paid my expenses to travel, but not to stay over. This was fine for York, and I managed it in a day, but not so good for Hull. I took the train from Kings Cross, with no plan at all about what to do. I changed at Doncaster. By the time we reached Hull, and I had to leave the cosy fug of the train, it was gone 11 at night, and very cold on Hull Paragon Station. After weighing things up I thought sleeping in one of the empty trains was the best bet and found a place to curl up with my bag for a pillow, but it was very cold. After a time someone came along. I thought I was going to be turfed out, but he only wanted to tell me that I'd be a lot better off in the waiting room, where they had just lit the fire. So that was where I spent the night, sitting up next to a blazing, roaring fire, and I slept fitfully as dark shapes elsewhere in the room snored occasionally as they too waited for the day to break and the trains to start up.

This worked to my advantage in an unexpected way. The professor who interviewed me was, rather typically for 1960s social scientists, impressed by my poverty-driven night on the station, and when I received a very good offer I realised that gritty southern realism could work to your advantage just as well as the northern kind.

I received good offers from both York and Hull, but the best offer was from Manchester, where I was grilled at length but seemed to fit the bill for their course on Social Administration. I had not thought it went very well, but my commitment and motivation were strong, and I was thrilled when I found out that I did not have to do any more than pass my 2 'A' Levels in the summer. To some extent I found it hard to believe, and in any event I was too insecure about things to let up my efforts, so I kept hard at Gladstone, Disraeli, the Chartists, the Marriage of Figaro and all the rest of it.

Soon after my interviews came my mother's long-awaited court appearance at the County Quarter Sessions in Aylesbury. My father went off with her on the bus, and I was left at home to look after my brother Bryan. I had no idea what to expect or whether she would come home. I knew it was serious – as well as the Christmas Club money there was the receiving of stolen beer. We had no phone, and nobody had told me what to expect. I waited through a long and very anxious day, trying to play with my brother and read, but finding it hard to concentrate on either. I was hoping hard, but unsure about what could happen and what might happen to her if she was sent away. I remember an aching and appalled feeling that unpleasant things might be done to my mother and that I would be able to do nothing about it. It is a particularly unpleasant type of helplessness, and I have never forgotten it.

In the late afternoon, just when I had almost given up hope and feared the worst, they came back. She had been given probation. They were relieved rather than elated, and it had been a hard and very public experience for both of them. The seeds were sown then, I know, of my own long career in probation, though I did not really have that specifically in mind for a long time yet. I did meet the Probation Officer once or twice. She always visited my mother at home, and seemed to concentrate on practical things. She found us a second-hand Baby Belling stove when our oven gave up the ghost, and it was used as long as my parents were in the house. Many years later I had a job in Buckinghamshire Probation and worked up the courage to look at my mother's file. The records sounded nothing like my family – terse and rather judgemental, with absolutely no apparent sense of any problem with alcohol at all. The lady concerned inevitably had operated a huge caseload at that time, but it was sad to see all my mother's determination, desperation and sense of humour, let alone her real needs, unrecognised and unresponded to.

I went on working towards the exams. In May I had the French oral. I had never had any direct experience of conversation in French except some practice in class, and I had never been anywhere near France. The examiner spoke reassuringly slowly, and she smiled a good deal. I was able to work my way into the predictable themes of my interests and rehearsed vocabulary – 'Je suis socialiste' I remember saying, but that is all I can remember. It certainly seemed to go well enough.

The main exams started early in June. I was so full of facts and essay plans, vocabulary and French quotations that I felt ready to explode, so that when the papers were placed on the desk in the College Main Hall it came as a release. In the intensity of it all I managed to keep my head and wrote on and on for three hours every time. At the end, after the final exam, I came home and had an exhaustion headache for the rest of the day. I felt great relief but also a strange sense of anti-climax. I went to bed early and fell asleep almost immediately, but next morning, as the sun came up, I woke with a huge, calm, sense of release and relief which lasted all day.

It worked. I got high grades, and the college was very pleased. It was the first year the place had been open, and I had turned to it for a second chance. It was a relaxed and encouraging setting for me, with enough structure to keep me on track, and actually a far higher standard of teaching than I had generally had at Ston. I took that for granted at the time, burrowing along in my preoccupied way once I had got the bit between my teeth, but I know that the college did much more than help me get my 'A' levels. It made me feel reasonably normal, rather than a strangely clothed outsider struggling in yo-yo fashion between the oppressions of school and the emotional assault course of home. While I was coping with mixed feelings of responsibility and guilt about life with my parents College allowed me to be my age alongside other young people, as well as enabling me to take direct responsibility for my work and my future.

As for life at home, it was still often difficult and painful but at least I was there, informed, and able to respond, so that there were no dreadful mysteries shielded from me by absence. I had never found the boarding school years of being rescued from home and then regularly dipped back into it easy to cope with. I learned in my year at the college that I always coped better facing problems directly and trying to go forward, and have never lost that feeling.

I took a factory job in the summer, working at the Moorhouse Jam factory in Aylesbury, rolling fruit barrels round the yard and dodging the showers of a fairly damp summer. I was able to pay my way at home and bought some clothes. There was the football to watch, and at the end of July everyone saw England win the World Cup. My grant was sorted out and I got the full amount possible. This, and the money from vacation working, was enough, I soon realised, to make me self-sufficient – much more so than many of my middle-class peers, who had to lean hard on parents to make up the shortfall on their smaller grants.

I applied for accommodation in Manchester and heard nothing, but did not care. Soon enough the day came and suitcase packed I hugged my mother goodbye and went off to the bus stop. At that moment I was independent at last. Although it took a very long time to lose the worst of my anxieties, and I came home for most of the vacations, I really was free from that point onwards, and began to find my own way and make my own life.

Chapter 32

WHAT HAPPENED
TO EVERYONE?

———————

S omehow my parents stayed together for years after they had
left the bright bar. There was a short separation in 1973 when
my father, having started a relationship with a married nurse,
made a sudden break for freedom and left to live with her in a
flat in Maida Vale, pursued by her irate policeman husband. In
London he took a job as an attendant at Madame Tussaud's,
where to the delight of American tourists he would confidently
improvise English history. It did not last for long, and under great
emotional pressure, after a day of great wrangling and turmoil,
she went back to the policeman. After a few weeks my father
returned home and the old patterns of mutual recrimination and
sporadic warfare resumed as before.

About 18 months later, on the back of a legacy from my
father's aunt, they were able to buy a house in Manchester and
moved to my mother's old childhood area of Chorlton. The money
had come down from Aunt Win's brother Cecil, always known

as 'Moss'. He had sold land to the Milton Keynes Development Corporation when the new city had begun galloping towards Newport Pagnell. Moss' smallholding had by now vanished into Milton Keynes, and the money meant that my parents and Bryan could make a fresh start. My father and mother were 52 and 49 at this point, young enough, you would have thought, to be able to start again.

When it came to the move my mother went on ahead, and two days later I arrived at the old house with a hired Bedford van to help my father pack up the furniture they were taking and drive up to Manchester. My father's delight in getting away was quite clear as we bumped and bashed remaining bits of furniture down the stairs. We got there by mid-evening. Sadly, it was clear that my mother had been drinking, and an argument began to rumble within moments. The house was a pleasant 1930s semi, much better than I had imagined, but my mother barely seemed to notice these new surroundings. I left early the next morning, feeling sad about the ways things were, and certain in my heart that this could never be a fresh start. I was sure too that my mother's drinking and general health had worsened. In the end I was just relieved to be away down the motorway.

The Manchester move was driven, I realised later, largely by my father. My mother was less keen on the prospect, though as with much else in her life she went along with his wishes. She had more to lose. Work in the village had given my mother an energy and companionship after the pub had gone. Although her heavy and secret drinking continued she was able to remain positive and optimistic, while unprepared to accept that she had a problem. The move to Manchester, and on the face of it an easier life, lost her the props of routine and purpose that had kept her going. She made a few friends in Manchester but saw little of her own brothers and sisters, who had dispersed over the years, and seemed disinclined to get involved. In the next year or so their relationship in Manchester became ever more angry and bitter. Yet still my parents stayed together, so bound up in mutually destructive rancour that there was no energy left to consider further attempts at escape.

It all ended in April 1977 when my mother died suddenly from heart failure at the age of 52. My father phoned with the news early on a bright spring day. She had, despite all, died in his arms at home. In many respects I felt that I had lost her a long time before that. We had always been close, but my early marriage and parenthood had taken me away, and she seemed to find this strangely unforgiveable. It seemed very much that her spirit, with its warmth and openness, had died well before her body did, killed off with British Sherry, and a refusal, desperately upsetting to me, to allow anyone to help. I thought about her almost unconditional love for us, and the endless pressures of coping with my father's illnesses, the loss of her sons to a boarding school life she never came to terms with, and the humiliation of the final times at the pub. Somehow she kept going through it all with great courage, but less and less awareness of the wider world beyond those problems, or any sense of hope in the future.

It took me a very long time to come to terms with her death. For years the pain of it came back, especially as my own children grew and I knew how much she had missed. My mother was not there to enjoy being a grandparent. She was not there to share in our successes, or worry about the bad times, or remind us of our childhoods, and I still wonder what she would have thought.

My father, still able to be outgoing and attractive when the mood took him, went on for many years and did succeed in making another life. He and my brother Bryan, still at Ston, moved to a flat and quite quickly he married again, so that I acquired a young stepsister. In the years that followed there were still signs in this marriage of the old John Victor with his emotional demands and abusive behaviour, but he did try his best. For him this was undoubtedly a better life, and he finally managed to join the football world properly as a senior gateman at Maine Road, where on Manchester City match days he would proudly march around the ground with an escort collecting the takings.

He continued to take a good deal of medication but it was as if his old illness had burnt itself out, leaving occasional echoes but nothing worse. He remained scared about hospitals and operations, and did not seek help until it was too late for anything to be done about his eventual liver cancer. It was only later that I realised how much this had rested on the shock of losing his mother 'under the knife' as people used to say. He only went into hospital two days before he died, and there was no operation. He was 76 – not a great age in modern terms, but he had lived much longer than might have been predicted in 1960, and managed to keep clear of alcohol until the last year or two, when he acquired a taste for white wine on family occasions and it seemed too late and too unkind by then to say anything.

John Victor remained very stubborn to the end. The last time his three sons were with him was at home, just before the end. We stood around the bed arguing with him about the need to get some help, because at that point he was refusing even to consider going to hospital. 'You're right in all you're saying' he croaked, 'but I'm not going'. I noticed that a bit of the old Bucks accent came back as he said it, but soon afterwards he was too weak to resist and went calmly enough.

I have often wondered in later life about how life might have been for my parents if they had not gone into the pub in the first place and resisted my grandfather's great plan, or if they had been able at least to leave it sooner. Even more crucially, how they might both have fared if they had separated from each other. Though they both came from a generation less prepared to consider divorce, many people did manage it, but there was a powerful glue of mutual dependence and fear of the unknown which kept them together despite all the disasters. On my mother's part particularly, this had a great deal to do with keeping a home together, and she had a huge investment in her three sons. Certainly our beginning to live our own lives left a big gap in hers and she never seemed to recover from this. My father's alcoholism and then mental illness made a carer of my mother, and when she needed care herself my father was unable to give it in the same way. In any event she would not accept it from him or from us either. Her own depression and alcoholism remained stubbornly untreated however much we tried. All of this, I know, will be very familiar territory to grown-up children of alcoholics – a status which you never really lose however old you may become.

It is sad to think of what they both lost, or never found. I remember my father's enthusiasm when he showed us as small children a thrush on the nest on a walk near Waddesdon. He could play Fats Waller stride style on the piano brilliantly (a style of playing in which the right hand plays the melody and the left hand plays a bass octave on the strong beat and a chord on the weak beat, developed in Harlem in the 20s from ragtime), but gave it up for no good reason. He wanted to search for the bright lights, which he did at least find eventually at Maine Road.

My mother, soft, and too caring of others for her own good, had an intelligence and warmth which had vanished by the age of 50, so that you were only left with memories of her gentle lullabies and tales of her childhood in Manchester before the war. It must have been especially tough for my youngest brother Bryan. David and I always had each other, and all of us have, in our own ways, done well. My father at least had the benefit of knowing that, and being known to his grandchildren, but my mother missed all of it and I am still very sad about that, particularly each April as the year rolls around again.

So how have the boys from Ston and the bright bar got on? David, three years younger than me, is without any doubt the most courageous person I have ever known. As we played together in the pub back room and car park his brittle bone disease meant that he had already had numerous fractures and spells in hospital. He always had a leather shin guard over his left leg, which had bowed badly. It affected his walking but not his determination to play football and cricket. Eventually, while at Ston, he became old enough for the big operation to straighten his leg, which had been talked about for years. He was in the Royal National Orthopaedic in Stanmore for ages. On Sundays I would go to see him at the hospital, taking the chance to get away from school.

David showed great courage and resilience, separated from home and school, but the operation was a big success. Later we were for some time, until I left, in the same house at Ston. Wrapped up again in my own feelings and preoccupations I did not give him much thought when I walked out in my last year, but he coped, and his ability to make friends and get on with people, together with his determination and general gutsiness, made him really very popular.

David remained at school through most of the crises at home after I had left, and was less caught up in the chaos and general dysfunction. I missed him in that, but he had seen enough over the years, and had endured so much personally, that I was glad he was spared some of it. He is the only witness left to the life we had behind the old bright bar, when he played cribbage with the old boys and we were given snuff for head colds and port wine to replace the blood if we cut ourselves. He was given a start by old Giddy Blake, the Ston Careers Master, and went to live in lodgings in London, beginning a long and distinguished banking career. In the early years he took time to go round the world and made lifelong friends in Australia and New Zealand. Later on he married, and he and Janice have two lovely daughters, both now grown up and married with their own successful careers. David kept his cricketing interests going and founded his own club, which I occasionally played for. He never let his brittle bone disease rule his life, and although injury ended his playing days he has never given up on sports generally and his beloved Manchester United in particular.

Bryan was born during the first year that David and I were away at school. He must have represented hope and the future to my parents, this Lammas Lamb. David and I did not get to meet him properly until we arrived home at the end of that term. We got used to pushing his pram around the village, anxiously at first and then with a fair degree of pride. I remember us all making that first family trip to Manchester with him, and him being shown off to the Williams clan.

As is clear from earlier chapters Bryan's early years in the pub were neither easy nor particularly comfortable. He eventually started school at St Mary's across the road, just as we had. Later they got a dog for him, I remember. It was a long -haired collie, Lassie like, with a long nose and sizeable energy. As might have been expected my parents just hoped for the best and provided very little training. After it wandered and then worried sheep it was thought best to arrange for it to 'go and live on a farm'. To this day Bryan thinks this may have been a euphemism for a less happy solution. Bryan acquired the family love of football early and I remember during holidays taking him to see Oxford at the Manor, travelling there and back on the bus as we had always done.

Bryan duly went off to Ston, long after David and I had left, and stayed there for the rest of his schooling. My father retained the staunch belief that, as with us, this was the best choice, though my mother had to go through a fresh loss and separation, which must have been very hard. There was no doubt that things at home remained fragile, unpredictable and occasionally violent. After the move to Manchester, during a school holiday, my parents' warfare had spilled onto the street outside, and Social Services were called. They contacted me and I tried to be helpful, but it was clear that there was real concern for my brother. He was 14 or so at the time, so his age and my reassurances to the social worker meant no further action was taken, but it was very worrying. It was a tough environment for Bryan, both physically and emotionally, and when my mother died it was heartbreaking for all of us, but Bryan was closest to it at 16 years old. I worried about him in the days and months that followed. I was so wrapped up in my own family and work at that time that I felt I could not do very much direct to help, but he came to stay with us for several weeks and at least we got to know him better.

Bryan left school and went to college in 1976. He always enjoyed Manchester, despite the problems of family life, and has gone on to have a successful life, despite all the difficulties of those early years. He married Kay and they have two sons, both now grown up, so like David, he has enjoyed a very different family life from the one we all grew up with behind the bright bar.

As for me, life changed radically with university. I found my feet easily enough and friends and freedom too. For a mid-60s student I was more diligent about work than most, and never wanted to risk what seemed to me to have been a very hard-won second chance. I had plenty of good times as well, though, and met my future wife in my final year. When it came to a choice of career my family experience and very basic wish to help people drove me towards the Probation Service. I trained in Liverpool before working for almost 40 years in the Thames Valley and London. I felt a passion about this work, driven by my parents' problems and my feelings about the need for a better and more caring response from society. It was not difficult to get into probation, and apart from the course interview there was very little challenging of individual motives for probation work. I did not share much about mine then or for many years. Once in post, while I worked hard to help my clients share their feelings and gremlins, I held on to mine tightly as a private possession and the source, which continued to power my work. I found it very hard in the early years to work with alcoholics but matured into it and later on campaigned successfully for new services for substance misuse and mental health.

I did eventually manage to share with colleagues what had always driven me, but this was right at the end, almost at retirement, and I wish now that I had done it earlier. I have not changed my view, though, that there will always need to be a special place in services like Probation for those whose vocational commitment is inspired primarily by direct life experience.

The early years and the yo-yo life have both had other long-term effects on my passions and choices, though it took me a long time to see that. My fear of boredom and need to make things happen certainly goes back to the stultifying village summers of my childhood and the massively regulated life at Ston. I have founded drama groups, a festival, campaigning groups and a charity working to deliver development projects in Mali, West Africa, which has enabled me, over the past 20 years, to have a direct stake in the lives of rural people in one of the poorest countries on earth.

This has all been great – though often done at the expense of family life and with a recklessness about time and energy. This passion to make things happen has much to do with another personal driver – a determination to stick two fingers up to the experts and sceptics, who want to tell you all the time that it won't work here, or can't be done that way. Proving them wrong eventually provides a special if perverse satisfaction.

A similar tendency that clearly came from my childhood was an inability to walk away from anything I saw as unfair or unjust. Whether confronting yobbos on trains, calling out racists or sticking up for various categories in underdog, I have always been impelled to do something. Probation over nearly 40 years provided plenty of opportunities, and I came close to serious trouble in the later stages taking action as a whistleblower about various iniquities in Wormwood Scrubs prison where I was working.

I was heavily involved in the labour Party for a number of years, organising elections and then fighting a 'no hope' seat in Mid-Oxfordshire in 1989. I worked hard and had a good response, but we were all blown away by the scale of the Thatcher victory and the beginning of a long and bleak period for most of the things I believed in. I knew having fought that campaign that full-time politics was not for me, and that I was too thin-skinned and emotional to make it a sensible career choice!

For many years I did not experience anything like the depression which drove me to run away from school as a teenager. I had glum periods, but they seemed to pass. It was not until my mid-thirties that I had my one serious depressive illness. I was told that it might well be a genetic gift from my father. The trough of that illness, lasting almost a year, was an incredibly painful experience, and certainly included periods of wandering in a fog of misery and considering how I might kill myself. It lasted for ages and I was away from work for many months. Even later as I began to trust my feelings again, I had many self-doubts and a strong feeling that I had been very damaged and might never fully recover.

I was able to see later how little personal time I had allowed myself to mourn the death of my mother some two or three years before. As I rushed on with life, those feelings of grief and of low self-worth could not be kept at bay by endless activity, however worthy it might be. For a long time afterwards I was very scared as to whether that level of depression would come back. It never has, which is testament to modern medication, the understanding of my employers and the patience and commitment of my partner. It served to give me some late insight into my father's predicament and courage, and my mother's perseverance and patience for most of that time. We still have big problems with the stigma surrounding mental illness, not least among people who should know better. I remember in the aftermath of my own illness being able to sort my colleagues into sheep and goats in terms of how they responded to me as members of a supposedly caring profession. It was often surprising to discover which of these flocks they actually belonged to.

Fundamentally what has kept me functioning through that crisis and everything else is my marriage. It was wonderful to find a partner, just before I started training, who was neither shocked nor put off by my account of a family life which I was initially anxious about sharing. It emerged soon, in fact, that she too had had plenty of that childhood experience of domestic violence and an alcoholic parent, so we both knew the issues. We have supported each other ever since, through all the ups and downs which might be expected, and have both realised that those family experiences have a long-lasting and somewhat ingrained ability to colour perceptions and impact on judgements, however you may feel that you have outgrown them. There is a bonus, though – a gift which should be claimed by everyone who had a tough childhood. It is an optimism that things can and do improve, that you have, for the most part, the resilience to cope, and that it is all so much better now than it was then.

Finally, what happened to Haddenham and Ston – those two very different worlds? Haddenham was always a big village and is bigger still now. It is not really a place any longer for the 'little old boys', and you will be unlikely to hear the old accent from anyone less than 70 years old. It is an expensive place to live, and you can commute to London, though the modern station is a mile or so up the road from the old one where David and I used to spend hours watching the trains. That has completely vanished.

The C of E Primary School was made into a village centre long ago and there is a new successor school further up the village. Haddenham still has some pubs, but no longer the Red Lion, which is now a private house. It faces a more manicured-looking green, though the church is the same as ever. I know no one there now, but I imagine some of the old families are still to be found.

Going away to school began the fraying of our connection, and it broke altogether with my parents' move to Manchester.

And Ston, the school, has gone as well, though the buildings remain. The place has meandered through several alternative careers after the school closed, and still rears up on television as a rather promiscuous ghost pretending to be an ancient college, crime scene, or sombre courthouse. Its latest and probably final identity is as an extremely expensive and gated community of luxury apartments known as Connaught Park. That name is the only vestige of Masonic identity left, recalling Edward VII's brother, who laid the foundation stone in 1903. As the northbound west coast main line trains from Euston flash past Bushey station you can just see the great clock tower in the distance, and this glimpse is still enough to bring back my schooldays and that strange old institution with all its beauties and horrors.

Chapter 33

LOOKING BACK

I have written this account in my early 70s. I share with most of my generation lucky enough to have got this far the idea that everything will be different for us. If you look back at the expectations of older people in the 1950s and 60s it already is, but trying to place memory in sequence also jolts your sense of distance. Ston's foundation stone was laid less than 60 years before I went away to school, for all that the place seemed so ancient. Actually for all the fuss about a new Elizabethan age, jet travel and 'you've never had it so good', that England of the early 1960s, and certainly life in the bright bar, had much more in common with Edwardian England than with England now. Similarly my parents' apparently endless and turbulent marriage, which ended with my mother's death, lasted only for 30 years, though for both of them very often it must have seemed much longer. What they seemed to have was an extraordinary but often destructive interdependence, but there must have been commitment and passion as well.

What did I really know of my parents' lives and secrets? I realised as I tried to write about them how young they had actually been through most of this story. Home from the war, my father married at 23 and had two sons by the age of 27. He had lost his mother by 1950, supposedly to a botched cancer operation in the days before doctors deigned to explain very much. My mother, married at 21, became a mother at 22 and was a pub landlady by the age of 28 – so young, so busy and so far from her own large family in Manchester.

By the age of 34 my father, having masked his illness with alcohol for years, was diagnosed with manic depression and only with hindsight can I see the full extent to which that illness redrew not only his life but everyone else's as well. The illness, and sometimes the treatments at times threatened his very life, let alone the way he was able to live it. Although he was blessed to live in an age when new approaches were coming in, his illness and the revolving hospital door affected the whole family. It hammered down our financial and emotional security, and left huge burdens on my mother. The stigma was so strong and so clear to us as children that it made us wary and defensive. I can still recall the time when he was away one summer, before we went to school. The boredom with nowhere to go and the grubbiness of our life in the pub back room seemed all the more unpleasant because of the heat and light of the long summer days.

This all began 60 years ago, but depressingly much has not changed. Treatment has continued to improve, but stigma remains a major problem and families still seem to be marginalised. This is very hard for children. No one ever explained what was going on to us, and for many I do not think that has changed very much, so that the defensiveness and loneliness are just handed on for a further generation.

Booze ran through my childhood. We lived in a pub and both my parents had major alcohol problems. My father eventually became sober, but the eventual consequences were much worse for my mother. It was a long and slow process, with the problem slyly increasing year on year from Guinness to a heavy and supposedly secret dependence on the dreadful British Sherry, which powered respectable alcohol misuse for many women in those days. For all her work to keep us together through the worst years, including the whole painful final times at the pub, her drinking killed her eventually. We knew that actually we had lost her long before the end came. There were few services in those days, and reluctance to 'push' or challenge behaviour. I tried very hard to get the family GP to at least talk to her about it, but he would not, and he should have.

We now have much cheaper alcohol, available almost everywhere, but there is a strange national self-delusion and denial which manages to ignore all the health advice on offer. Perhaps the generation coming up will have a clearer and healthier attitude to it all, but the picture to date is not very encouraging.

I now see more clearly why my father so wanted us to go away to Ston. For him it was our rescue – one that he could claim through Freemasonry as his own. He was so committed to his great plan that he just carried my mother along and bullied away her doubts and fears. It changed everything for me, and even now I am not sure whether it saved me from misery and disaster at home and day school or saddled me forever with an anxiety about separation.

Certainly my brothers and I were spared the day-to-day problems of a chaotic and sometimes violent home life. It had already begun to corrode my schooling before I went away. It is true also that the years at school had much that was funny and happy in them, but it was a drastic solution, and Ston was a hard school. The yo-yo experience between the two was always painful and never got any easier as time went by.

I remain deeply sceptical overall about boarding education. It may well have improved in recent years but it still involves, at least for younger children, an enforced separation, a requirement for stiff upper lips and a loss of the community you leave behind. I am not sure that the damage done is ever quite put right. If you doubt that, I suggest you talk to people from my generation, boys and girls, who went away to school very young – you can usually trace fairly quickly the effect, not often very positive, on their choices and later life relationships. It was always assumed at Ston that the regime would put you right and keep you going without any need for pastoral care or personal choice. Given the reasons most of us were sent away, this now seems extraordinary to me.

Being 'rescued' and sent away, however well intentioned, left me with some long-lasting feelings and assumptions. I have never lost the need to face things directly and try to go forward, rather than just hope for the best, even when realistically that was the only sensible thing to do. Knowing that things were bad at home, and not being there, bred a stress and anxiety which lay behind my eventual running away and sense of hopelessness. The visits home for holidays just reinforced this, and through my adult life I have always wanted to have the good news and the bad news at the same time.

My childhood, at home and school, was marked by assumptions that I did not need to have problems explained. In reality children suffer far worse when secrets are kept and lies are told about difficult things. I hope it is clear from my memories that children always see more than adults realise, and that exposure to heavy arguments, emotion and physical violence leave a long-lasting mark. The only balm for those wounds is talk and explanation. Kindness without these is just not enough. If families cannot address the unresolved pain and emotional damage themselves, then they need help to do so. For children bland reassurance, or simply removal from the scene, are not of themselves going to help. While it is true that children are more robust than they are usually given credit for, and that survival through difficult things can give real resilience, this is not always true. What you cannot do is clamp a lid over feelings which need to be expressed, because they will not simply fade away in time, as my own later depression and insecurity confirm. The fact is that no one at any stage sought to help our family as a family.

Finally, what about the Masons and their charity? My brothers and I never joined the Old Masonians. Once I had left, the experience overall was not one I wished to recreate or celebrate with others. The distance between school life and the exciting freedoms of a new and challenging world outside felt like a million miles. Most of us wanted to get on with life and forget the grey-suited regimentation of school. Consequently, over the years, I only went back twice. First, and reluctantly, to see my youngest brother in the 1970s, and then that final visit just before the developers finally took over. Singing the old hymns in the chapel surrounded by all those grey and white heads was inevitably poignant, but overall I did not think I had missed very much by avoiding all those years of rose-tinted and honey-flavoured gatherings.

For all my negative feelings about Ston, I still have ambivalent and conflicting feelings about our benefactors. With great generosity they provided a whole education at no cost to any of the parents in the belief that they were helping the sons of lost or troubled brothers. It would be cheap to deny their genuine and sustained commitment. Our patrons were always in evidence at high days and holidays, with visits from different contributing lodges and Worshipful Grand Masters. I know that we were neither educated for Freemasonry nor educated by Freemasons. The influence was subtler than that and did, I am sure, rely on a sense of gratitude and recognition from a mixed bag of Stonic alumni. It is very hard to dismiss those feelings, despite my having really had no say about becoming the recipient of the Masons' generosity. If secretly it was all meant to provide a conveyor belt of new Brothers, that has never been evident to me. If a softer process of engagement through gratitude was intended, then the business of actually living through the Spartan and regularly militarized regime at Ston proved enough to harden most hearts in our generation against coming to the square ourselves.

By the time I left in the mid 60s, Ston seemed to stand for values which were already unfashionable. The most obvious Masonic assumption, beyond a general commitment to law and order and the status quo, was summed up in the school motto Audi, Vide, Tace, or Hear, See and Be Silent. It was not a very healthy educational message but spoke instead to the mysteries of apprenticeship and secrecy. It is a rotten maxim, and although I have not always been very good about sharing my own feelings I have always tried to speak out as plainly as I could about causes I cared about and injustices which I have seen. This has not always been easy when it came to prisons, courts and injustices, but I am proud that I have never followed the old Stonic rule and kept silent.

Printed in Great Britain
by Amazon